BETWEEN HEIDEGGER AND NOVALIS

Northwestern University
Studies in Phenomenology
and
Existential Philosophy

General Editor Anthony J. Steinbock

BETWEEN HEIDEGGER AND NOVALIS

Peter Hanly

Northwestern University Press
Evanston, Illinois

Northwestern University Press
www.nupress.northwestern.edu

Printed in the United States of America

10 9 8 7 6 5 4 3 2 1

Library of Congress Cataloging-in-Publication Data
Names: Hanly, Peter, author.
Title: Between Heidegger and Novalis / Peter Hanly.
Other titles: Studies in phenomenology and existential philosophy.
Description: Evanston, Illinois : Northwestern University Press, 2021. | Series: Northwestern University Studies in phenomenology and existential philosophy | Includes bibliographical references and index.
Identifiers: LCCN 2020049838 | ISBN 9780810143241 (paperback) | ISBN 9780810143258 (cloth) | ISBN 9780810143265 (ebook)
Subjects: LCSH: Heidegger, Martin, 1889–1976. | Novalis, 1772–1801—Criticism and interpretation. | Relation (Philosophy) | Relation (Philosophy) in literature.
Classification: LCC B3279.H49 H273 2021 | DDC 193—dc23
LC record available at https://lccn.loc.gov/2020049838

For Anaïs

I am a friend of the migrant birds even though, to put it mildly, they adhere to dubious philosophies—perhaps even wrong ones. And even though it is stupid and dangerous and indeed downright criminal to fly across the ocean on those useless little wings, the golden plover has a lovely song in spring . . .

—Halldór Laxness

Contents

Acknowledgments

This book began its journey at Boston College, and so the most immediate debt of gratitude is owed to the many, many people who have supported and encouraged my endeavors there. In the first place I would like to thank John Sallis sincerely for his inspiration, unfailing support, and generous encouragement in many different directions and over a period of many years. And while there are so many from whom I have learned and received encouragement, the hours spent with the late William Richardson, S.J., deserve special mention. Fueled as they often were with copious quantities of sherry, the lengthy conversations I was privileged to have with him were formative and inspirational; and they are sorely missed. Equally, though, an immense debt of gratitude is owed to the special network of friends and colleagues at Boston College whose generosity and care has inspired me on many levels. They are certainly too numerous to list, but I would like especially to mention Frances Maughan-Brown, Teresa Fenichel, Vanessa Rumble, Gustavo Gómez-Pérez, and Martín Bernales for their genuine friendship over many long years.

Several segments of this work, both on Novalis and on Heidegger, evolved from preliminary explorations, over the years, in conferences and seminars. In particular, several panels at the Nordic Society for Phenomenology in Reykjavik, Oslo, and Stockholm, and a 2011 seminar at Södertörn University on "Loss of Grounds" left a distinct mark: I am immensely grateful for the quality of listening that I experienced there.

This book has been ten years in the making; and over that time there are many with whom I have crossed paths who have inspired, encouraged, and provoked its direction; and others who, simply by the virtue of friendship, of kindness, have enabled it to come to fruition. Among those whose presence and conversation have marked this work, often in unexpected ways, I would like in particular to mention Ben and Yolande Vedder, Gert-Jan van der Heiden, Sanem Yazıcıoğlu, María del Rosario Acosta López, Claudia Baracchi, Andrew Mitchell, Alejandro Vallega, and Daniela Vallega-Neu. And among my musical colleagues, I owe thanks especially to Aija Silina and Lisa Hennessy for their kindness, their friendship, and for tolerating my endless distraction in rehearsals and performances. But in particular, it is my dear friend Marcia Sá Cavalcante Schuback that I would like to thank: it is from her that the first thought of writing about Novalis came, and she has been a kind and generous interlocutor at every stage of the book's development. Over the years her friendship, and that of her wonderful family, have sustained me in more ways than I can count.

Finally, for all that this book has been many years in gestation, it must be said that it would certainly never have been completed if it were not for literary historian Anna Razumnaya, my beloved Anaïs, who somehow manages, along with her wonderful son Leo, to lift every single day into celebration.

BETWEEN HEIDEGGER AND NOVALIS

Introduction

Heidegger, Novalis, and the Between

Points of Contact

This book is a study in relation. This is meant in two senses. On the one hand, it aims to consider the nature of the relation between two thinkers of radically different sensibilities and philosophical orientations, Martin Heidegger and Friedrich von Hardenberg, known as Novalis. On the other hand, the book will be concerned with relation itself, with how we might better understand both connectivity and difference by exploring and interrogating the category of relation. It is in respect of both these senses that the "between" of the title is intended. This is because it turns out that, in the broadest sense, what will govern the relation between Heidegger and Novalis *is* the particular sense of a "between" and the concomitant possibilities it allows for exploring the nature of relation itself. To be more explicit, the figure of the "between" at play in both Heidegger's and Novalis's work is one that introduces a dynamic tension into the category of relation by conceiving it in terms of contradictory energies of separation, dispersion, pulling-apart, and gathering or converging. This figure, in turn, can be understood as derived from a specifically Greek understanding of *harmonia*, one given voice in a particular way by Heraclitus. Because this conception of *harmonia* differs in radical degree from the senses of the word "harmony" that are more familiar to us, this book undertakes, in part, something like the retrieval of a forgotten thought, and asks at the same time why that thought may be so elusive, and what the stakes might be in its elision or its retrieval.

Imagined thus, it is possible to think of Novalis and Heidegger as sharing a common ground of thinking, despite chasms of difference, conceptually and contextually, between them. It is this strange affinity, or elusive harmony that, I believe, accounts, on the one hand, for the interest and curiosity, but also, on the other, for the ambivalence that Heidegger almost invariably displays on the rare occasions that he addresses Novalis directly. The first thing that will be undertaken here, then, is to give an account of those points of contact: the moments at which the figure of Novalis emerges as a concrete presence for Heidegger, one whose importance, it will be seen, entirely exceeds its quantifiable reach.

The question of contact is not the same as the question of influence. The latter aims at isolating genealogies of concepts, exposing the operations of a shadowy and, presumably, hitherto concealed presence in the work of one or another writer. To claim Novalis as an "influence" on Heidegger would be to claim for the former a formative presence, to present his work as an "ingredient," as it were, in the assemblage of ideas ascribed to the latter. Such a claim does justice to neither Novalis nor Heidegger, in that it tends to reduce the former to the status of "forerunner," and the latter to the uninspiring position of "afterthought." Despite their lure, then, analyses of "the influence of X on Y" bury rather than shed light upon their subject. And in the case of both Novalis and Heidegger, such a proceeding would be particularly inimical, not just because it would fail to do justice to the originality of either, but because it would trample over the dynamic and engaged sensitivities that both reveal with regard to questions of history itself. By contrast with the study of influence, then, the question of contact makes no claim for a continuous presence. There will be no attempt here to argue for the inclusion of Novalis among the list of canonical presences with whom Heidegger is often said to be in dialogue: Hegel, Hölderlin, Nietzsche, Aristotle, and so on. Instead, the intent is to allow Novalis a voice in the margins of Heidegger's work, a borderline presence, one that looms up only on occasion, neither explored at length nor dismissed out of hand, a presence indistinct and ambiguous. In the 1957 *Freiburg Lectures*, and at the precise moment that he will introduce Novalis to the stage, Heidegger speaks of a "flashing up" (*aufblitzen*) of thought, and of the "estranging" (*befremdlich*) encounter in which we "catch a glimpse of the afterglow of such a flash" (*GA* 79: 173/163). A flash of thought, an afterglow, a sense of the glimpsing of something strange and untoward: these indeed are images deeply akin to the way in which Heidegger appears to experience Novalis's thinking. To explore the question of contact, then, will be to attempt to do justice to this explosive strangeness.

If we then move to examine the concrete instances in which Novalis's work enters within the horizon of Heidegger's, and does so with sufficient force to obligate acknowledgment, we can see that the reception of these instances attests to a particular kind of ambiguity. On the one hand, references to and quotations from Novalis's work amid Heidegger's writings span over four decades, from an epigraph in the *Habilitationsschrift* of 1916 (*GA* 1: 399/62) through a significant presence in *Unterwegs zur Sprache* of 1959 (*GA* 12). Despite the intermittence of these appearances, this temporal span alone makes clear that the marginal presence of Novalis was in some fashion accessible to Heidegger throughout most of his writing life. On the other hand, there is—quite evidently—no substantial or sustained address to Novalis's thinking, or indeed to the thinking of Jena Romanticism, in Heidegger's work.[1] There is, of course, the overwhelming presence of Hölderlin; but, though connected, Hölderlin was not part of the circle of the Jena Romantics, and—more importantly—the general direction of Heidegger's attention is to consider Hölderlin as exceptional, as the exclusive source of a thinking that leads beyond metaphysics. His work is thus framed as being set apart from the social and intellectual milieu in which he flourished, a context that thereby falls away the more his insights hold sway in Heidegger's thinking. Thus, the presence of Novalis seems, despite its repeated emergence, outside the mainstream of Heidegger's thinking as it relates to Hölderlin, and equally outside Heidegger's relations to the central philosophical axis that guides his engagement with the historical period of Hölderlin's poetic output: Kant, Schelling, and Hegel.

Nonetheless, as we examine the references to Novalis's work that lie scattered across this forty-year period, we discover that the recourse to Novalis is generally undertaken with a specific flourish, a special kind of emphasis that makes the quotations far more than ornamental. Rather, they seem often to mark points of crisis in the text, and in so marking, propel the writing forward. Novalis, then, is not so much cited by Heidegger as he is "invoked"—introduced with a certain solemnity, a sense of authority that, however, remains unexplored. For example, in the *Fundamental Concepts of Metaphysics* (*GA* 29/30), Heidegger brings Novalis on to the stage to announce that "philosophy is properly homesickness [*Heimweh*]; the drive to be everywhere at home" (*W* II: 675).[2] This summoning, though, is followed by a curious, almost theatrically rhetorical gesture in which Heidegger makes a grand play of refusing to "provoke an argument over the authority and significance of this witness" who is, he explains with a slightly labored irony, "merely a poet, after all" (*GA* 29/30: 7/5). The sense, then, is of an authority without authority, an invocation of seminal and decisive import that never quite abandons its reserve, even its caution. This caution or reserve can be measured, too, in the verdicts—always terse, undeveloped, but intriguing—which do on occasion attach to his "witness." In *Der Satz vom Grund* of 1955–56, for instance, Heidegger calls Novalis "the poet who was also a great thinker" (*GA* 10: 20/13). Given the weight that the appellations of "poet" and "thinker" acquire for Heidegger, we can assume that their use is measured with extreme precision; but it is never elaborated. The ambiguity of the invocation can easily be seen elsewhere, too, for instance in the *Freiburg Lectures* of 1957 (*GA* 79: 82–176/ 77–166), and again in *Unterwegs zur Sprache* where despite, and following, its summons, Novalis's thinking is nonetheless cursorily rejected on the grounds of a too easily assumed proximity to Hegel. The honored guest is invited to the table, only to be summarily dismissed.

In Heidegger's early *Habilitationsschrift* (*GA* 1: 399/62), it is as an epigraph that Novalis's name appears, marking a movement from the domain of Scholastic inquiry toward an engagement with Hegel. The epigraph takes up the first of Novalis's *Blüthenstaub* fragments, and reads: "we *search* everywhere [*überall*] for the unconditioned and *find* only the conditioned" (*W* II: 226). The sense here is of an endlessness, a desire that is and must remain unresolved. And it is precisely this same sense of an endless striving that Heidegger also discovers in Novalis when he first engages him actively in the body of his writings. This, then, is in the lecture course of 1929/30 (*Fundamental Concepts of Metaphysics*) where Heidegger cites, with elaborate but curiously unexplained approbation, the following fragment from Novalis: "Philosophy is properly homesickness [*Heimweh*]; the drive to be everywhere [*überall*] at home" (*W* II: 675). It is the sense of the "everywhere," in both this fragment and the epigraph, which governs the restlessness and radical dissatisfaction of the "search" (in the first fragment) and of philosophy itself (in the second). This means that philosophy is to be understood not as a ubiquitous force of appropriation, somehow making itself "at home" everywhere, but rather as unresolvable longing. More importantly still, the "everywhere" in both cases indicates a force of dispersal rather than a "longing for home." In relation to this sense of the "everywhere," we can observe that Novalis, exploring the complex mechanisms of reciprocity between positing subject and countering force that fascinate him in Fichte, and which we will examine, writes: "*the point is everywhere* [*überall*]" (*W* II: 41/*FS* 34). This is intended to indicate the paradoxical situation of that which is at once specifically local and indefinitely dispersed: this paradox deflects any of the usual senses of "direction" that the thought of "longing for home" might suggest. The "drive to be everywhere" must be understood in terms of a dispersive energetics, and not those of a singular directedness; and the "at home" is to be understood as the locus of a stability where philosophy, precisely and constitutively, *is not*. Thought from out of this homelessness, for which the pain of longing, of searching, is constitutive, what belongs most properly to philosophy is precisely this restlessness—an unease, uncertain and unsettled.

It is from out of this sense of primary homelessness, then, that we must understand Heidegger when he claims, toward the close of the *Freiburg Lectures*, that "we remain settled upon this earth in relationality" (*GA* 79: 175/165). This "relationality" clearly says something other than "being in relation with." To be "in relation with" implies polarities, an otherness, the distinct otherness of that with which we are "in relation." To be "settled in relationality" implies by contrast a state of betweenness, the discomfort of operating continuously *from within* a field of relation. It is, in that sense, a state of homelessness, a not being "at home." In this way, philosophy—and this is true in different ways for Heidegger and Novalis—will come to be paradigmatic of this not-quite-belonging, of this relational "between" that we are said to inhabit. In Novalis's case, we can see how this betweenness is expressed if we consider again the first of the *Blüthenstaub* fragments, which Heidegger used as an epigraph for his *Habilitationsschrift*: "we *search* everywhere [*überall*] for the unconditioned [*das Unbedingte*] and *find* only the conditioned [*Dinge*]." As is often pointed out, the translation of the opposition *Unbedingte/Dinge* as unconditioned/conditioned, while capturing the aural and semantic resonance of the terms, misses the fact that *Dinge* means "things" in a sense that is concretely material, something not evident from its translation as "the conditioned." Thought in its original sense, the between-space, in which we find ourselves uncomfortably lodged, will have everything to do with our relation with the things of the world, or more specifically with the difficult and unresolvable tension between an ideality of thought and the experience of the world to which it remains inextricably bound. As it turns out, it is *language* that will come, in a certain way, to reside in this between-space. But not in an easy way: not in a way that would suggest, for instance, that the word just "fills up" a space between, or acts as a mere connective, the facilitation of a passageway. In the *Freiburg Lectures* (*GA* 79) Heidegger expresses this between-space of language as follows, in a way that could be construed as a commentary on Novalis's first *Blüthenstaub* fragment:

> We would first have to experience and withstand what is most estranging: that before all being and thinking, and before the belonging-together of both of these, the essence of language is the play, oscillating in itself [*in sich schwingende Spiel*] of the locus, within the reach [*Bereich*] of which the saying hands over [*überreicht*] all things and beings to one another, and thus extends them toward us, such that we everywhere encounter or miss them. (*GA* 79: 173/163)

It is precisely the tension-filled space of an "oscillating" between that this book will set out to describe, and to which it will return again and again. In Heidegger's first expressions of his encounter with Novalis's thinking, then, what we see is that it is philosophy itself which is to give voice to the unsettlement of this between, to the "relationality" in which we are "settled upon this earth." If philosophy is to be the voice of this unsettlement, this

Unheimlichkeit, it is precisely within the horizon of the tensed attunement of this in-between that it can most properly flourish. This is the sense in which the experience articulated first by Novalis is appropriated by Heidegger in such a way as to belong equally to both.

Following the encounter of 1929/30 which takes place in the lecture series *Fundamental Concepts of Metaphysics* (*GA* 29/30), there is a gap in Heidegger's engagements with Novalis, one of close to thirty years, a hiatus after which references resurface boldly and with some frequency in various series of lectures in the late 1950s. The relative frequency of these later reappearances suggests that we can reasonably conclude that it is at this time, between 1955 and 1959, that Heidegger is considering Novalis most carefully. It is now that the contact becomes particularly vibrant and fecund; and it will be valuable to consider its instances.

The first of the several occasions, in the 1950s, in which Novalis appears on the stage, is in the lecture course entitled *Der Satz vom Grund,* which Heidegger delivered in Freiburg in the winter semester of 1955–56. The first lecture directs his listener toward a kind of obscurity that attaches to the principle of ground, or reason:

> Wherever we may look, the situating of the principle of ground becomes obscure with its very first steps. And that is how it should be. For we should like to elucidate the principle of ground. What is lucid and light needs the obscure and shadowy . . . (*GA* 10: 13/9)

Should not the principle of reason, Heidegger asks, be equally a principle of light? If so, whence the obscurity that attends the question of the ground? In the second lecture, Heidegger wants to show that what casts a shadow over this principle of light is in a way its self-evidence, its imperviousness to question. In insisting on its own validity—"nothing is without ground/reason"—the *Satz vom Grund* is nonetheless unable to supply its own ground, its own foundation: "what is the ground for the principle of ground?" asks Heidegger (*GA* 10: 17/11). The difficulties we fall into in addressing this question, he surmises, are twofold: on the one hand, we might say that the principle of ground has no ground. If we say this, though, we are placing the principle *outside* of its own jurisdiction. Alternatively, we might supply a ground for the principle, but in doing so will open ourselves to the threat of infinite regress. The investigation into the principle of ground, then, far from an experience of self-evident clarity, has become fraught with danger (*Gefahr*), threatening at every moment to expose itself to a kind of dissolution; to "run aground" (*zugrunde gehen*).

It is at this moment that Heidegger calls upon Novalis, "the poet who was also a great thinker." What Novalis is called upon to supply is a kind of reinforcement: not, evidently, the securing of a self-evident clarity, but rather the opposite. Addressing once more the "commonplace but dubious opinion" that a principle must needs be "patently stabilizing for thinking," Heidegger suggests that Novalis "knew otherwise." This authority, then, is summoned forth at a critical juncture precisely to articulate a radical instability, to give voice to the "danger" into which the investigation has plunged. In giving voice to this peril, it will be Novalis who shows the way forward: he is to show how this fundamental instability might be embraced rather than shunned. Heidegger cites, therefore, a fragment of Novalis from the series known as the "Logological Fragments":

> Should the highest principle not contain in its task the highest paradox? To be a proposition that would allow no peace—that always attracts and repels—that would always become incomprehensible anew, as soon as one understood it? That ceaselessly stirred our activity—without ever exhausting it or ever becoming familiar? (*GA* 10: 20/13; *W* II: 314)

It is important to mark precisely what it is that draws Heidegger's attention here, and what allows him to utilize Novalis to push forward his own investigation into the radical destabilization of the principle of reason. We note, then, that the central operation of the "highest principle" that Novalis envisages is precisely a double movement of drawing-together-pulling-apart that we have claimed already as the guiding thought of this book: rather than resting in the security of ground, the highest principle would be one that engages an indefinite restlessness and instability. What is envisaged is something we could call a "principle of distress," one that would at once "always attract and repel," and that would hover on the border of comprehension, slipping tirelessly across that border the moment it appeared graspable: situated at the very edge of the *logos*, always both within and without, ekeing out a half-life at its limits. This is the space of the "between" that we have set out to map. It is also the node of contact between Novalis and Heidegger.

Heidegger closes the lecture series *Der Satz vom Grund* with the following:

> The question remains, whether we, hearing the movements [*Sätze*] of this play, play along and conjoin ourselves to the play [*mitspielen und uns in das Spiel fügen*]. (*GA* 10: 169/113)

Earlier in the series, Heidegger had repeatedly emphasized and explored the polysemy of the word *Satz*, a polysemy that thereby takes on the aspect of a point of access to this same play. He writes:

> If we fully think through the polysemic word *Satz* not only as "statement," not only as "utterance," not only as "leap" but at the same time also in the musical sense of "movement," then we gain for the first time the complete connection to the principle of ground. (*GA* 10: 132/89)

It is Novalis who first opens up this field of play in Heidegger's text. And it is no less true that the destabilization intimated by Novalis at the heart of his "highest principle" works itself out through the lecture series in terms of a continuous dispersion of the senses of the word *Satz* across a broader and broader semantic field. If, then, the impulse for this dispersive endeavor is provided by Novalis, it should not be surprising that, when Heidegger again turns in his direction, some eighteen months later in the summer of 1957, it is within the aspect of questions of ground, but also of questions of language, that he will make another appearance.

The Freiburg lecture course of that summer, entitled *The Basic Principles of Thinking*, is strongly linked thematically with the 1955–56 lectures on *Der Satz vom Grund*. It is also the locus of the most persistent presence of Novalis in Heidegger's work. In addition to two important quotations—of the entirety of the "Monologue," and of a late fragment closely connected with the citation in the 1956 lectures—Heidegger on two occasions mentions Novalis alongside Hölderlin as figures who give "poetical" voice to the philosophical thought of their environs (*GA* 79: 82/78 and 140/132). In addition, we find an unattributed quotation from a late poem written for a projected continuation of the novel *Heinrich von Ofterdingen* (*GA* 79: 157/148);[3] and it seems also quite possible that the brief discussion of the *Märchen*, or fairy tale, in the fifth lecture of the series is occasioned by a reading of Novalis, for whom the form had a particular significance.

Given the persistence of this presence, then, it is noteworthy that this lecture series, and these quotations, also begin to mark out the territory of a resistance to Novalis, a divergence—even a miscommunication. The nature of this resistance has to do with Heidegger's insistence on bringing Novalis into close proximity with Hegel. This approach occurs right at the outset, when Heidegger (somewhat strangely) draws both Novalis and Hölderlin into the frame of Hegel's thought, claiming that their "poetic mindfulness [*Besinnung*] . . . likewise moves about within the precincts [*Bezirk*] of dialectic" (*GA* 79: 82/78). The sense of this "precinct" is somewhat ambiguous, particularly as Heidegger will elsewhere strenuously resist the idea that Hölderlin's thinking is in any way caught up in the dynamics of Hegel's thinking; but the push toward a conflation becomes more explicit toward the close of the lecture, where Heidegger cites Novalis once again. The first lecture of the series has focused on the *Satz des Widerspruchs*, or "principle of non-contradiction," and has oriented itself toward Hegel who, Heidegger says, has brought forward the question of contradiction into a central position: "contradiction tears [*reißt*] life and death asunder, it is the tearing [*Zerissenheit*] of the two" (*GA* 79: 87/82). It is at this juncture, then, that he summons Novalis once again, citing the following late fragment:

> The annihilation [*vernichten*] of the principle of non-contradiction is perhaps the highest task of higher logic. (*GA* 79: 88/93)

Heidegger, however, claims that, despite appearances to the contrary, Novalis here says "*exactly the same* as that which Hegel thinks" (*GA* 79 88/83, emphasis added). Now, the difficulty with this direct assimilation of Novalis's to Hegel's thinking will rest upon an understanding of the *vernichten*, or annihilation that Novalis introduces. This fragment will be addressed later on, and when we do so it will be in order precisely to wrest Novalis's thought away from this appropriation to the structure of the dialectic, an appropriation which suggests that what is at stake in Novalis's *vernichten* is something like the reabsorption of contradiction. Instead of this Hegelian appropriation, then, this fragment is to be understood in accord with the fragment that Heidegger had quoted in the lecture series of 1955–56 on *Der Satz vom Grund.* We have seen that what drew Heidegger's attention toward Novalis's account of a "highest principle" was the way in which it appeared to suggest a radical motility of ground. Here, too, in a similar way, the "annihilation of the principle of non-contradiction" must be understood as being directed not at all toward a reconciliation, a cancellation or an elevation, but rather toward the embrace of an instability, the insistence of a between.

Close to the end of the final lecture of the series, Heidegger returns once more to Novalis; the question now has turned toward language, and Heidegger, voicing, as we have seen, a sympathy with this strange "flashing up," quotes the entirety of the "Monologue." Having done so, and measuring both the proximity and the distance of Novalis's words, he then continues:

> Much remains dark and confusing in this monologue of λόγος, especially as he thinks in another direction and speaks in another language than the one attempted in these lectures. (*GA* 79: 174/164)

To some extent, it will be to this difference, and to this strangeness, that the first part of this book is dedicated; to the endeavor, in other words, of finding in Novalis's writing something entirely other, something indeed "dark and strange." Heidegger well understands, here, the tangential and difficult relation he must sustain with this thinking: approaching and coming into contact, but always with the sense of an elusive remainder, a trace of something fugitive, something not quite to be assimilated. By the time, though, that Heidegger returns to Novalis's "Monologue" in the final text from *Unterwegs zur Sprache* (*GA* 12: 254/134), it is to this assimilation that he commits himself. Here now, having opened his lecture with the first words of the "Monologue," Heidegger will explore the text in ways that are quite consonant with Novalis's text; until, that is, the close of the lecture, where Heidegger arrives at the notion of language as *Aufriß*, as an upsurge eventuated by a tearing-apart, an irruption. Now he is decisive:

> The monological character of the being of language has its ordinance in the *Aufriß* of language, with which Novalis's thinking does not and cannot coincide. This is because Novalis understands language from within the field of vision of absolute idealism—that is, dialectically, from out of subjectivity. (*GA* 12: 254/134)

Again, it will be the aim of the first part of this book to contest this assimilation as firmly as possible, and to offer for Novalis's thought a space governed by an entirely different field of vision than the one Heidegger wishes to choose for him; a field, moreover, from within which Heidegger's own thinking can be readdressed. On the way toward that space, Novalis's experience with language will be explored, and it will turn out that, after all, this experience is not as far from Heidegger's *Aufriß* as the latter appears to think.

Harmonia: Heraclitus and the Between

> Here, between agitation and motionlessness, everything becomes more complicated.
>
> —Nicole Loraux

The threads that run between Heidegger and Novalis are, in historical terms, tentative, fraught with hesitation and ambivalence. In this regard, we can see in the relation between the two an echo of the figure of thought that will dominate the conceptual framework of the study that follows. There is a kind of convergence between them—a gathering, a hesitant approach—and also a radical separation, a gulf: of history, of sensibility, of intention. It is this sense of a convergent separation that allows for a thinking of their relation, of what might transpire in the dialogue between. And as it turns out, this figure of tensional, oppositional gathering is not merely the occasion for an exchange between the two, but can *in itself* be understood to undergird both of their endeavors. An agonistic figure of separative gathering, in which a "between" can emerge that is neither mediating connective nor a palliative of primal difference: this is the figure of which we are in pursuit, and which the work of Novalis and Heidegger can in different ways enable us to expose. It is in this sense that we can understand both Novalis and Heidegger's thinking as emerging from a common source; and this source is a strange thinking of harmony, or *harmonia,* that emerges first in the fragments of Heraclitus. It is a thought of harmony as a tensional dynamic of original dissonance, a thought that seems to emerge in the history of philosophy only with difficulty and on occasion. It is equally to this occasional and difficult emergence that this book is devoted: both Heidegger's and Novalis's work is, in different ways, to be understood as a manifestation of this undercurrent. And it is in the light of this Heraclitean thinking of originary dissonance that their thinking can be brought together. And thus it will be necessary, at least briefly, to outline this thought of Heraclitean *harmonia,* and to note some of the difficulties that its long history has encountered.

We can present the figure of this strange original dissonance as Plato does when, in the *Symposium,* it appears under a (necessarily) negative light. It is, then, the doctor (Erixymachus) who introduces us to the figure of Heraclitus, and does so in the following terms: "About the One, he says that 'in variance from itself it agrees with itself, like the harmony of bow and lyre'" (187a). The good doctor is dismissive, thereby initiating a gesture that will be reenacted repeatedly in the history of philosophy. Such an idea, he claims, is preposterous: it is impossible for something to be at once at variance and in agreement. To say such a thing, he says, is an *alogia,* an absurdity: it is entirely without reason, it lacks *logos.* Evidently, says Erixymachus, what Heraclitus must have meant is that what is *first* at variance, *then* comes into an agreement, just as "rhythms are produced by fast and slow, which first were at variance, and later came to agree" (187c).

First one, and then the other: the deflection of this central Heraclitean figure into a sequentiality, into a mode in which it can be subsumed beneath principles of change and alteration, reappears—strikingly—in Aristotle. On two occasions, in the course of formulating what will become known as "the principle of non-contradiction," he calls Heraclitus to the tribunal, only in order to dismiss him summarily. The second of these occasions, in *Metaphysics Kappa*, involves the insistence "that it is impossible for the same thing *at one and the same time* to be and not to be, and for the other things that are opposite each other in that way to belong to it" (1062a). In asserting a thought which appears to run counter to this principle, "about which there is no demonstration," Heraclitus—says Aristotle—was clearly not listening to his own words: "he took hold of this opinion without understanding what his own words meant" (1062a 35). In a beautiful recent study of Heraclitus,[4] Eva Brann suggests that indeed this is precisely the case: was it not Heraclitus, after all, who enjoins us to listen "not to me, but to the *logos*" (*DK* 50)? The question before us, then, will be the following: what kind of listening does Heraclitus's thinking of harmony require? What kind of *logos* will be heard in this listening?

This deflection of opposition into sequence will enforce as its primary gesture the dominance of a linear temporality. First one; and *then* the other: and indeed, is this not also the model for a sequential unfolding of propositions, of "argument"? Thought in this way, the figure of Heraclitus that emerges in the pages of the *Symposium* is indeed *alogon*, and is so in a precise sense. This might give us occasion to wonder, then: what is it that is being resisted in the subsumption of this oppositional tension to a model of linear change? What is refused, it seems, in this insistence on a linear unfolding, is the possibility of the *simultaneous* emergence of difference. This is because such a spontaneous emergence would evoke the specter of its irreducibility, the danger that opposition might not be gathered into a unity, the risk that the stable presence might appear as riven, in an always anterior way, with a kind of instability. What threatens to emerge from this thought is the figure of difference as a constitutive dynamism: the dynamism of a tension that is neither quite in motion, nor at rest; no longer "on its way," but also never-yet arriving.

In the *Symposium*, though, Erixymachus takes a step toward the dismissal of these possibilities that is still more decisive. Expressing his distaste for the Heraclitean thinking he himself has invoked, Erixymachus explains that such a thinking is impossible because "harmony [*harmonia*] is *concord* [*symphonia*]; and concord is agreement [*homologia*]." Heraclitus's difficult *harmonia* of opposition, then—the figure of the One at variance with itself, internally riven and restlessly differentiated—is to be reconceived as *symphonia*, as concordance: it is only thus, on condition of this move, that this *harmonia* can properly enter into the *logos*. The stakes of this apparently innocuous and, for us, generally self-evident explication of harmony in terms of concordance are very high: much will rest on this. This is because what is intimated here is that harmony must necessarily involve the absorption of difference; not perhaps its collapse, but at the very least its joining-together in agreement: harmony will no longer articulate the dissonance of an opposition, but will insist on gathering that opposition into reconciliation, into a higher and more completely unified One.

There is, for the most part, a consensus that Erixymachus's version of Heraclitus's utterance involves a conflation of two separate fragments.[5] First of all, then, we have fragment 51, which contains the idea of the harmony of bow and lyre, a tensile harmony of difference. The second fragment (*DK* 10), though, contains a startling formulation, one that condenses in a very deliberate way the oppositional gathering that is at stake in this Heraclitean *harmonia*. The formulation is "*sympheromenon—diapheromenon*." The two Greek words are juxtaposed without reserve, without interruptive qualification: we can translate the phrase as something like a "drawing-together-tearing-apart." What is at stake in this formulation has to do with the nature of the gathering in which these opposites confront one another. The attempt is being made to think a kind of conjoining of opposites which resists in some manner the dominance of the first term, the drawing-together (*sympheromenon*), insisting instead on the full equivalence of the tearing-apart (*diapheromenon*); a conjoining, in other words, which refuses the slippage of harmony into concordance—*harmonia* into *symphonia*—and instead retains the integrity of opposition. How would one characterize the tensile figure of this drawing-together-tearing-apart? Eva Brann writes that Heraclitus's thinking expresses a "tautly vital, twangingly alive, strainingly static cosmos."[6] And indeed, a vision forged from this tension would have to embrace the difficult and fugitive thought of movement in stasis,[7] and the attendant unsettlement that follows in its wake.

But how is it possible to address oneself to a thought that, by its very nature—as Erixymachus well understood—is utterly resistant to the *logos*? What will need to be pursued in order to effect this address, and to expose the operation of Heraclitean *harmonia* in its, as it were, un-reformed state, are the edges of that resistance, the moments of its flashing-up (its *Aufblitzen*, to use Heidegger's term once more). If the *harmonia* of opposites will always tend to be drawn toward a *symphonia*, toward the reabsorption of difference, then an address to the Heraclitean insight can only occupy the edges and limits of thought, those that precede or exceed that reappropriation. What is required to explore this terrain is a language that anchors itself, paradoxically, in the fugitive, the transitional; and the opening onto such a possibility presents itself in the midst of fragment 10, precisely in the phrase we have already cited: *sympheromenon–diapheromenon*. This is because what this figure, in its gathering of opposites, allows us to think is the *between*, the space in which the two polarities conjoin and transact. *This* is the fugitive between-space of which we will be in pursuit: and the hope is that, if the thought of this between is always to be under pressure, and will always for that reason be elusive, it may nonetheless be possible to uncover fragile and intermittent means through which it might be accessed.

The aim of this book, ultimately, resides in an attempt to expose occasions in the subsequent history of philosophy in which this tentative thought of the "between" has been able to reemerge; and to grasp and articulate that exposure. Novalis and Heidegger will be addressed, then, not just because of the odd and tentative approach that the latter makes toward the former, but because their work can be understood as very different manifestations of a possibility of thought that is first made accessible in the *harmonia* that Heraclitus's fragments expose, and whose operation we have outlined. Just as in the figure itself, then, between the two very different historical moments in which Novalis's and Heidegger's thinking appear, it will equally be a question of convergence and divergence: no simple identity or repetition, no imitation or replication, but rather a more subtle play of echo and reconfiguration. If, then, in respect of their convergence, it will be on the ground of a recovery of this Heraclitean harmony that they will meet, their divergence will be equally pronounced. This divergence expresses itself not merely with regard to the conceptual framework within which their thinking of a "between" transpires, but equally in the affective possibilities that attach to this same between: for Novalis, the "between" is a fertile, fecund space, the possibility of emergence, proliferation. By contrast, this same "between," for Heidegger, is agonistic, a space of pain. In respect of this divergence, then, the book is divided into two parts. The first will address Novalis, and stress the way in which the tensional figure of a between emerges as the agent of proliferative increase, of fertility. The second will address Heidegger, and the way in which the same figure is inflected instead in ways that emphasize absence, pain, and loss.

Part 1

Novalis: The Fertility of the Between

> "It is considered unwise to whisper one's secrets to the wind," I said. She looked at me after long reflection and asked somberly, "Are you the wind?"
> "Part of it," I said.
> —Halldór Laxness

1

Fecundity, Proliferation, and Exchange

Seed: The Drift toward Metaphor

The very first figure in which we can trace the outlines of a *harmonia* of tensional difference is one which courses through Novalis's work from the moment that his writing begins to engage with the natural world: "All is seed," he tells us (*W* II: 352). Decisive in tone, yet strange, and concise to the point of hermeticism, the claim nonetheless does contain, like the seed itself, a precious pointer of future possibilities. This is because the figure of the seed will turn out to be possessed of a double set of tensions, which play in and around one another in insistent fashion. The first of these has to do with the dynamics of seeding, with its attendant images of gathering and dispersal, and with the seed itself, its metamorphoses and transformations. The second has to do with the linguistic register in which the figure of seed is maintained: a register at once literal, descriptive—in which sense seed and seeding are observed and engaged as events in a natural landscape—and at the same time metonymic and metaphorical, a disposition in which "seed" comes to elaborate structures of meaning that leave explicit natural observation behind. It must be observed, too, that it is not by accident that seed becomes, here, a starting-point: even the adopted name "Novalis" opens on to such a possibility, Novalis being the Latinate version of a medieval name of the Hardenberg family that has connotations both of the cultivation of fields, and of striking out into new territory.[1]

What Novalis is engaging, when he claims "all is seed," is first and foremost the sense of proliferation that seed implies: a capacity to explode and to flourish into something entirely other. In this sense, and in relation to the germinating seed, Goethe writes that "its coverings . . . are left more or less behind in the earth, and in many cases the root establishes itself in the soil before the first organs of its upper growth . . . emerge to meet the light."[2] The seed thus abandons its first "coverings" and begins to emerge, splitting apart to sink its roots into the ground as it opens onto the visible appearing of the plant: to claim that "all is seed" is to think not merely about scattering and dispersion, but also about emergence and splitting open. However, Goethe also goes on to say that "the phenomena of convergence, centering and anastomosis[3] are not peculiar to the flower and fruit alone."[4] Thus, he claims, convergence, gathering-together, and the forging of connections belong as intimately to the processes of the plant as do the phenomena of dispersion and splitting open. If seed and seeding are indeed to be considered a central image in Novalis's work, this is because the image of the seed revolves around a dynamic tension of splitting-apart, dispersing, scattering, and convergence, gathering. And it is in terms of this central dynamism that the figure of a "between" will appear.

The first image of a "between," then, which comes to us from Novalis is one that is deeply rooted in the natural world. The image of the seed, though, operates not just as an invocation of natural process but also as a metaphor. Thus, on the one hand, Novalis's fascination with the matter and the fertile processes of the natural world is insistent and actual. On the other hand, though, that same thinking can be understood as a series of reflections upon metaphoric structures of meaning that belong inherently to language. It is this that allows the word "seed" to operate as both more and less than a descriptor of a natural object. Natural referent and metaphorical elaboration will be seen to play around one another in his work, opening up a peculiar terrain of exchange and intertwinement: a "between" space.

It is the adoption of the nom de plume Novalis, with its connotations of seeding that lends a particular resonance to the title of the first collection of fragments published by the Schlegel brothers in the *Athenaeum* journal, which marked the first occasion of the appearance of the name "Novalis." The collection is called *Blüthenstaub*, or *Pollen*, and carries the motto: "Friends, the soil is poor, we must scatter abundant seed, so that even a frugal harvest flourishes for us" (*W*II: 227). The thinking of seed, then, moves in and around Novalis's work, and centrally: splitting, scattering, germination, and pollination are among its central operations, as are processes of gathering and convergence. A reading of the texts gathered under the name "Novalis" will thus be best undertaken with an ear that is open to their fecundity, which attends to their proliferation; an ear, above all, that listens for the effects of dispersal, scattering, growth, and connectivity that emerge there. We can also say that a reading which attempts to stay with the thought of seed and seeding is one that will address the flower, the plant, or the tree, but that will do so without losing sight of its processes of emergence and splitting apart, the severance that attends its flourishing.

The first temptation that emerges from this approach, though, presents itself immediately in the form of a question that appears spontaneously enough: "What exactly," we want to ask, "does Novalis really *mean* by 'seed'"? The most immediate answer to this question would probably be that "seed" in some way metaphorizes "idea" or "thought": the association is commonplace. If we first make this assumption, then we will shortly, too, find ourselves asking about the broader conceptual frame in which this metaphor has a place. Presuming we are able to describe this frame, we are likely then to want to know what it is that is intended to proliferate from the scattering of the "seeds." What is the mechanism of the scattering? How is the "seeding" effected? And, most especially, one wants to know what is meant by the "ground" upon which the seeds are to be scattered? These questions appear obvious: "seed," we assume, is being used as a kind of "poetization," clearly metaphoric in operation. But it is precisely the reduction implied in such a "clarity" that poses the danger here, implying as it does that these terms are operating solely at the level of metaphor. This would mean that the vocabulary of "seed" is being used to stand in for, or in some manner instantiate other, deeper concerns. Even the mere fact that we are reading the words "seed," "seeding," and "ground" enclosed by inverted commas can serve as an alert that we have trivialized and reduced their field of operation to one of simple substitution: for these mechanisms of reading, metaphorical substitutes are to be seen through by an interpretation which is to aim at the exposure of the conceptual apparatus underpinning and validating their deployment.

What if, though, it is this very insistence that terms such as seed and ground are to be reduced to metaphor, which a reading that is attentive to processes of proliferation needs to refuse? What if it was necessary instead, rather than taking this drift toward metaphor for granted, to question the movement in which the term "seed" becomes merely emblematic, the processes in which "seed" comes to stand in for something like "thought" or "idea"? What would be necessary, under such conditions, would be an attentive observation of the transmutation, the shifting of meanings across a semantic field. It would be a kind of observation that would not content itself with the assumption that when the link has been observed, and the word "seed" has mutated to mean "thought/idea," its "core" significance will thereby have been accessed. It would mean instead that this reading must be alert to a different kind of equivalence altogether between "seed" and "idea," or between the "soil" and "ground." The mutations and drifts of meaning would, then, no longer be measured in terms of a hierarchical depth, for which conceptual meanings underpin their poetic elaboration, but in terms of new forms of convergence and looser kinds of analogical connectivity. The movements of meaning will be lateral and tangential rather than hierarchical and reductive; and it will be this kind of movement that will prove key to an understanding of the mechanisms of Novalis's thinking.

The Elasticity of the Soul

It is possible that it is the operations of these lateral and tangential movements of meaning that Novalis has in mind when he follows the first of his *Blüthenstaub* fragments thus:

> Signifying through tones and marks is an abstraction worthy of wonder. Three letters signify *God* to me; a few marks a million things. How easy it is to manipulate the universe, how graphic the concentricity of the spiritual world. Grammar is the dynamic of the spiritual world. One word of command moves armies; the word "freedom"—nations. (*W* II: 227/*PW* 23)

What this fragment calls for is an attention to the movement of what Novalis himself refers to as "abstraction": those movements by which the "tones and marks" of words transmute. This does not mean an attention to language per se, but rather an alertness to the processes of movement that are manifest within it; a reflexive attentiveness which never allows that movement to remain unnoticed or unremarked.

To begin with, then, we can observe that in Novalis's writing certain terms and ideas thread consistently through the texts, weaving in and out in ways that do not so much offer keys to a definitive decipherment as they do a particular kind of continuity. "Seed" is certainly among these, but in addition we would have to list the terms "cohesion," "dissolution," "elasticity," "fluidity," and "crystallization." It is of immediate importance to note that these figures operate quite precisely as descriptors of physical and chemical processes. And this is unsurprising: after all, Novalis's involvement with the science of his day is well-documented, and both his studies at the Mining Academy in Freiberg and his extensive explorations in the fields of physics and chemistry are evidently crucial to his development. Indeed, they form the basis of much of the work of the "Encyclopaedia" project and its surrounding notebooks, to be explored in chapter 3.

Reading the notebooks, however, it is evident that these terms are moving in directions that alter and distort their application to natural scientific processes. What seems to take place is an operation in which the term in question is subjected to a kind of pull, to the pressure of a kind of deviance that renders its status uncertain. "Elasticity," to take one example, operates, under this pressure, as a description of material flexion with a precise home in the sensible domain: elasticity, thus, is indeed treated as a sensible quality. In the same gesture, though, and simultaneously, the term becomes the index of a thought that reaches out into entirely other, speculative dimensions. Of course, in one sense, this mode of abstraction is familiar: to speak of an elasticity, or of a cohesion or a fluidity beyond material referents—the fluidity or cohesiveness of thought, for example—is far from unusual. But what lends the operation of Novalis's thinking its unique quality is the strange freedom with which he moves within the passage between material and speculative dimensions. This means that, on the one hand, insisting in the corporeal, Novalis is able to lend his speculative ideations a peculiar and discomfiting literalness. On the other hand, and at the same time, physical description performs and plays in a domain that transforms its materiality into something far more speculative than its material referent might seem to warrant. This is where the pull is felt to retreat from speculative density under the cover of the "metaphoric," from behind which it might be ascertained which are the "real" senses and uses of these terms and which are simply metaphoric substitutions. In other words, one might want to take comfort in the thought that what is going on is a kind of "poetization" of the material. The text, however, refuses to allow the comfort of such a refuge—preferring to allow terms like "elasticicity" to hover in an uncertain in-between space in relation to both their material referents and their speculative elaborations. At stake, then, is not a "poetization," or simply an "imaginative elaboration" of the given, but rather an osmotic and uncertain process of exchange, in which the sensible is exposed to operations of a speculative elaboration to the same extent that this latter reengages the sensible by being rendered literal.

If we continue to take the complex sense of "elasticity" as an example, we must emphasize once again that elasticity belongs within an array of terms that indeed connote a concrete materiality. This array of terms is one that is often, in Novalis's thinking, related to forms of tactility, occupying consequently a position on a spectrum between pure liquidity and impenetrable solidity: they are words of fluidity and viscosity, but equally of rigidity or crystalline density. However, we can also observe that this array of terms is simultaneously allowed to wander from the domain of the determination of sensible experience into a domain that would ordinarily be described as figurative, as metaphorical transposition: it is in this sense, for example, we notice that a late fragment calls, not unambiguously, for both an "elasticity of thought" and a "thinking of elasticity" (*elastisch zu denken*). An "elasticity of thought" might be powerfully descriptive of the kind of thinking that is necessary to a reading of Novalis: the endeavor we have already summarily described indeed involves such a flexibility—a stretching beyond expected parameters. For such a thought, "elasticity" seems an adequate descriptive term. But at the same time, the term operates equally within a field of pure tactile observation: "elasticity" refers, in Novalis's work, just as often to empirically observable phenomena as it does to metaphorical speculation. What is remarkable, then, is the shifting and interweaving of registers such that a movement of exchange takes place, one in which the relations between concrete determination and ideational figuration seems to dissolve. In the "Encyclopaedia" notebooks, for example, we find the following note, which begins:

> Application of the concepts of *elasticity*, brittleness—softness—hardening etc. to the body, and the explication of their appearances. (*W*II: 642)

Now this note, part of a larger fragment, certainly seems to function rhetorically as a suggestion for a project of scientific observation:[5] in that sense, "elasticity" and "brittleness" operate here purely as potential descriptors of observable sense data, such as might belong to a medical notebook. However, the fragment continues:

> The soul = a *spring* [*Feder*] = maximum effect of a spring—exaggeration—understatement [*übertrieben—untertrieben*].

What is striking here is the way in which the observation of sensible properties is immediately transferred to a conception of the soul, which—it is suggested—shares somehow in the elasticity of bodies. What we find, then, is a curious and porous exchange—an osmosis, a reciprocity in which terms shift resonance in such a way as to dissolve the borders that would like to demarcate the domains of both. Concrete particular and speculative ideation have, in this writing, a unique intercourse and play which will work not just toward the dissolution of conceptual boundaries but, as we shall see, toward an exploding of the integrity of the text itself.

In making use of the terms "dissolution" and "explosion" as a way of addressing the processes of Novalis's thinking, it is clear that we are thinking in relation to modes of chemical process. To speak of words as "dissolving" or "exploding" is to address them as if they were somehow enigmatically subject to the instability that besets certain kinds of physical matter under condition of interaction. This is to say, then, that what we are dealing with, in considering Novalis's work, is a kind of chemistry of words. In reading Novalis, we are obliged to consider not merely an engagement with chemical processes themselves, but also the way in which those processes are enacted at the level of the writing itself, in the operations of the text. And thus it is that language becomes the object of inquiry—not in the sense of a discrete domain open to its own description and analysis, but precisely because it is in the elasticity of words themselves that the process of exchange and infusion between material and ideational is enabled. What will be at stake in Novalis's writing is an entirely other relation between word and sensible experience, one neither allowed in the classical formulations of meaning and expression, nor one that is readily available to many of the revisions and interrogations of the classical model which the history of philosophy has made possible. It is in this spirit that Novalis will write, in *Die Lehrlinge von Saïs*, of

> new kinds of perceptions, which seem nothing else than the delicate movements of a colorful or noisy pencil, the wondrous drawing-together and figurations of an elastic liquidity. (*WI*: 220/*NS* 74–75)

These, then, are some of the ways in which Novalis's writing brings into play a kind of conceptual fecundity that treats of the physical world as a domain in which the imagination travels freely and without hindrance. This means that when Novalis writes, in one of the late fragments, that "physics is nothing but the doctrine of fantasy," he is not indicating just the arbitrary application of imaginative flourishes to a given empirical domain, but rather the porosity of an open passageway, the mutual and reciprocal processes of exchange with which his writing is always involved. The operations of the imagination, of poetic sensibility, are never absent, or in any way inhibited in this exchange. On the contrary, they are quite explicitly evident in every gesture of Novalis's writing. What will have occurred, instead, is a kind of saturation of the imagination, such that the borders that delimit its domain begin to be effaced. In this new space, the classical lines of demarcation that surround the notion of the poetic will have to be reconfigured—and with this reconfiguration, the domains it helps to define will also suffer transformation.

Intertwinement: The Poetry of Matter

The operations of "seed" and of "elasticity" in Novalis's work can be said to be paradigmatic of the way in which the boundaries that separate orders of discourse enter in his thinking into a free osmotic exchange: the materiality of the things of the earth enters into a free play of intertwinement with abstract speculative ideation. In this exchange it is no longer possible to talk of the "poetic" over against the material: instead, it seems as if the borderlines have become opaque, fuzzy. The lines that would separate out the domain of concrete description and allow for speculative elaboration to be labeled "metaphorical" are being elided. Instead, what is exposed is a movement of exchange, the free flow of a passage between.

The question thus arises: what is it that enables this intertwinement, this collapsing of boundaries? What is it that permits Novalis's thought to flow so freely between speculative ideation and material observation? In order to address these questions, we need to explore the generative philosophical core of his thinking—a thinking in which the borderlines and relations between what he will refer to as the domains of "real" and "ideal" will be relentlessly interrogated. In this interrogation, what will appear as "poetry" is the negotiation of the between-space of these domains: poetry will be the mechanism that opens the communicative passageway between abstract speculation and concrete sensible.

To that extent, what is at stake is the question of another between—that of philosophy and poetry. No longer the polar opposite of philosophy, poetry can also no longer be seen as the subordinate to philosophical speculation in the archaic Platonizing sense. However, it must be equally clear that what is to be effected is not a simple reversal, a reordering of hierarchies that would simply favor the "poetic" over against a notion of philosophical rigor: to reverse a hierarchy is to keep its coordinates intact. What we are in pursuit of, rather, is a kind of mechanics of displacement—a mode of thinking in which the ordering of "real" and "ideal" is subject to a sustained interrogation.

In this interrogation, both will be altered and transformed, "as if an alkahest has been poured over the senses of man," as a late work of Novalis's puts it (*W* I: 201/*NS* 3). In this alchemical transmutation, what will be at stake is the language that negotiates the passage between concept and the sensible particular. And in the arena of this between, the lines and border-crossings that would want to delineate different arenas of thinking will become obscure, untraceable. In particular, then, the line between philosophical and poetic language will be complicated to the extent that neither can continue to occupy its terrain in an unquestioned manner. If Novalis will continue to refer to the categories of philosophy and poetry in his later writing, it will be only as subject to an incessant program of redefinition and reconfiguration. When he writes, for example, that "philosophy is the poem of the understanding" (*W* II: 321), this thought emerges from an investigation in which the parameters and possibilities of both philosophy and poetry have been entirely reorganized.

What is to be considered now is the working of this "between" of the poetic in respect of one particular and paradigmatic image. The aim here will be to find a way back to the philosophical genesis of Novalis's processes of thinking, and address the philosophical milieu in which it arises. However, it is important to insist that, in pursuing the philosophical grounds of Novalis's thinking, we are not in any way aiming at a covert restoration of the precedence of philosophical thought. When Novalis, in the image of which we will shortly treat, writes that "like us, the stars hover alternatingly between illumination and darkening" (*W* II: 408), we will certainly have to see this as something other than a merely colorful elaboration, a "poetic ornamentation" of a more weighty philosophical thought. The point, however, is that if this alternate terrain or between-space is to be mapped onto a ground of a philosophical abstraction, it will still always be necessary to consider this newly formed geography in relation to that ground, even as it is being forsaken.

The passageway back to these philosophical origins can be opened by considering what is at stake in the fragment just cited, the German of which runs "*wie wir, schweben die Sterne in abwechselnder Erleuchtung und Verdunklung*." In respect of this image, there are several observations that can be made right away. The first and most obvious is that the fragment evidently desires to set up some sort of equivalence between we ourselves and the stars: *wie wir . . . die Sterne*. The second observation is that this equivalence, however it is to be understood, is described as a kind of "*Schweben*," or hovering. Now, the use of this word is very far from incidental: *Schweben* has a very particular history, as we shall see—one crucially bound up with the philosophical thinking of the imagination. Its use here evokes that thinking, evokes the expansion of the role of the imaginative. The third observation to make is that this hovering (*Schweben*), in which both we and the stars are immersed, appears to be in some sense a matter of "exchange," of reciprocity—again, the word *abwechselnder* and other cognates of *Wechsel* (change, variation, alternation, exchange) will figure decisively in the philosophical explorations that provided the soil whose seeding issues in the landscape of Novalis's writing. Fourth, and finally, this hovering seems to involve a kind of reciprocity of opposites, a mutual involvement of light and dark, such that both we and the appearing of the night sky can be thought of as a gathering together of appearance and occlusion, of the visible and the invisible, of light and dark.[6]

Considering further this fragment, and moving, now, further in the direction of a historical and philosophical genesis, we can focus on the mutual involvement of our own selves and the night sky, on the reciprocity that the fragment brings into play. Time and time again, Novalis will orient his writing toward the moment of exchange, toward the moment in which thought, addressing the phenomena of the natural world, appears itself to be addressed by them. This, in Novalis, is the complex osmotic intertwinement of what he calls "inner" and "outer," terms that lose much of their classical valence in their intertwining. What will come to interest Novalis most, then, is neither the inner nor the outer, but rather the point of contact, *Berührung*: the between, the touch of that otherness which marks the point of exchange.

It is this same domain of contact and exchange that is engaged in the following, though now removed to a more theoretical register:

> Thus earthly life springs from an originary reflexion, a primitive ingoing, a gathering into the I. Conversely, spiritual life in this world springs from breaking through [*durchbrechen*] that primitive reflexion. Spirit unfolds once more, spirit goes out to itself again, again to some degree raises up [*aufhebt*] that reflexion, and in that moment says for the first time—I. One sees here how relative is the outgoing and the ingoing. (*W* II: 245)

What will engage Novalis, then, is not the plenitude of sensible experience, the complexities of its description or iteration, but a process of transformation, the alchemical mutation that what he terms "real" and "ideal" perform upon one another; and the point at which they meet, the shifting nexus of their intertwinement, this particular movement of the between, is the locus at which his strange and fragmentary writing will unfold. If, on the one hand, for Novalis "language is never too poor but always too general" (*W* II: 322/*AB* 54), it is nonetheless also true that he will find in this generality the space for a kind of wandering, an itinerance that negotiates its way between the registers of concrete and abstract.

It is clear that, in describing the workings of the "star" fragment, we have moved already from the concrete sensible toward a form of abstraction, from the specificity of the stars to the thought of the "outer world" in general. Maintaining this general direction of thought, then, we can say that, in Novalis's thinking, movements belonging both to an internality and an externality are manifest in many registers. It seems, though, that the reciprocity of the movements, their intertwinement and mutuality, has meant that they have become relative to one another: the very sense of inside and outside is challenged in their contact. This is why Novalis will tend to surrender up the vocabulary of inner and outer in favor of a dynamic of forces, writing, for instance, in the "Logological Fragments" that

> centripetal force is the synthetic striving of the spirit—centrifugal force is the analytic striving of the spirit. Striving toward unity—striving toward diversity [*streben nach Einheit—streben nach Manichfaltigkeit*]. (*W* II: 378/*AB* 79)[7]

The vocabulary of this fragment points more clearly now in the direction of a genesis because, however strangely invested, the term *streben* inherits a thinking that is associated with Fichte, in particular the Fichte of the 1794 *Wissenschaftslehre,* based on the lectures by which Novalis, along with an entire generation, was entranced during his period of philosophical study in Jena. This dynamic movement of exchange, the reciprocity between what is termed an inside and an outside, is key to what Novalis calls, in the aforementioned fragment, "a gathering into the I" (*W*II: 245). This "I," then—following the movement of emergence that the fragment describes—is uttered and made articulate at the point of contact, in the movement of exchange, in the dynamic collision of a force of opposing directionalities. "I," in this formulation, does not seem to be an origin, but rather the instant of collision, the sign of a shifting coalescence. The "I," indeed, seems possessed here of an unusual transience, an almost provisional character, as if its mark might be as easily dispersed as coalesce into an appearing ("One sees here how relative is the outgoing and the ingoing"). And if the "I" retains some sort of punctuality—the punctuality of contact—it nonetheless no longer appears to have the quality of ground or origin. In reflecting upon the genesis of this "I," then, we have moved into the arena of philosophical discourse that formed the crucible of Novalis's work: we must look into that crucible.

Abstract Origins: The Engagement with Fichte

In order to address the question of genesis, we will have to consider aspects of the mechanics of Fichte's endeavor as Novalis experienced it, laboring intensively through a tumultuous year upon an extraordinary series of notes that have become known as the *Fichte Studies.*[8] In order to mark the end-point of the trajectory we must trace, we note the following strange and problematic remark, which dates from 1798—two years beyond the closing of the notebooks that make up the *Fichte Studies*:

> I = Not-I. Highest principle of all science and art. (*W*II: 331/*PW* 59)

There is a dramatic reduction involved in the almost casual adoption of a formulation, derived from Fichte, that is now made to operate not just as the grounding proposition or principle (*Satz*) of knowing (*Wissenschaft*), but equally of art. By 1798, then, this principle has been so entirely appropriated and absorbed as to find itself the grounding principle of poetry as much as of philosophy. It is this principle that will in turn allow for the strange crossing between domains that is the distinctive feature of Novalis's thinking.

However, what will detain us here is not in the first place this crossing as such, but rather the first moment of the fragment. In particular, what needs to be considered is the potency of the = sign. "I = Not-I": what kind of equivalence is at stake here, what kind of identity? A great deal rests on this question, as it will enable us to mark the proximity of Novalis's thinking to Fichte's, but also the possibility of a divergence.

The proximity emerges in that the experience of thought involved in this equivalence belongs directly to the working-through of Fichte's *Wissenschaftslehre*, both in its first version (1794), and still more explicitly in the so-called *Nova Metodo* of 1796/99. In the former we find the following:

> Thus I does not equal I, but rather I = Not-I, and Not-I = I. (*SWI*: 109/107)

Fichte's derivation of this surprising proposition can be outlined only briefly here. The proposition belongs to the third moment or principle of the *Wissenschaftslehre*, whose first moment establishes a formal principle of identity: A = A. The "necessary connection" that this identity reveals (between A and A) is described by Fichte as a "judgment," which he refers to as X. Now, insofar as X—the "necessary connection" involved in the principle of identity—is a judgment, it is exposed as already having been "posited": it reveals an act, an activity of positing, and thus the prior operation of what he is already able to call "I." In that sense, the identity revealed in A = A is equivalent, for Fichte, to the statement "I am":

> In it [X—the "necessary connection"] the I is posited, not conditionally, but absolutely, with the predicate of equivalence to itself; hence it really is posited, and the proposition can also be expressed as *I am*. (*SWI*: 95/96)

Hence, according to Fichte, despite the formal quality of the principle of identity (the absence of existential content), its very self-evidence nonetheless expresses the existential claim of the I, qua positing activity. In fact, such is the intimacy of the link between the two that the progress of Fichte's argument will show that "it is not the 'I am' that is based on 'A = A,' but rather the latter [that] is based on the former"—the claim of identity is grounded in the "already-having-occurred" positing activity of the I.

The extension of this principle of formal identity that Fichte endeavors to establish in his "second principle" involves the equally "perfectly certain and established" claim that "Not-A is not equal to A." Now, even if, says Fichte, we are able to formulate this proposition as "~A =

~A," this, too, would reduce to the principle of identity—and indeed, it is clear that ~A = ~A is equivalent to A = A, that it engages the same principle of identity. However—and this is the crucial maneuver that Fichte makes from the point of view of what follows—despite its pure formal equivalence, the new formulation has nonetheless introduced into the sameness of the principle of identity a difference: it has introduced what he calls the "category of negation." It might be said that it is from out of this gesture that the entire text of the *Wissenschaftslehre* unfolds. This is because this second principle, which Fichte comes to refer to as the "principle of opposition," appears to install the "category of negation" in a tangential relation with the principle of identity: the proposition ~A = ~A is a statement, on the one hand, of the principle of identity, but on the other hand, it has at the same time introduced an element that exceeds that principle: the negation, one might say, both belongs and does not belong to the principle. It is this dynamic of excess and inclusion that will be played out most dramatically in the text: to the extent that the principle of identity has revealed the activity of the I in its always prior gesture of positing, this moment of negation will at once belong to and exceed that activity. The peculiar operations of the "Not-I" in Fichte's text work out this dynamic movement of inclusion and excess in radical degree: but it is essentially this fundamental inclusivity within the activity of the I that enables Fichte to establish the claim of the third principle, namely, the curious equivalence involved in the claim "I = Not-I." In the later, 1796 version of the *Wissenschaftslehre*—the *Nova Metodo*—this equivalence is more fully expressed, less strained: there, Fichte writes that

> the opposing terms are one and the same, merely viewed from different sides . . . The[y] simply represent two, inseparably linked aspects or ways of looking at the same thing, for the I must be a subject-object.[9]

A little later in the same text we also encounter the following formulation, significant for the direction in which it will take this inquiry:

> The Not-I is thus nothing other than another way of looking at the I. When we consider the I as an activity, we obtain the I; when we consider it in a state of repose, we obtain the Not-I. (*WNM* 133)[10]

Now, although the expression of the relation of I and Not-I here is interestingly divergent—in its indication of a dynamic of activity and passivity—from the 1794 version of the *Wissenschaftslehre*, in which the not-I is referred to consistently as a "counter-positing," nonetheless, the "reciprocal interaction of I and not I"[11] here remains fundamentally a question of reaction: in one sense or another, the "not-I" responds to the "I," whether as passivity or counter-thrust. In fact, in both instances, the dynamic of the interaction as it unfolds in the text will be one of limit—a setting of limits, a mutual limitation, the divisibility that derives from the instituting of limit:

> How can A and ~A, being and non-being, reality and negation, be thought together without mutual elimination and destruction?
>
> We need not expect anyone to answer the question other than as follows: they will mutually limit each other. (*SW* I: 108/108)

At this point, though, it should be noted that Fichte makes an interesting parenthetical gesture, which appears to circumscribe the connection between the formal logical abstractions involved in the principle of identity and the operations of the self-positing "I" upon which the opening of the text had been at pains to insist. Instead, he now claims that "the manner of the possible unification [of I and not-I] is by no means implicit in these principles, being governed, rather, by a *special* law of the mind, which the foregoing experiment was designed to bring to consciousness" (*SW* I: 108/108). It seems, thus, that the formal derivation of the proposition has reached a limit, which seems to be marked by the point at which the reduction of formal abstraction has to be considered less than necessary, less than fundamental, and has become something else—an "experiment," a procedure designed to express or exemplify a "special law of the mind" that is not in fact reducible to purely formal principles.

As the *Wissenschaftslehre* of 1794 develops, it will become clear that this "special law" of the unification of "I" and "Not-I" and of the operations of their reciprocity is none other than the *imagination*, and it will be our purpose later to explore this "special law" in order to gain a vantage point from which to investigate certain aspects of Novalis's thinking. But even before we undertake this, it is already possible to glimpse a key element of that thinking by returning to the operations of the opening of Fichte's 1794 text, the source and origin of much of Novalis's experience of Fichte's work.

The point, then, has been the establishment of a certain equivalence, a sameness or identity such that Fichte is able to formulate, in one way or another, the proposition "I = Not-I." We have tried to indicate the way in which Fichte understands this proposition, in particular the kind of equivalence that binds I and not-I together in the proposition. Now, it has been determined that central to even the preliminary determinations of Fichte's text is the sense of activity, described as a "positing." The I, in its self-determining activity, will have posited itself, and the absolute inclusivity of this positing movement, as we saw, will also govern the introduction of a negation. To say, then, that "I = Not-I" is to say that Not-I is in some sense *included* in the I. For Fichte, then, the = sign of the formula reveals a certain priority: the not-I, the principle of limitation or of opposition, is always to be thought as already having been posited by an I. This priority governs the vocabulary of reaction that Fichte deploys consistently: however Fichte envisages the dependence of the self-positing I on a limit or on the moment of its negation, that moment is always described either as productive of a *counter*-thrust, a *counter*-positing, or as a certain kind of passivity of resistance.

It is in the primacy of this self-constituting activity that the limits of formal reduction are encountered. These limits are evident in that the formula "I = Not-I," from a formal standpoint, obviously does not allow for anything like a priority or precedence: a pure equivalence would necessitate the kind of absolute reciprocity that the vocabulary of positing and counter-positing cannot sustain. If the I is thought, rather, as it appears to be, as *positing* the not-I, then the equivalence of I and not-I is not merely limited to a gesture of inclusion: decisively, this reciprocity has been allowed to become a *movement.* In becoming a movement, a *temporal difference* is introduced into the proposition; and it is this that cannot be contained by the idea of pure formal equivalence. This temporality, then, may indeed be the element that resists the reduction to formal principle, the element that limits the operation of the first principle (the principle of identity) in the unfolding of the *Wissenschaftslehre.*

The limits and strictures that appear to have been placed around the simple equivalence of "I" and "Not-I" in Fichte's text may be said to be the point at which Novalis intervenes, following rigorously and elaborating the lines of implication that the former establishes. How, then, does Novalis understand the proposition "I = Not-I"? And in what way does the identity that it proposes become the "highest principle [*Satz*] of science and art"?

In order to elaborate a response, let us first say that clearly, for Novalis, the equivalence or identity of I and not-I is no longer limited—at least not entirely—by the mechanics of a "positing." This will mean that the equivalence of I and not-I—the = sign of the proposition—is no longer to be thought of as an "enclosing." Instead, the sense of "production" that dominates Fichte's model is to give way to a thought of *exchange*: the equivalence of I and not-I begins to be thought by Novalis more purely as a replaceability, as a dynamics of substitution. In other words, in Novalis's thinking, the = sign of our proposition is deployed to institute, rather than negation and limit, a process of exchange, an activity of mutual transformation. Now, the consequences of this change are substantial, and will dramatically affect every aspect of Novalis's project. Among these consequences, we will consider the following three:

(1) In this new thinking of equivalence, which replaces a vocabulary of production with a vocabulary of exchange, Novalis will retain the sense of the primacy of activity, and therefore of movement that comes to light in Fichte's account. However, if the sense of activity is no longer thought in terms of the primacy of the I, but belongs—in this new equivalence—to a movement that flows equally across both sides of the proposition, then the experience of action and reaction is detached, removed from the primacy of a subject becoming conscious of itself. What we will find in Novalis, instead, is more of an energetics, an exploration of force and the dynamics of experience that floats free of structures tied to a particular model of consciousness. When Novalis asks, then, early on in his notes on Fichte: "Has not Fichte packed too much into the I? With what warrant?" (*W* II: 12/7), this points to an experience of a thinking that is generated from a resistance to the unilateral appropriation of the central proposition of equivalence that we see operative in Fichte's text. What we will see instead is a dynamics of reciprocity and exchange that will allow us again to assert the operation of a dissonant *harmonia,* in the sense already articulated, at work in this thinking.

(2) The continued insistence on movement, on the motility of the exchange between I and not-I that governs their equivalence, will mean that Novalis, like Fichte, will be restrained from identifying the activities of this equivalence with formal logical processes. Nonetheless, the refusal to allow the first moment of the equivalence ("I") to dominate the second ("not-I") means that Novalis is able, to a degree greater than Fichte, to play within the domain of pure logical equivalence. In this sense, what will come to dominate Novalis's thinking, in relation to the "highest proposition of science and art," is the exigency of its *paradox*—the thought, contained in the proposition "I = not-I," of an impossibility, of an excess, of a pushing beyond the boundaries of rational, logical containment. Consider, in this light, the following thought, which comes from the 1798 "Logological Fragments" and one that, as we saw in the introduction, drew Heidegger's attention in a significant way:

> Should not the highest principle contain the highest paradox in its operation? To be a proposition [*Satz*] that would allow no peace, that always both attracts and repulses . . . (*W* II: 314/*PW* 49)

It seems from this fragment as if the dynamic of movement exposed beneath the play of equivalence in Fichte's work has found a way to strike at the heart of the formal conditions that (at least ostensibly) governed the progress of the argument: the security of the proposition itself is to be subject to a force of destabilization, a momentum of disquiet, in which the only constant will be a sense of unsettlement.

Consider also this second fragment, from a notebook dated 1800, composed thus in the final year of Novalis's life:

> To undo, to nullify [*vernichten*] the principle of non-contradiction is perhaps the highest work of higher logic. (*W*II: 767)

The work of undoing, of the unseating of fundamental principles will belong to this endeavor of thinking: such an undoing, we are told, *is* indeed the work of thinking. If we think these fragments together, we might envision the work of undoing, this un-working of the grounding principle, to be a matter of destabilization, of dissipation into an interminable restlessness. The ground, in such a thought, would not be the static and certain foundation of an unshakeable structure, but the locus of insatiety, of a quivering uncertainty, a force of threatening collapse.

(3) In the first *Introduction to the Wissenschaftslehre* of 1797, Fichte will write:

> A finite rational being has nothing beyond experience . . . the philosopher stands necessarily under the same condition; it seems, therefore, inconceivable how he might raise himself above experience. But he can abstract; that is, that which is bound together in experience he can separate out through the freedom of thought. (*SW*I: 425/8)

Fichte's enterprise is in fact wedded to this process of "abstraction," by which is intended not merely a withdrawal from the concrete, but a literal ab(s)-traction, the drawing-out or -away from the coordinates of lived experience. This, indeed, *is* the philosophical project for Fichte: if philosophy is to expose the ground of the "system of experience" (*SW*I: 423/6), it will do so in exercising a freedom which in a certain sense runs counter to its grain. It will "separate" what is "bound" in the system, remove itself from the warp and weft of experience, and perform its work by untying that fabric. If philosophy, then, stands outside experience, it stands, too, outside the system, exposing its ground in this activity of withdrawal. Now Novalis's thinking, too, will be entranced by the thought of "abstraction." However, as we have already begun to see, the sense of abstraction is not, for Novalis, dominated by unilateral movement inward, toward the punctuality of a self-positing I. Instead, within the domain of equivalence that is set up by his understanding of the "highest proposition of art and science," "abstraction"—and with it "philosophy"—will come to mean something other than a gesture of reflexive withdrawal. Abstraction, for Novalis, will instead come to be identified with the transformative working of thought, "alternately raising and lowering," effecting "logarithmic change" upon both the obduracy of the sensible world and the ideality of the I (*W* II: 324). This operation is what Novalis will term "logology." In this new thinking, if philosophy is to retain a reflexive sense, it will be not the reflexivity that turns back upon the positing of the originary I, but the movement that turns to reflect upon itself, upon its own possibility.

Once again, then, we are confronted with a sensibility that replaces the unilateral movement of the I with a movement of exchange, and the reduction to the singular with the intertwinement of multiplicity. It is in this sense that, for Novalis, the gestures of thought and language all have to do with the dynamic of a double movement, a play of conjoining, combining, and separating. Thus he writes, in the *Blüthenstaub* fragments:

> Before abstraction everything is one—but it is one as chaos is—after abstraction everything is again unified [*vereinigt*]—but this unification is a free binding of independent, self-determined beings . . . chaos is transformed into a manifold world. (*W* II: 270/*PW* 40)

The movement of abstraction, thus, does not operate by separating itself from the dense weave of experience in order to travel along a trajectory of withdrawal from multiplicity toward a singular point of origin. Rather, the movement of abstraction is a movement from one kind of multiplicity to another, from one sense of a dynamic interplay of singular and multiple to another, from the unity of chaos to the multiplicity of "world."

The effects of these alterations will be radical: in this intertwinement, in this dramatic transfiguration of multiple and singular, entirely new possibilities are opened up for a kind of thinking in which what will have been called poetry will invest and intensify what will have been called philosophy—and vice versa. This new kind of cooperation will express a fecundity and volubility quite at odds with the intent of the philosophical "abstraction" from which it arose. It will contest the rigor of a withdrawal to ground with an alternative rigor of variation and combination; and the articulation of this rigor will manifest itself not as a drive toward the integrity of system so much as an opening on to the indefinite expanse of a "romantic encyclopaedia."

* * *

We were directed on the way toward a philosophical point of origin by the fragment that began "*Wie wir, schweben die Sterne . . .*" and the strange equivalence between the stars and ourselves that it appeared to posit. Evidently, from the vantage point we have now reached, we can construe the image as an elaboration of a process of thought undertaken in response to an engagement with Fichte's thinking of the I and the Not-I and their strange equivalence. However, in following this path back through the Fichtean legacy in Novalis's writings, it might well seem as if we have followed a trajectory determined by models of abstraction which belong precisely to that philosophical orbit: the experience of a regression to a ground. In doing so there is a risk that, counter to the pull of Novalis's thinking, we might end up falling into the trap that emerged at the outset of this chapter, as we considered the manifold sense of "seed": the trap of reducing the experience of the thought-image of this fragment to an expression or elaboration of its "conceptual underpinnings." The fecundity and vibrancy of the experience of Novalis's words would thereby be hollowed out in pursuit of their philosophical ground, and reduced to the status of ornament or example. It will be necessary to respond, then, to the simplification that would want to dispose of the question of these words merely by attaching to these images the label "poetry." If we are to ask in a meaningful way what Novalis intends in articulating this strange equivalence of ourselves and the stars, then we cannot allow ourselves the anodyne comfort of a label that would find in these words merely a colorful and quixotic elaboration of a more serious idea. On the contrary, it is crucial to an understanding of Novalis's process that this image, and others like it, are not reduced to the status of "poetic elaboration." If we are to interrogate seriously the thinking of which the example we cite here is an occasion, then it will be necessary, too, to take equally seriously the work that this "poetizing" undertakes in relation to its conceptual ground. In the following chapter, then, we will reenter the arena of philosophical origin, but will take our clue from the word that occurs centrally in the thought-image, a word that appears to describe the mode of equivalence Novalis is establishing: that word is *schweben*—to hover, to waver, to oscillate—a word that has a history complex enough to allow it to negotiate the passageways between philosophy and poetry, passageways that Novalis will make his own. Occurring in multiple registers of thought, *Schweben* will be a term that makes for *itself* a kind of between-space, one that enables the kind of transmutation that, for Novalis, institutes our own very peculiar belongingness—with the stars, that hover.

2

Hovering at the Edge

Oscillation, Indeterminacy, and the Between

Imagining the Between

The verb *schweben* can be said to be the name of a problem, a problem having to do with the imagination, with its distribution and operation. More precisely, the indeterminacy or restlessness that the term implies invokes what is difficult about the imagination. Lodged indecisively, uncomfortably, somewhere between passivity and activity, *schweben*—a hovering, wavering, or oscillating—comes to be the unstable point around which transformations and reconfigurations of the imagination occur at the close of the eighteenth century.

In relation to the imagination, the term *Schweben* emerges first of all under an entirely negative sign, within a field of proscription: it is a term that Kant engages in the first *Critique* to mark, not a positive attribute of the imagination, but its entirely illegitimate deployment. From these fearful and proscriptive beginnings, which we will explore, the story of the transformation of the sense of the verb *schweben* will trace out, and in a certain sense enact, the explosive reconfiguration of the imagination that occurs in the wake of the critical project. A discussion of the central installation of the idea of *schweben* in Fichte's 1794 *Wissenschaftslehre* will then enable us to see more clearly the way in which its difficulties and unresolved complexities open possibilities that Novalis will pursue, perhaps more fully than anyone else. We will be able to see how the seed that Kant reluctantly plants in the garden of the imagination becomes the force that will overwhelm it entirely, outstripping any containment, dissolving even the borders it was to have delineated.[1]

Fundamentally at stake here are the ways in which this central indeterminacy operates to configure the between-space of I and not-I, and to articulate their interconnectedness. We will see how the *Schweben* of the imagination comes to name that between-space, but also the kinds of constraints under which Fichte's account finds it necessary to place the instability that this between-space engenders. In that sense, we will be able to understand Novalis's reading of Fichte as a way of appropriating the instability of this between-space, precisely by taking up the difficulties that Fichte encounters in his attempts to delimit it. In Novalis's appropriation, then, such will be the intensity of the interrogation of this "between" that the sense of "hovering" or "oscillating" will loosen the ties of the polarities it was to have kept in place. In this new account, "imagination" qua capacity, or faculty, will be absorbed into the indeterminate interplay of I and not-I: indeed, Novalis writes but rarely of "imagination" per se.

To begin to weave together this fabric, then, we can commence with Kant's proscriptive delineation of the *Schweben* of the imagination, addressing ourselves to a moment from the first *Critique*. This is the moment, toward the close of the "Transcendental Dialectic," when Kant turns to the concept of the Ideal. What the ideal is to represent—but only within certain limits, and subject to certain specific restrictions—is a kind of "individuation" of the idea. Not exactly a concrete instantiation—such a thing would be impossible, says Kant—but rather an "archetype" (A 569), an *Urbild* that appears to hover on the edge of instantiation. His example is the "ideal" of the Stoic, the "wise man" who "exists only in one's thoughts but is entirely congruent with the idea of wisdom" (A 570). To presume, even in those thoughts, or in words and images, to actively instantiate such an *Urbild* would be, Kant says, "preposterous and unedifying." Thus, for example, to imagine that one might "realize the wise person in a novel" would instantly render the archetype "suspect." We are dealing, then, with an instantiation without an instance, an individuation whose imaginative articulation is expressly proscribed.

We can certainly wonder about the status of this "archetype": an image that remains "exemplary" by resisting instantiation, that has its very being in that resistance, is one that necessarily seems to have already entered into relation with that which it will resist—to depend upon it, in a sense. There seems to be an anxiety, here, connected with the sense of instantiation: and it is in the paragraph that follows that we begin to understand that this anxiety is in turn connected specifically to questions concerning the status of the imagination. Here, the function of the ideal of reason as *Urbild* or archetype is distinguished with vitriolic determination from those mere "creatures of the imagination" which "painters and physiognomists claim to have in their heads," "shadow-images" (A 570) incapable of concretion, but in a way that is different—utterly different, Kant assures us—from the *Urbild* of reason. Kant describes these dubious and shadowy formations as "*monograms.*" This is a word that explicitly invokes the language of the schematism: there, the possibility of experience is said to rest upon the "secret art" of the schema, which operates, Kant says, as the "*monogram* of the pure a priori imagination" (A 142). Thus, we might have reason to assume that the "shadow-images" which Kant invokes share in the operation of that faculty, and thus might be detached only with difficulty from their more "legitimate" function—hence the scorn that Kant evinces. Be that as it may, we note that at the height of his proscriptive anger, Kant will describe the kinds of imaginative operations that are most to be resisted, the forms of thinking that most incite his scorn, as "*schwebende Zeichnungen*"(A 570). And thus it is that *schweben*—the sense of a hovering, oscillating indeterminacy—enters into the vocabulary of the imagination. Operating, at first, entirely under a negative sign, it is this very term that will be transformed, first in Fichte, and then more radically in Novalis, into a kind of rallying cry for a new centralization of the imagination. This, then, is the direction in which we shall follow.

To carry these threads of inquiry further, we recall that we have seen earlier that Fichte's attempts to resolve the relation of I and not-I into formal abstract terms runs up against a limit: the third moment of his argument, in which the I comes to confront the not-I in a kind of equivalence, was after all possible only on the basis of a kind of lopsidedness. In other words, I = not-I is intelligible in Fichte only to the extent that the = sign expresses a kind of productivity: the not-I is equivalent to the I insofar as it belongs to the primacy of the positing I. Eschewing pure formal equivalence, Fichte instead claims that, after all, "the manner of the possible unification [of I and not-I] is by no means implicit in these principles, being governed, rather, by a *special* law of the mind, which the foregoing experiment was designed to bring to consciousness" (*SW* I: 108/108). And as we saw earlier, this "special law" turns out to be the operation of the imagination, which takes up the role of instituting and governing the relation of I and not-I. Indeed, the entirety of Fichte's text might be said to unfold as an abstract drama of the engagement of this pair, taking the form of the clash and mutual embrace of limit and unlimit, of finite and infinite. What is always most difficult, though, in this drama is not the opposition, but rather the "uniting"—the bringing-and holding-together of this opposedness. And as we shall see, it is the difficult sense of their conjoining that will necessitate the formulation of a dynamic and fluid conception of the I, one that is in some measure at odds with its own drive toward foundational stability, and which will push us once again in the direction of a *harmonia* of difference. But in order to see this strange conjoining, we first need to investigate the question of "limit" which, in Fichte's thinking, the opposedness of an I and a not-I has originarily brought into play.

Fichte's Geometry of the Imagination[2]

Deep within the core of the *Wissenschaftslehre,* we encounter the following expression of the intertwinement of I and not-I, construed here as the relation between an infinite positing activity and an experience of limit: "No infinity, no limiting [*Begrenzung*]; no limiting, no infinity . . . infinity and limiting are united in one and the same synthetic component" (*SW* I: 214/192).[3] However, the notion of boundary or limit has been embedded from the outset of the *Wissenschaftslehre,* through the original gesture by which "a not-I is opposed absolutely to the I"—the so-called "principle of opposition" (*SW* I: 105/105). This founding opposition sets in motion the complex rhythms of determination and indetermination that flow through the labyrinthine edifice of the text. The gradual narrowing of focus that constitutes the movement and direction of the argument leads to an increasing preoccupation with the precise moment in which the mutually determining and self-limiting I and not-I can be thought of as confronting one another. This narrowing of focus, the insistence on the encounter of finite and infinite, limit and unlimit, leads Fichte to articulate the instant of that encounter, to give name to its force. He calls it *Anstoß,* a "check" in which the infinite outward movement of the I encounters its own limit, and is determined—qua infinite—in that encounter. It can be said, then, that the articulation of the I depends on a counterforce in reference to which the intrinsic unboundedness of its activity can differentiate itself. Reciprocally, though, the "check" can only be understood in relation to the activity of the I: "No activity of the I, no check . . . no check, no self-determination" (*SW* I: 191/175).

If we think of the *Anstoß,* the check, as expressing a limit, then it is there, in that moment of block, of stoppage, that some sort of reciprocity of finite and infinite, some sort of belonging-together is to be thought: the *Anstoß,* after all, is the point of their encounter.[4] Thus, when Fichte writes: "if the activity of the I did not extend into the infinite, it could not itself set limits to this activity . . . moreover, if the I did not bound itself, it would not be infinite" (*SW* I: 214/192), he is indicating the sense in which the infinite activity of the I is intertwined, entirely, with its own limiting. We can say, then, that the I is determined in and as the experience of the irresolvable exchange of finite and infinite. The I, in this sense, *is* this reciprocity, this intertwinement of limit and unlimit: and as the exchange, the reciprocity of finite and infinite, limit and unlimit, the I becomes—quite paradoxically—neither. Instead, this exchange or uneasy reciprocity will lend to the I a particular restlessness, a motile dynamic of flow and inhibition in which the I recognizes its infinite activity, its indefinite momentum of positing, only in the self-thwarting of that very activity. We can even wonder whether, in view of this restless interplay, the entire possibility of determination itself is not itself forestalled: and indeed, such an uneasy question can be seen to lie at the heart of the unfolding of the text.

Here is how Fichte describes this restless exchange:

> The interplay [*Wechsel*] [of finite and infinite] consists . . . in conflict [*Widerstreit*] with itself, and is self-reproducing, in that the I endeavors to unify the un-unifiable [*das Ich unvereinbares vereinigt will*], now attempting to take up the infinite in the form of the finite, now driven back, positing it again outside the latter, and in that very moment seeking once more to take it up under the form of finitude. (*SW* I: 215/193)

There is a struggle, then, a conflict; but one that belongs to the unity of the self-positing I: "If the I did not bound itself, it would not be infinite" (*SW* I: 214/192). Stretched out on the rack of this conflict, the I "posits itself at once as finite and infinite." We might understand the restlessness of the I, as activity, as a fluid complex of opposing directionalities: the interplay of these directionalities generates a continuous dynamic of excess and lack, with the I reaching for a beyond which is at the same time not a beyond. What this dynamic movement seeks—and what escapes it—is the secure ground that is capable of determining the course of the movement even as it eludes it, indeed *in* and *as* that very eluding. The name that Fichte gives to this dynamic is *imagination* (*Einbildungskraft*), and to the complex of movements through which it opens itself to description—*Schweben*: "the spirit [*Geist*] lingers in this conflict [*Streit*] and hovers [*schwebt*] between the two—hovers between the demand and the impossibility of its fulfillment" (*SW* I: 226/202). Buffeted between the irreconcilable and yet mutually determining demands of finite and infinite, the I discovers itself in this "hovering" of the imagination, which is thought here precisely as "a faculty that wavers in the middle between determination and non-determination" (*SW* I: 217/194).[5]

In addition to the incessance of this movement, however, it will also be apparent that the model thus far described rests upon a kind of tension. This tension has to do with the relation between movement and interruption, between flow and block, striving and its arrest. If, on the one hand, the self-determination of the I rests upon a dynamic movement, such a movement is manifestly possible only on the basis of the check, the *Anstoß*, which arrests and inhibits its free flow. It is this tension between movement and its restriction that will lead Fichte to offer two opposing metaphorical models, neither of which will resolve into the other, but nor yet will separately satisfy their own demands. In what follows, these two models will be described, and an attempt made to indicate both their limitations and their incompatible exigencies.

We have seen that, from the outset, the interaction of I and not-I—despite the intensity of their intertwinement—is governed by a model of action and reaction: the force of a positing I is confronted by the counterforce of the not-I. We noted, too, that whatever the kinds of equivalence Fichte will attempt to establish between these two polarities, the tendency of this model will be to draw toward a hierarchical dominance of the first term. However, there appears now a further consequence to measure, one that has to do with the pressures that this model exerts toward a particular kind of geometry. This geometry is derived quite explicitly from the metaphorical gestures with which Fichte describes the activity and processes of I and not-I—a geometry of line and point, whose rigor will be at odds with the dynamic instability of the imagination that is to draw them toward a unity. We need to look more closely at this geometry.

Let us begin by locating a moment at which Fichte explicitly conceives the activity of the I as a movement of pure linearity, even if such a conception is consciously engaged as metaphor: Fichte writes that "one should represent to oneself the infinitely outreaching activity [of the I] in the image of a straight line stretching from A through B to C, etc." (*SW* I: 228/203). In this structure of pure linearity, though, the interplay of infinite and finite cannot, of course, be conceived in a unidirectional sense: the I can never be a pure unfolding, but—in encountering a limit—will recoil upon itself. Thus, the "infinitely outreaching activity of the I" will involve engagement with limit in the form of the check (*Anstoß*) which forces a reversal, a rebounding of the movement of the I back upon itself. Fichte is explicit about the symmetry of this return; and it is precisely the symmetrical structure of line, point, and reversal that enables the specular metaphors—the metaphors of reflection and reflexivity—to proliferate. The activity of the I, then, will invite a reversal which must travel, Fichte tells us, along an identical axis:

> The infinitely outreaching activity of the I, in which nothing can be distinguished, precisely because it reaches into infinity, is subjected to a check [*Anstoß*]; and its activity, though by no means extinguished thereby, is reflected, driven inwards it takes *exactly the reverse direction* . . . the I's activity from A to C is reflected from C to A. (*SW* I: 228/203, emphasis added)

The restrictive linearity of this model, though, poses something of a challenge to the wavering indeterminacy that marked the process of unifying that the imagination was to have effected. This *Schweben* of the imagination is to be construed, as we have seen, as a holding-together of the finite and the infinite within the I. However, within a structure constrained by pure linearity, it is not clear where and how such an indeterminacy would operate—where, as it were, the *Schweben* would have room to move. The linear metaphor will have limited the hovering or wavering of the imagination, placing its instability outside of the very movement or activity that it was intended to ground.

Thus, the linear model which grows quite naturally from the first gesture of positing that defines the activity of the I runs into difficulties when it needs to maintain a dominance over the between-space of the imagination: the gesture that would subordinate the between to the polarities that occasion it is precisely the gesture that Novalis will challenge. However, the resources of Fichte's text are by no means exhausted in the geometry of the straight line. The limits of the linear, bidirectional model of reflexivity are indeed such that the movement of *Schweben* will be constrained to the point at which it will tend to become inoperative. But at this point, and for these reasons, when Fichte describes the instability of the imagination itself, he will adopt an entirely new figure—exchanging, now, the constriction of the straight line for the fluidity of the *circle*. He writes:

> The ultimate ground of all consciousness is an interaction [*Wechselwirkung*] of the I with itself, by way of a not-I. This is the circle, from which the finite spirit cannot escape, and—unless it is to disown reason [*Vernunft*] and demand its own annihilation—cannot wish to escape. (*SW* I: 282/248)

The figure of the circle, of circularity, allows for a flow of movement that is, quite literally, unchecked—a continuity and reciprocity which offers Fichte possibilities unavailable within the (dominant) linear reflexive model.[6] To conceive of the interaction of I and not-I as movement within a circle allows him to move beyond the limits of the static, punctual confrontation of the *Anstoß*, and opens up a way of understanding the *Wechsel* of I and not-I, the reciprocal binding of finite and infinite, as both fluid and continuous. Accordingly, with this refiguration, new possibilities are opened up for the *Schweben* of the imagination: the holding-together of finite and infinite, the lingering within the demand of an impossible unity, can finally now become determinative of the movement within the circle. The exchange, the interplay within which the imagination hovers becomes, indeed, the fullest sense of that movement: one can say, indeed, that the *Schweben* of the imagination is what holds the circle together. The *Wechsel* between I and not-I which is constitutive of the circle and its movement is possible only on condition of its binding, its holding-together: the imagination will be what keeps the circle whole.

However, it is precisely at this moment, at the point at which a conceptual mechanism has been brought into play that will finally begin to allow the imagination to take up its central, constitutive role, that another difficulty arises in the text; and this is a difficulty which will entail an intervention that will once again—this time definitively—limit or restrict the movement of *Schweben*. The image of the circle has indeed provided Fichte with a fluidity of movement, an incessance of reciprocal interaction that makes possible the centralization of the movement of the imagination. But paradoxically, it is this very fluidity, the uninterrupted flow of the movement within the circle, which becomes immediately problematic. The problem with the consistency of the circular movement is precisely the absence of fixity; a circular movement implies a continuity, a lack of differentiation, which makes impossible the very stability upon which a "foundation [*Grundlage*] of theoretical knowledge" is to be grounded. Fichte writes:

> In this inquiry we clearly have no fixed point, and are revolving endlessly in a circle, unless intuition, in itself and as such, is first stabilized . . . the possibility of solving the problem posed above is dependent on the possibility of stabilizing intuition as such. (*SW* I: 232/206)

But such a stabilization cannot be effected within a structure determined by the uncertain movement of the imagination. Indeed, the thinking of *Schweben* here entails that *intuition itself* be thought in terms of this hovering instability, as the movement of exchange, of interplay. This, indeed, is what Fichte tells us, in exposing the dynamics of his difficulty: "but intuition as such is in no way stable, consisting, rather, in a wavering [*Schweben*] of the imagination between conflicting directions." What will be necessary, then, is an intervention, the activation of a "dormant, inactive power" lurking, impossibly, both within and beyond the circle—within because the very possibility of such a power cannot be thought outside the circle, but beyond, in that the circle itself contains no such mechanism of interruption. This "dormant" power, which will rise up to arrest the flow of the imagination, is "understanding"—"the power," writes Fichte, "wherein a transiency is *arrested, settled,* brought to a stand" (*SW* I: 233/207).

Given that the very possibility of intuition rests upon the *Schweben* of the imagination, the "arrest" that understanding will effect will be a precarious one—an interruption from within, as it were. It will necessitate granting to the "stabilizing" of intuition the sense of an "as if"—the quality of the provisional. The understanding will seize hold of the instability of the imagination in such a way as to bring to a stop the fluidity of exchange within the circle, but only on condition that such a stoppage retain at every instant the trace (*Spur*) of the *Schweben* it will have subordinated—a trace that will be neither incidental nor arbitrary. Rather, the trace, the remainder, will paradoxically constitute the entire possibility of the arrest itself. Here is how Fichte describes the problematic:

> That it should be stabilized, is to say that imagination should waver [*schwebt*] no longer, with the result that intuition would be utterly abolished and destroyed. Yet this must not happen; so that in intuition there must at least remain the product of this condition, a trace of opposed directions, consisting in neither but containing something of both. (*SW* I: 233/207)

Despite, then—or rather *because* of—the central indeterminacy of *schweben*, the projecting of a foundation will require a difficult subordination of the hovering of the imagination to a moment of fixity, an instant of blockage within the movement of the circle. To conceive of intuition as fixity will, inevitably, run the risk of lapsing into a "dogmatism" of the object. Fichte must, ultimately, circumvent this problem by insisting that the stabilizing of the intuition, its fixity, is yet to be contained within the I itself. This will necessitate that the moment of intuition is made, as it were, to "curl back" upon the I—that the fixity which both threatens and is threatened by the imagination come to rest within the I itself. The foundational dynamic of Fichte's project thus requires that the fixity, the paradoxical stabilization of intuition, ultimately become the self-intuiting of the I. A pure spontaneity, the I that intuits itself in reflexive immediacy will place itself beyond and before the temporal dislocation that belongs to the metaphorical structures of the movements and processes which have determined the unfolding of consciousness, and which had maintained, however precariously, the movement of the imagination as the unstable center of that unfolding. Two years later, in 1797, in the *Second Introduction to the Wissenschaftslehre*, Fichte will have called this foundational spontaneity "intellectual intuition."

Let us sum up. What we find in Fichte's 1794 text is an account of the subject in which the demand of the ground will insist upon a determination of the I as at once *origin* and *destination*. The internal displacement generated by this demand necessitates the unfolding of a structure in which the I can be understood both as internally differentiated *and* as radical unity. The tension generated in and between the different "moments" of the I—its "infinite outward striving" and its spontaneous reflexive return—resolves into a complex topology, a paradoxical geometry of circle and line. But neither of these figures, on their own, can sustain the demands of the I as absolute foundation *and* as interplay, as origin and exchange: each figure will require the intervention of the other to uphold its integrity. Now, then, we must turn back to Novalis, to see something of the transformative appropriation that his thinking will perform upon these tensions.

Unhinging the Between: Novalis Intervenes

What binds together the geometrical models around which Fichte's discourse revolves can be said to be a particular kind of relation between movement and arrest, between a streaming-forth and its curtailment, its blocking, its inhibition. In the linear model, which is clearly central in the text of the *Wissenschaftslehre*, the arrest takes the form of the *Anstoß*, the check in which the Not-I forces the striving I back upon itself. The circular model, by contrast, requires a kind of inhibition, the temporary cessation of a flow of movement whose incessance would threaten the foundational stability of the positing I. In both cases, then, the term *Schweben* is introduced in order to describe a movement, a process of exchange between the I and its limits. But we can see that this movement—essential for the grounding of the generative principle of the I—at the same time introduces an instability that neither geometrical model is able entirely to contain.

The question that arises, then—the question that Novalis will want to pose—is: what might happen if we were *really* to allow to the movement of *Schweben* the centrality that Fichte's account implies? What if we were really to take seriously its determinative instability, and orient our account around the effects that such an uncertainty introduces? Such a move would necessitate a complete rethinking of the structural opposition between I and Not-I, and a reorienting of our account of the dynamics of experience that would fully make room for its provisional and indecisive character. In effect, Novalis's studies of Fichte can be read (at least in part) as a kind of extended experiment with such a reorientation. The elusive character of the thinking, and in particular the unstable, protean use of terminology in these notes derive from an attempt to discover a vocabulary, a thinking language that would give voice to this redistributive experiment. This same protean quality renders impossible any attempt to gather this thinking into one fold. An attempt to trace out each movement of the text would founder on this instability: to follow the warp and weft of the text entirely would produce only its replication.

What is possible, however, is to indicate some of the moments in which this instability comes into focus—moments at which the mechanics of this reorientation—or disorientation—become themselves visible, and suggest ways in which a more complete reading of the text might be attempted. In addition, an address to these moments would allow us a better understanding of the process of thinking that informs the direction of Novalis's thinking as it unfolds in the years that follow the composition of these notes.

In one sense, that direction is established on the very first page. Composed in the white heat of that encounter, Novalis's opening gesture confronts Fichte's primary insight with a dramatic question. In order to see this, we might present the initial unfolding of Fichte's text as a movement of expansion and retraction: the I is declared and established on the basis of a proposition (A = A). If so, the I can be said to stretch itself across an equivalence, only in order to withdraw, to return; it is in this return that it will become what it has always already been. One might speculate that without this stretching—the movement by which the self-identical stretches itself across the breadth of a proposition—there would be no text at all. And this first opening is the very place at which Novalis will intervene, calling a halt, forestalling that movement with a question. Let us consider a passage from the opening page of the notes. Reflecting upon the principle A = A, Novalis writes:

> The essence of identity can let itself be presented only in an apparent proposition [*Scheinsatz*]. We abandon the *identical* in order to present it. Either this occurs only apparently [*scheinbar*]—and we are brought by the imagination to believe it—that which is *occurring*, already is—naturally through imaginary separation and unification—Or we represent it through its "not-being," through a "not-identical"—a sign. (*W* II: 8/*FS* 3)

The establishment of identity, then, involves a movement of abandonment and retrieval: it requires an articulation, and such an articulation is possible only on the basis of a separation: A is separated from A in order to present itself as self-same. It appears, thus, to Novalis that the affirmation, or grasp of the identical can only take place on the basis of a replication, the introduction of a multiplicity.[7] Implicitly, this multiplicity introduces a kind of difference, installing division at the core of identity. Neither pure singularity nor absolute divergence, the replication that the proposition of identity represents engages the = sign of the proposition A = A as the bearer, not of formal abstract equivalence, but of a dislocation, a disturbance which allows a kind of "temporal spread" to enter into identity: insofar as it is accessible from out of this proposition, identity, then, is not quite itself: "we abandon the identical in order to present it . . . what is *occurring, already* is."

From the outset, then, we see that the status of this foundational proposition, whose difficult co-option by Fichte we have already engaged, is interrogated by Novalis in such a way as to bring the apparent "innocence" of the proposition into question. If we find, later in Novalis's thinking, extravagant developments of this idea—developments that play with astonishing vibrancy in complex modes of "equivalence"—it is valuable to note that these derive from a question that unfolds from the very first moments of his philosophical engagements.

So, the "spread"—as we have called it—of the proposition A = A introduces a kind of dislocation, a particular kind of difference at odds with its semantic intentions: this is why Novalis claims that the proposition possesses the quality of semblance—it is a *Scheinsatz* in the sense that a gap is operative between its appearance and its effects. The real effect, then, of this gap—of the difference that it installs—is to introduce a motility into the proposition of identity: articulating identity and difference all at once, the proposition will simultaneously gather toward a unity and force that unity apart. This is why, several times amid the first pages of Novalis's notes we find scribbled the phrase "dividing and uniting," suggesting therein the force of double movement which will become emblematic of his manner and process of thinking.

As the passage proceeds, Novalis says that the displacement, the double movement of "separation and unification," might be construed as indicating the operation of an imaginative process—we note, in passing, that at this early stage Novalis is still engaged with the idea of "imagination" as a distinct element of experience—but, he says, it might equally indicate a negation: "or, we represent it [the I] through its 'not-being,' through a 'not-identical'—a sign." This is, in a sense, a curious way of introducing the second moment of Fichte's exposition (the "principle of opposition"), but what Novalis intends to express is that what is crucial, at the core of the proposition, is the operation of difference—the separation that belongs to the unification. In that it is difference that remains decisive, it might be said that in the very dislocation, in the slip from one side of the proposition to the other, a moment of negation is introduced: expressed otherwise, the separation is the negation of the unification, and vice versa. In either case, Novalis wants to say, whether thought via the power of imagination, or conceived as the operation of a negation, the figure of difference in unity remains decisive. A thinking that wishes to engage with the self-experiencing of the I in its activity cannot do otherwise than gather itself around this unstable core. It is this constitutive instability, the irresolvable play of difference, which will be what Novalis calls *Schweben*. The term, evidently, has taken on a sense that leaves behind the limits within which Fichte had still wanted to confine it: if *Schweben* is still to describe a moving-between, it will do so only in an entirely volatile sense, one that unsettles and disorients the polarities it was introduced to negotiate—unhinging even the very notion of a "between."

Intertwinement and Reciprocity: Novalis's *Fichte Studies*

From the opening of his investigations, Novalis sees that if we are to understand that the I is always radically divided from itself, then what is in play is essentially a dynamic of intertwinement, an interplay of action and reaction. In this dividedness, what counts is the force with which the components move against one another, a play of determination and indetermination. Right from the start, indeed, static terms of reference, such as "I" and "Not-I" will tend to be surrendered to this fluidity. This is the sense in which Novalis will ask, as we saw earlier: "Has Fichte not arbitrarily packed too much into the I? With what warrant?" and suggest that perhaps "the I has a hieroglyphic power" in the sense of being a merely emblematic construction that represents and stands in for the operation of a more fundamental process (*SW* I: 12/7). In this way I and not-I become not so much mutually determining poles, mediated by a "between" space that binds them together, but rather markers, points of coalescence in a perpetual movement of exchange and displacement that is not governed by any geometrical model, but defined by its chaotic motility. From early on in his notes, Novalis will begin to call these points of coalescence "signs," developing for them a complex theory of their exchange and reciprocity.[8] From out of this dislodging of stable referents into domains of force will arise a perspective on language that we will come to consider later on. But for now, we need to look more closely at the effects of this reciprocal exchange, the displacement of the foundational moments of consciousness into an unstable play of differential signs, or marks. To this end, what is necessary to explore more fully is the sense of *relation* in the *Fichte Studies*—the rapport, the movement of exchange between I, not-I, and their belonging-together. What needs to be exposed, then, is the dynamism, the sense of flow between zones of determination and indetermination that—in multiple ways—seems to mark out the domain of what Novalis will call "life" (*W* II: 12/*FS* 6).

Adressing the question, not merely of opposition, but of the binding-together of what is opposed, Novalis writes:

> The act by which the I posits itself as I must be connected with the antithesis of an independent Not-I and of the relationship to a sphere that encompasses them—this sphere can be called God, and I. (*W*II: 12/*FS* 6)

As we have seen, the I is expressed here in terms of difference—in terms of a fundamental and irreducible splitting. I and Not-I are components of a consciousness that is accessible only in terms of their relation. In this way I and Not-I are mutually dependent correlates, each occupying, at different moments and always relative to one another, relative domains of determination and indetermination. As interdependent, however, they are only conceivable insofar as they are gathered together into a belonging. Although a terminological instability will belong constitutively to the play of this structure, and to the identification of its zones of determination and indetermination, Novalis will term it with some frequency the "original schema," deploying a familiar triadic structure: "There has to be a not-I, in order that I can posit the I as I. Thesis. Antithesis. Synthesis" (*W*II: 12/*FS* 6). In Novalis's thinking, this "original schema" operates in a way that runs entirely counter to any sense of a rigid structural hierarchy: on the contrary, it is a vocabulary that is introduced rather to open than to close, to introduce the structures of thought to a flexibility inaccessible to the polarized dualities of "I" and "not-I." The terms of the "original schema" come to substitute for the directedness of the latter model a mode of thought that allows a new sense of mutuality and reciprocity: thesis and antithesis are the intertwined moments of an indefinitely mobile and uncentered structure, locked in a play of determination and indetermination that is accessible only in relation to a "feeling of limit" or unlimit.[9] Synthesis is the element of their conjoining, their gatheredness, but never in the sense of a hierarchical absorption of difference. Indeed, what becomes both puzzling and remarkable is Novalis's insistence that, given their interdependence and the mutual interplay of their determination and indetermination, *all three positions* must possess an absolute equivalence. This equivalence implies, fascinatingly, that they exchange positions: I and not-I, and the sphere in which they are both to be thought together, become interchangeable:

> Every one of these is all three, and this is proof of their belonging-together. The synthesis is, or can be, thesis and antithesis. The same with the thesis and the antithesis. Original schema. One in all. All in one. (*W*II: 14/*FS* 9)[10]

In order to better approach the sense of exchange that Novalis is attempting to articulate, we must first endeavor to understand the extent to which he is intent from the outset on interrogating, and ultimately moving beyond the structural grip of opposition. We have seen how Fichte's model—despite its radicality, despite the significance of the moments in which he appears to step beyond these limits—is a model that is fundamentally based around such opposition. From the very first moments of his reading, by contrast, Novalis will already have begun to interrogate this oppositionality: "how are I and not-I opposable?" he asks early on (*W* II: 12/*FS* 6). For Novalis, the interdependence of these internally differentiated aspects will immediately begin to suggest new kinds of belonging, new ways of reciprocal involvement and mutuality whose description entails the abandonment of a formal and static structure of opposition. Not that, of course, "thesis" and "antithesis," I and not-I, are anything other than oppositional concept-pairs. But for this very reason, Novalis will want to interrogate the exigency which appears to oblige us to think always in oppositional terms: "why dichotomous oppositions everywhere?" he exclaims (*W* II: 78/*FS* 68).

Reflecting elsewhere upon the play of wholeness and dividedness, unity and separation whose undecidability has, from the outset, determined the course of his reflections, Novalis speculates:

> The I is absolutely united in two absolutely divided parts—but as such it is representable and therefore we can represent reason for ourselves, in a certain way, because all opposition can be thought. Because *everything* is an opposite, *everything* can be thought. (*W* II: 165/*FS* 152)

Opposition is, thus, it seems, a requirement, an exigency of representational thought. Without the articulation of opposition, without its frame, then, there is no thought—or at the very least, without pushing toward such a structure we risk undermining the very ground of our representations; this is why Novalis will also declare that "we must seek the dichotomy everywhere" (*W* II: 201/*FS* 187), an imperative that expresses not so much a program of engagement as the basis of a question. Interrogating the nature of the "opposite" per se, then, Novalis observes that the "opposite itself is a relational concept—but here [i.e., in the domain of opposition] all relation should be abstracted from" (*W* II: 112/*FS* 50). It is this sense of relation that Novalis will want to restore, working across a domain in which what becomes most central is *connection*, connectivity, transition—the moving-between, such that "the particular mark of the opposite" becomes part of a broader, mobile reticular field. Of this "particular mark," Novalis will conclude that, conceived outside a more general structure of relationship: "Its essence is namelessness—therefore every word must drive it away. It is a non-word, a non-concept" (*W* II: 112/

FS 98). For Novalis, then, it will be connectivity, the transverse movement of conjoining, relation, combination, that drives and spurs on infinitely the fecundity of language and of thinking: a structure that is locked into the oppositional will tend always toward silence, toward an unutterability, a blank.

The reason this subversive interrogation of the oppositional dependency of thought is of huge importance is that it is in relation to this questioning that Novalis conceives his sense of "synthesis." Synthesis is the holding or binding-together of thesis and antithesis, of I and not-I—it is the "sphere" in which their relation becomes possible. However, if I and not-I are no longer to be thought from out of the framework of an opposition, then their "belonging," too, must be differently conceived. If I and not-I can be thought otherwise than oppositionally, then the element of their synthesis—"absolute sphere without boundary," as Novalis strikingly claims (*W* II: 44/*FS* 36)—will be thought rather as a domain of connectivity, the arena of their coincidence, their fluidic merging or transient overlapping. This is the arena of thought that Novalis will term "absolute relation," the groundless space of a conjoining.[11] Thus we might say that, for Novalis, that which "we" are can no longer be apprehended from out of the absolute necessity of a pure, punctual origin. Rather, this point becomes the domain of an abyssal convergence, the shifting ground of an indefinitely unstable structure: "this point is everywhere in us—everywhere where thesis, antithesis and synthesis are, that is, where we ourselves are" (*W* II: 41/*FS* 34).

Evidently, with the unsettling of the polarities of I and Not-I, the "between" of the movement of *schweben* will also have to be rethought: without the binding of limits, the polarity of oppositions will melt away—and with it, the "between" that sustained and mediated the polarity. Instead of a "between" of I and Not-I, then, Novalis's imagination will become this "power of exchange"—*Wechselkraft* (W II: 94/*FS* 83). The *Schweben* of the imagination will be the movement that effects the exchange, distribution, and interplay of determination and indetermination, subject and object, I and Not-I. In this redistribution, the mechanics of the relations between the oppositional pairs has altered entirely: in place of a structure determined by a positing and a counter-positing, which is to say by an active propulsion and a resistance, we have a relationally fluid process, in which object and subject gather and coalesce, configuring and reconfiguring their separation and their unity. Of this new structure, Novalis writes:

> The circle can be interrupted at any point—the pole of intuition and representation can be placed and displaced at any point. Imagination

> manifests itself as insight/interruption [*Einfalls*] and inhibition [*Hemmkraft*]. (*W* II: 98/*FS* 88)

I and Not-I have become, then, interruptive articulations that manifest the movement of imagination, the nodes into which it crystallizes, distributes itself. What has entered into play is a way of reinscribing and redistributing a dynamic of movement and arrest, of flow and stabilization. Instead, then, of an imagination that wavers between determinate limits, conjoining but also ultimately controlled by them, we have a movement that is no longer subordinate to those polarities. Rather, the points of arrest, whether these belong to subject or object positions, are merely the temporary alighting moments in which the indefinitely fluid movement of the imagination articulates itself, in inhibition, in interruption. As Novalis's thought develops, it will be this sense of interruption, of "crystallization,"[12] of temporary convergences of a fluidic movement, that becomes the dominant model, both for his explorations of natural phenomena in the scientific notebooks and for his understanding of language, of the convergence of word and thing.

It is in this manner that the "between" comes to the fore in Novalis's thinking: the constitutive instability and uncertainty of the between-space of I and not-I, identified by Fichte with the hovering or wavering of the imagination, has become the index of a groundless free play. What Novalis calls "the highest proposition of all art and science"—the special equivalence of I and Not-I—is now to be understood as the operation of a space of relation. So fully has this relational "between" become the generative heart of Novalis's thinking that it comes to be identified with life itself:

> Should there be a still higher sphere, it would be the sphere between being and not-being—the oscillating [*Schweben*] between the two—something inexpressible, and here we have the concept of life. (W II: 11/*FS* 6)

One of the central moments from the studies, a moment that provides a dramatic perspective from out of which this reorientation can be seen, appears quite late in the text, and concerns this very hovering, or *Schweben*. The passage reads as follows:

> All being, being in general, is nothing but being free—hovering [*Schweben*] between extremes that necessarily are to be united and necessarily are to be separated. All reality radiates from this light-point of *Schweben*—everything is contained in it—object and subject have their being through it, not it through them. I-ness [*Ichheit*] or productive power

> of imagination, the hovering—determine, produce the extremes within which the hovering occurs—this is a deception, but only in the realm of ordinary understanding. Otherwise it is something thoroughly real, because the hovering, its cause, is the source, the mother of all reality itself. (*W* II: 177/*FS* 164)

We can see here that the enshrinement of indeterminacy and a groundless motility has become sufficiently central to set up a series of equivalences: "Being" is equated with the freedom of a play which is no longer constrained within the limits of a determinate positing. In this space of movement, the only stabilizing instances will be the mutually exchangeable nodes of relation, the "extremes" whose structural necessity entails both that they belong together and that they are kept apart: "united" and "separate" at one and the same time, in a tension that has become already familiar to us. The "between" is thus to be understood as the dynamic and fragile space that not only articulates the opposition of I and Not-I but generates their interplay: "all reality streams forth from this light-point of *Schweben*," as Novalis writes. No longer can this between be understood purely as the corollary of the necessary polarities of consciousness. Now, instead, "object and subject have their being through it [*Schweben*], not it through them." The polarities are merely the transient expressions of a dynamic movement, the uncertain shadows of a "light-point" whose motility cannot be circumscribed by the spatial metaphors that the notion of a "between" implies. Indeed, in the pure productivity of this movement, spatial metaphors will collapse in on themselves. The "light-point" of *Schweben* produces and sustains the play of crystallization and dissolution; so much so that, in a sense, the structure that has oriented the investigation of *Schweben* becomes dissolved. "Imagination," to the extent that it remains tied to an account of "powers" or "capacities," is no longer an adequate notional receptacle for an instability that thereby becomes originary. Instead, we must speak—as Novalis begins to at the very end of his reflections on Fichte—of *creation*: "because all creation is about being, and being is *Schweben*" (*W* II: 178/*FS* 165).

The *Fichte Studies*, then, are guided by a central tension, pursued relentlessly throughout, between "separation and unification" (*trennen und vereinigen*). Attempting to follow along this track, we have been led to the sense that the element—or as Novalis calls it, the "sphere"—of belonging, far from representing an ultimate fusing or ab-solving of what is divided, is given in the abyssal in-between of the tension that plays in the double movement of "dividing and uniting": it is the decisive presence of this figure that draws it into the orbit of this study, in which we encounter it as both echo and reiterated question. What becomes central, then, to the development of Novalis's thinking beyond the *Fichte Studies* is precisely this difficult figure of the between, the explosive gathering point of a dissonant *harmonia*. The preoccupations with combining, juxtaposing, and dissolving that are so evident in the scientific notebooks are all oriented toward its articulation; the sense of porosity between zones of visible and invisible, ideal and real is entirely driven by a demand for its recovery. What pertains most particularly to this between-space as Novalis conceives it is *movement*, a mobility that allows the between an infinite adaptability, while also ensuring that it eludes determination, articulation. To say, as Novalis does, that "synthesis is, or can be, thesis and antithesis" is to place synthesis in a domain of exchange, where it moves in the fluid dimension of a reciprocal play of determination and indetermination. What is foregrounded in this play is precisely the movement, the passage of the between, which thereby becomes both utterly fundamental and fragile to the point of inarticulacy. Novalis will work endlessly to expose this zone of fragility, pulling at the edges of the determinate in order to open its motility, its porosity, its volatility. And it will be in relation to observations of the natural world that the complex relationality of I and not-I will find its most vivid expression.

3

Writing the Book of Nature

I, crystal
—Paul Klee

We have isolated, and explored at its point of origin, the emergence of a fertile between-space in Novalis's work, associating it with a distinctive elaboration of Fichte's insights into the interrelation of I and not-I: the between of these two has emerged as a generative nexus which refused to either polarity the primacy of an origin. However, as we observed in chapter 1, it would betray the energies of Novalis's thinking if we were to assume that his later fragments can be reduced to merely "poetic" elaborations of these philosophical abstractions. We have said that what speaks in Novalis's work is a captivation with the world, with the sheer materiality of things. This means that nothing in Novalis can be addressed in terms of an exemplarity: the ruminations and speculations of, for example, his studies of Werner are far from mere "applications" on the basis of a theoretical framework, even if the development of the notion of *Schweben* can be understood as the generative core of these speculations. The task, then, will be to seek and to articulate the osmotic relation, the sphere of "the idealreal and realideal," as the *Fichte Studies* would have it (*W* II: 19/*FS* 13), and to map this territory of the between, first elaborated in the readings of Fichte—the territory of "separating and uniting"—onto the objects of the earth, the things of the world, as they reveal themselves in that movement. The work of the fragments will be this work of mapping, an articulation of the chiasmic intertwinement of sensible and imaginary, inside and outside, visible and invisible.

This is how Novalis expresses this intertwinement in one of the 1798 "Studien zur Bildenden Kunst," a fragment we have already cited:

> All that is visible clings to the invisible. That which is audible to that which is inaudible—the felt to the unfelt. Perhaps the thinkable to the unthinkable—. (*W* II: 423)

It is this "clinging" which most powerfully expresses the thoroughgoing interpenetration of inside and outside in the fragments, an interpenetration that refuses to allow an opposition to ossify into a settled structure. Instead, what we find is a particular kind of belonging, a sense of the visible as haunted by the invisible, by that which lies beyond its grasp, the audible haunted by what is silent, thought by what is unthought.

It is in this light, too, that Novalis's famous exhortation from the "Logological Fragments" is to be understood: "The world must be made romantic [*Die Welt muß romantisiert werden*]. It is thus that one can find again originary meaning" (*W* II: 334). The source of that meaning, and of the transformative project that will rediscover it, is a work of thinking with and in the interpenetration of ideal and material, in the space between. The work of *romantisieren* is the alchemical penetration of idea and object: not merely a one-sided "elevation of tone." True, Novalis says that in this transformation the commonplace is "given a higher sense, the everyday an obscure aspect, the known the worth of the unknown, the finite the appearance of the infinite." But this transformation is to be matched by its paradoxical reverse, by a downward movement such that "the process for the higher, the unknown, the mystical, the infinite is the inverse . . . it receives an everyday expression." The endless osmotic exchange of higher and lower forms the central node of Novalis's thinking at the point at which it was able to integrate itself with the interests and endeavors of the Schlegel brothers and the *Athenaeum* project, even if the rigor and intensity of Novalis's undertaking is such that the manifesto-like quality of that opening was not able to enclose it.

From the start, Novalis's particular preoccupations have been with the question of exchange, of the "moving-between" in which the domains of ideal and real gather, interpenetrate, and split apart. As Novalis moves away from the commitments which forged the *Athenaeum* journal, it begins to be in the scientific notebooks that we rediscover an acute address to the thought of a between. It is here that Novalis develops a vocabulary—appropriating the vocabulary of the empirical sciences in which he had immersed himself—with which he can engage the transformative movements to which Fichte's work had already provided access.

Above all, it is in the notes collected under the heading *Das Allgemeine Brouillon* that Novalis begins to push the consequences of the experience of thinking that his intensive involvement with Fichte had initiated, and to move in the direction of entirely new possibilities. This direction, and these new possibilities, have to do with the exigency of the fragment, as it emerges in relation to the *Athenaeum* project. This is because what the fragment brings into play, more than anything, is the question of the whole, the question of completion and of totality. It is here, then, in the "Encyclopaedia" notes that this question forces itself most fully upon us, and it is this question that will return us still more vividly to the experience of a dynamic of "separating and uniting," of conjoinment and dispersal which we will see as central to Novalis's endeavor, as to the endeavor of this book.

In respect of the "Encyclopaedia" project, there is, of course, one kind of approach that would find it easy to avoid the question of "the whole" entirely by presenting the text in biographical terms: this approach would maintain that, although Novalis certainly had the intention of creating something like an encyclopedia, the unfortunate brevity of his life prevented him from doing more than accumulating preliminary observations and speculations. Accordingly, the notes that make up the text of *Das Allgemeine Brouillon* would have a status akin to the preliminary sketches toward a grand painting, the first tentative jottings of a melody for a large-scale symphony: signs, merely, of an abandoned dream. Thought in this way, the question of the whole—which is also the question of the project itself—is relegated to the domain of biographical curiosity, and the notes are read as a collection of disparate and ill-formed speculations.

There are several reasons why this approach, whether tacit or overt, impoverishes rather than encourages a reading of the notebooks. These are reasons that are not extraneous to the text, but rather present within it, both in terms of Novalis's explicit reflections on his own conception and in the working-out of the processes of the writing. In this respect, then, of most importance are the notes concerned specifically with the notion of completion, of beginnings and endings, of inclusivity and structure—thoughts, in fact, generated by the very idea of what he refers to as an "encyclopedistics." Especially germane in this respect is Novalis's striking preoccupation with systems of classification and ordering; his interrogation of the structure of connection; and most importantly, the way in which thematic engagements—in particular those concerned with the thought of the chemical, with crystallography and with mineralogy—invade the text not merely at the level of content, but in terms, too, of its structure. What we will try to expose, in what follows, and by addressing the text at the level of writing, is the way in which Novalis's "Encyclopaedia" project moves in a dimension that is caught indefinitely—and necessarily—*between* completion and incompletion. A book, in other words, that can nonetheless never quite be a book.

In the Garden of Orpheus: Musical Relation as Model

We will begin by returning once more to the image of the seed. We noted at the outset the persistence of this image: of the senses of germination, of pollination that abound in Novalis's work, and which are even implicit in his chosen authorial subscription. Novalis's insistence that "all is seed" has indeed manifold implications; but from the perspective of the idea of writing now under consideration, the sense of germination that is most pertinent involves the experience of a kind of proliferation. Seed, scattered upon the ground in ways that are either more or less controlled by the scatterer, flourishes in relation to the environment in which it is scattered, in relation to the soil in which it finds itself, in relation to the contingencies that beset it: its possibilities for growth and further pollination depend on the workings of complex external exigencies. More than anything, though, what seems to determine the seed is its potential for growth, for expansion, or, as Goethe would have it, metamorphosis. To think of a text as seed, of the written word as the initiation of a metamorphosis, is to think of those written signs not as repositories of meaning but as openings, occasions for the event of a flourishing.

This gathering-together of word and seed, so central to Novalis's project, clearly recalls the *Phaedrus* in the manner in which it plays with the possibility of thinking words as "organic" entities: a kind of productivity, a fecundity and a sense of unfulfilled openness also seem to belong to Plato's word insofar as it is "written in the learning soul" (276a), and not "sown in black water" (276c). In Plato these latter—words sown, seeded in a ground which is other than the soul—are granted only a kind of provisional quality, one that lacks a certain kind of "seriousness": the "garden of letters" is the appropriate locus only for a "reminding," for a storing up against the winter of age, and for a certain kind of pleasure in watching them grow in others (276d).[1] For Novalis, though, this botanical lexicon will be inflected entirely differently: here, the "garden of letters" is neither provisional nor secondary, but is rather the occasion for an openness whose primary site is the written text. The sense of seed remains—the sense of growth and germination—but the insistence on the productivity and fertility of the written word will force a dramatic effect upon the writing of the text itself. The insistence on metamorphosis, on the transformative potential of word/seed, obliges one to think differently about their operation: it suggests that the text may be written precisely with an ear not to its self-containment, its completedeness, but to its fertility and openness—like seeds which are to be harvested later, upon the occasion of their flourishing.

Such a possibility lends a very particular inflection to considerations that revolve around the question of the "completion" of a text, indeed of its status *as* a book, or a "work" in the sense of a self-contained and consistent endeavor. No longer will completion be thought in terms of the working-through of a structure of argumentation. Rather, if each word is to open onto a fecundity of possibilities that lie beyond linear argument, then a text that appears to labor toward an inclusivity or wholeness will be one that embraces a paradox at its heart, one which cannot avoid putting its own premises in question: the "Encyclopaedia" project of Novalis's *Das Allgemeine Brouillon* is such a book.

The set of problems that such a thinking poses for an "Encyclopaedia" project is twofold: first, how will the project generate a sense of closure? How, if each of the moments of its writing represents the gesture of a scattering, will this dispersion gather itself into a totality? How, in other words, can the openness of these gestures replicate the sense of inclusivity that an "encyclopaedistics" implies? And second, if each moment of the writing represents the opportunity for, as it were, independent avenues of growth, singular metamorphoses, then how is the connection, the coherence between these avenues to be conceived? What is its ground? How is this coherence to be engaged in the text? It is in this sense that we can read the following parenthetical note, from the middle of the notebooks, as being central to Novalis's thinking:

> (Ground of *cohesion*—of the belonging-together, etc. of thoughts—Observation on thoughts and image-making—their variations—interminglings, etc.) (*W* II: 662/*AB* 145)

The "ground of cohesion" is the question that each reflection, each attempt at an entry will bring in its wake; and at the heart of the question of cohesion will lie the question of the "belonging-together" of the disparate entries, of their connections, their "variations," their "interminglings." This suggests that the principal task of reading, the central mode of access to this body of texts, is via an address not so much to the fragments themselves, but rather to the space between them. What is required is a reading that addresses itself to the question of their binding, the question exposed precisely by their scattered and dispersive quality. At stake, then, in the "Encyclopaedia" project is what Novalis will describe repeatedly as a "*Combinationslehre*" or as a "*Verhältnislehre*." This project—the "classification of all operations of knowledge"—must take up the question of the binding-together of the dispersive, the disparate; and this is why Novalis will say that "the theory of combination [*Combinationslehre*] contains the principle of completion" (*W* II: 601/*AB* 100). It is the thinking of the belonging-together of the gestures of the writing, and of the between-space in which those gestures are gathered and separated, that will open onto the paradoxical thought of a totality.

The notebooks, then, will unfold as an address to the possibility of the project of an encyclopedia. But it is an address that occurs on two levels: on the one hand, Novalis explicitly turns his thoughts, and with frequency, back upon the project he is engaged upon, often under the heading "Encyclopedistics," or more often—though more curiously—"Philology." The inclusion of these moments not only implies that the encyclopedia project will necessarily be a reflexive activity whose inclusivity involves a consideration of its own possibilities; equally, and on the other hand, these moments allow for an opening onto a second level, in which the text is performative in nature, enacting in its unfolding the processes of gathering, cohering, and separating that are the dominant objects of its encyclopedic inquiry.

It is with regard to these questions that the following fragment presents itself, a detailed investigation of which will open up new avenues for an understanding of Novalis's purpose:

> The book is Nature put into strokes (like music) and completed. (*W* II: 605/*AB* 103)

The overarching question this strange statement presents will inevitably be the following: what is "nature," for Novalis, such that its "completion" is to be effected by the written word? But before this question can be properly asked, several observations must be made. In the first place, it is evident in this fragment that "the book" is not to be considered as a "representation" or "description" of nature or natural process. Rather, it is to be its fulfillment, the event of its achievement. Now, if the activity of the text is to "complete" nature, then the text must in a way step beyond the representation of nature, in order that this completion might be effected. In this sense, then, the book is both within and outside of nature. This speculation lends a peculiar intensity to the title of Novalis's own project, which thereby acquires an almost insupportable weight: an "encyclopaedia" will not only sustain the burden of inclusivity, but its act of composition must lend itself to that other completion, the completion of nature itself.

However one is to understand nature, then, with regard to this completion it is clear that the event of the written word has a very special belonging within it, a particular status that has little to do with a merely descriptive undertaking. Another way of expressing this is to say that it appears that, here, it is emphatically not the materiality of nature that is to be placed over against the ideality of the word, as complement: however the relation between word and nature is to be understood, it will not be configured on the basis of this opposition. Words, rather, seem to be wrapped up in their own peculiar materiality; indeed, we shall see that they are to become the nexus of an intertwining, a fertile kind of between-space.

The second emergent thought that this fragment initiates is the thought of music: the fragment says that insofar as the book can be said to "complete" nature, it will do so as strokes or marks (*Striche*), and this "putting" of nature into mark resembles in some sense music. This resemblance needs to be examined.

"Music," Novalis will say later in the same fragment, "sets all in motion." Thus, if we are to accept the analogy he proposes earlier between the gestures of language and the operation of music ("put into strokes (like music)"), then we should understand the "completing" of nature not in terms of the fulfillment of a static structure but in terms of movement, of a setting into motion. The semantic field of "achievement," "fulfillment," "completion" will have to be rethought in the face of this gesture, by which a motility is inscribed not merely into the process of completion or fulfillment, but into its very completedness.

The thought of music is never far from the surface of Novalis's thinking, and music offers itself to him often as a model for his own enterprise. More often than not, music provides the image of a certain kind of relationality, the motile and unstable connectivity whose articulation and production is close to the heart of his "Encyclopaedia" project: "perhaps all relations are musical relations," suggests a late fragment; and in the *Allgemeine Brouillon* itself we read, in an entry entitled "Musical Mathematics," that music "exhibits something of combinatorial analysis, and vice versa" (*W* II: 597/*AB* 96). What allows for the analogical possibility that Novalis indicates between, on the one hand, music, and on the other, writing in its connection with the natural world, is a thinking of music not as a given structure, but rather as the movement of relations that are capable of infinite permutation, infinite variation: movement in its moving, relation in its relating. The music that Novalis envisages will be what he describes elsewhere as a "chemical music" (*W* II: 671/*AB* 152), a music that pushes toward continual dissolution and internal reconfiguration, a music that effects ineluctable and gradual change in its material. Novalis ponders, at one point, the "musical nature of fever" (*W* II: 544/*AB* 57), indicating that a kind of rhythm operates across the whole field of the body, in its dissolution as in its maximalization. This is a rhythm that will invade the entire domain of nature and of thought, and the processes of exchange and interchange between them that we have already begun to establish. It is in this sense that Novalis claims that "Fichte has uncovered the rhythm of philosophy" (*W* II: 544/*AB* 57), because it is in the work that belongs to his earliest philosophical encounters that Novalis espies the fluid exchange of inner and outer, the intertwinement of materiality and ideality, the pulse of their movement. In this movement, as we saw earlier, we are to think no longer of the intransigence of limits and checks, but of rhythms of gathering and decay, concretion and dissolution. If then, as Novalis says, "all method is rhythm; remove the rhythm of the world, and the world itself is removed" (*W* II: 544/*AB* 57), this is said in respect of the motility in which modes of observation, inquiry, and articulation fuse and intertwine with their objects, the play of gathering and dispersion intimate to the experience of the world. If this is rhythm, it will be rhythm in the way in which Benveniste beautifully expresses it: "rhythm is . . . form in the instant in which it is assumed by what is mobile and fluid . . . the form as improvised, momentary, changeable."[2]

"Only then" writes Novalis, "when the philosopher appears as Orpheus, will the whole arrange itself together" (*W* II: 544/*AB* 57). What is at stake, for Novalis, when philosophy wears the garb of the musician—when philosophy makes music; when it sings, even[3]—is the experiencing of relation, of the between-spaces of thought, of thought as it negotiates the between; an anarchic relationality, unsubordinated to a governing principle. The encyclopaedia project, or the sketchbooks of *Das Allgemeine Brouillon* in which that project is both completed and rendered impossible, will emerge as a fabric of connections, a combinatoric play that is motivated by the intertwining of ideality with the materiality of the earth. If the book is to "complete nature" in a way that is aligned with this sense of music, its aim will be to expose the rhythms of that exchange, and at the same time watch the processes of connection and combination which unfold in that rhythm. The word, or more concretely the "strokes" (*Striche*) of writing, will become the locus of this exchange, the momentary fixing of this fluidity: "All *fixing* occurs by means of tying-together, connecting [*Verknüpfung*]" (W II: 665/*AB* 147). A thought, then, will achieve a definite articulation, will become in a certain way *fixed* in the gestures of the written word, but will achieve this fixity as a function of a reticular structure of indefinite mobility. This productive and fertile motility can be seen to develop and extend the discoveries of the *Fichte Studies* in respect of the *Schweben* of the imagination. Indeed, just as before, if one were to descry a governing thought in Novalis's encyclopaedia project, it would once again reside in this indeterminate pull between fixing and tearing-apart, gathering-together and dissolution, liquefaction and solidification, which we are associating with a *harmonia* of primary dissonance.

* * *

Our starting point here was a very particular sense of completion, a completion that is brought to nature through the gesture of writing. However, we see that the sense of completion is not to be understood as any kind of closure or closing-off, but rather as a kind of music, an infinite play of variations, the interweaving of sets of relations, the rhythm of connection. A text which is oriented toward this rhythm will be one that is attentive to the ways in which connections merge, emerge, and pull apart: it will be as attentive to the ruptures and lacunae that separate as it is to the movement of binding-together. Indeed, it will find its experience of totality in this tension between separating and binding. If the text appears to be interruptive, discontinuous, the figure that nonetheless most fully defines its operation is neither that of a purely continuous unfolding nor that of pure disruption, but rather a kind of continuity in interruption, a writing that gazes both at and across the points of rupture. Later on, we will see how it is the written word that comes, for Novalis, to operate as a nodal point in this tension of separating and binding; and we will explore how the word comes to appear as the moment of coalescence, the unstable point of gathering of the transformative exchange of real and ideal. But before this possibility can emerge, we need to explore further the mechanics of the "Encyclopaedia" project. This we will do, first, by considering the writing itself, taking as our starting point the idea of the fragment, though this idea will ultimately prove to have only a limited value in respect of an understanding of Novalis's undertaking. Secondly, we will address ourselves to the conceptions of order and classification that provoke Novalis's experimentation.

The Cut and the Join: The Way of the Fragment

It is the same dynamic structure which we have repeatedly identified—the irresolvable tension of binding and separation—that is central to the thematic of the fragment as it emerges in Jena in the 1790s. In this respect the fragment is an idea of considerable importance to Novalis, and one which must be explored even if, in the long run, and for reasons that we hope to make clear, it is not there that the central interest of Novalis's work resides. Despite these reservations, then, a consideration of the idea of the fragment, of its possibilities and limitations, will be germane to a better understanding of that work, and it is in this direction that we will proceed.

To begin with, and without recapitulating the entire history of its development, we can say that the idea of the "philosophical fragment"—though never explicitly theorized as such—belongs in a preeminent sense to the work of Friedrich Schlegel. Schlegel, as is well known, was influenced in this endeavor by his encounter with the fragments of Chamfort;

and although the possibilities of the fragment had already been developed in extremely interesting directions by, among others, Lichtenberg, it is noteworthy that the predominant domain of influence belongs to the French tradition that Chamfort inherits. This is significant in that this tradition evolved around conceptions of the "maxim" as repository of wit, of a certain kind of incisiveness, a cut. The brevity and closure of the maxim in this tradition have to do not so much with a provocation to thought, but with a reduction to silence: the maxim refuses dialogue, closes it off in a kind of peremptory brilliance, an overwhelming flash of style. In a sense, despite the fact that the fragment as it is reconceived by Jena Romanticism moves in entirely other directions, it is still true that its development and progress are deeply haunted by that history, and that the fragment per se will always include a kind of slipping-back to its origin.

This historical origin notwithstanding, the sense of the fragment developed for the *Athenaeum* seems motivated equally by a different need: by the movement toward an openness of response and co-respondence, something that Schlegel and the other members of his circle would call *sympraxis*. In this sense the fragment will want to be anything but definitive, will long to avoid the "statement," and will aim instead to embrace a sense of interruption, of constitutive uncompleteness that is far removed from the sense of an authoritative dictum that determines the wholeness and perfection of the maxim. It is very much within the tension of these two opposing directions that the Romantic fragment must be read. In an exquisite essay from *L'Entretien Infini*, Blanchot shows how the possibility of the fragment as conceived by Schlegel and enacted most visibly in the short-lived *Athenaeum* journal rests upon precisely this tension: that it belongs to the fragment to deteriorate, to fail in its ambition, for the interruptive to lapse into the closure of the sentence. Reflecting upon this necessary, constitutive failure of the fragment as "project," Blanchot writes that the movement of thinking to which Schlegel invites us "leads the fragment back toward the aphorism, that is, toward the perfect sentence." He continues, in a way that sets up clearly the tension between the ambition of the fragmentary and the decay that attends that ambition:

> This inflection is perhaps inevitable and comes down to: 1) considering the fragment as a text that is concentrated, having its center in itself rather than in a field that *other* fragments constitute along with it; 2) neglecting the interval (wait or pause) that separates the fragments and makes of this separation the rhythmic principle of the work at a structural level; 3) forgetting that this manner of writing tends not to make a view of the whole more difficult or the relations of unity more lax, but

> rather makes possible new relations that except themselves from unity, just as they exceed the whole.[4]

The passage wraps beautifully the promise of the fragment into a description of its deterioration; and does so in a way that coordinates closely with the kinds of operation we have observed in Novalis's work. For Blanchot, then, and in entire consonance with the structures of thinking we have identified in Novalis, the question of the fragment is the question of the between, the question of conjoining that interruption makes possible and thematizes. The question of reading the fragmentary would then revolve around the space or interval in which what Blanchot calls the "rhythmic principle" of the work would reveal itself. What it is necessary to observe, then, is that the central issue around which the idea of fragmentation revolves is not simply a mechanics of interruption or dispersion, but far more a complex reflection on the nature of *completion.* Thus, in the figure of deteriorative decay that Blanchot sets before us, the more difficult exigencies of the whole that the spacing of the fragment presents are sacrificed to a simpler kind of closure, to the resounding self-containment of the aphorism. By contrast, the possibilities that are opened up in the fragment, even if subject to this necessary decay, are far other: the question of completion becomes that of a wholeness able to embrace its own interruption, a structure that achieves itself in the openness of a between-space. Philippe Lacoue-Labarthe and Jean-Luc Nancy have shown that what is refused in the fragment—at least in its most aspirational moment—is not at all "completion," or perfection in the ordinary sense. Rather, what the fragment represents is not a sacrifice of closure to the whims of disintegration, but rather the bringing into question of a particular notion of "system." We will address this question of system more fully shortly, especially with regard to what might be termed the "system of nature." In a preliminary way, though, it is necessary first to note that the question that is raised by the fragment in relation to the idea of system is far more than a gesture of refusal, or the simple assertion of a logic of disruption over and against the mechanisms of organization on which the systematic might appear to depend. Far rather, what is at stake is an entirely other *sense* of system, a sense that harks back to its original meaning, one that revolves around the sense of holding-together, a placing-together in juxtaposition. Lacoue-Labarthe and Nancy write:

> It thus becomes necessary . . . to propose that fragmentation constitutes the properly romantic vision of the system, if by "System" . . . one understands not the so-called systematic ordering of an ensemble, but that by which and as which an ensemble holds together and establishes itself for

> itself in the autonomy of the self-jointure that makes its "systasis," to use Heidegger's term.[5]

Later on, we will have opportunity to revisit this sense of "systasis" in relation to certain aspects of Heidegger's work.[6] But for now, though, it is necessary only to observe that, thought in this way, it becomes possible to see in the fragment not so much the blank refusal of completion, but rather its startling reinvention. The completion that belongs to the fragmentary will be of a kind that embraces its interruption, that stares across the chasm that divides one thought, one articulation, from another, and—rather than insisting on "filling in" the lacunae that emerge in the passage between fragments—will lend itself to the peculiar openness of the between.[7]

The question of the fragment, then, as it emerges in what becomes known as Jena Romanticism is highly correspondent with the development of Novalis's writing. In particular, its idea of the fragment can be said to be strongly coordinated with the sense of completion that Novalis envisions for his "Encyclopaedia" project, so much so that it would be possible to trace out the development of this project precisely in terms of a response to the kinds of exigency that belong to this new thought of systemic completion, the sense of "fragmentary system." Evidently, the *Combinationslehre* that Novalis envisions in the "Encyclopaedia" responds to the thought of a between, of an opening in which the play of relation, of combination or connection can take place. Such a perspective is warranted by his close involvement with the Schlegel brothers and with the *sympraxis* of the *Athenaeum* project. There are many moments at which Novalis appears to offer reflections that are developed in relation to the reconstrual of the relation between system and fragment that was underway in that project: it is in this light, for example, that the following can be read, bearing in mind once again Novalis's involvement with music, and the insistent preoccupation with structures of relation which that involvement allows:

> Certain stops [*Hemmungen*] are like the fingerings of the flute-player, who stops now this hole and now that in order to produce different sounds, but appears to be making arbitrary combinations of silent and sounding openings. (*W* II: 228)

This thought can certainly be mapped onto a thinking of the drama of completion and interruption that the structure of the fragment brings into play. However, the idea of the fragment, while certainly germane to the development and operation of Novalis's work, cannot easily adapt itself to the fecundity and density of his thinking, in particular in the "Encyclopaedia" project and beyond. The problem—the limitation of conceiving of the fragment as central to Novalis's work—is opened up for us, though this time unwittingly, by Blanchot, who writes, again from his essay on the *Athenaeum* project in *L'Entretien Infini*:

> Unless one of the tasks of romanticism was to introduce an entirely new mode of accomplishment, and even a veritable conversion of writing: the work's power to be and no longer to represent; to be everything, *but without content or with a content that is almost indifferent*, and thus at the same time affirming the absolute and the fragmentary; affirming totality, but in a form that, being all forms—that is, at the limit, being none at all—does not realize the whole, but signifies it by suspending it.[8]

The passage once again delicately articulates and indeed extends the tension in the "completion" that the book represents. In that tension, we experience the indefinite multiplicity of avenues that the text opens up, avenues that conjoin and separate, interrupt and fuse in an entirely dynamic manner. In this dynamism is broached an entirely new sense of totality, one which foregrounds the notion of the "work," of the "book" as the gathering nexus of this multiplicity. This thought of Blanchot's, then, comes close to the quasi-organic sense of the "completion" of the book that marked the self-reflection of Novalis's project.

But here it is necessary to express a resistance, to offer Novalis's work as a counter to a tendency that seems inevitably to be generated in the thinking of system and fragment in Blanchot's work and elsewhere. This resistance has to do with Blanchot's insistence that the drive of the sense of totality that the "fragmentary form" engenders is toward a writing that is "without content or with a content that is almost indifferent." Thought in terms of a "contentless" play, the fragment enters a domain in which it is most fundamentally expressive of a sense of writing conceived in the most general sense. The concrete specificity of *what* is addressed within the fragment per se is thus reduced to the dynamics of the "book," to the complex interweaving of completion and incompletion that constitute the "work." Now, this engagement with writing is certainly apposite to Blanchot's own process and thinking, but it presents something of a problem when addressed to Novalis's work. This is because what this approach will tend to foreground is a force of abstraction, a force that withdraws from the specificity of the fragments themselves, pushing them toward a position in which their "content" is relegated to the status of the "exemplary," the mere illustration of a dynamics of the formal dance of writing.

Everything that we have so far observed in Novalis's work moves against such an idea. There is no question, as we have seen, that the seminal encounter of his philosophical life was with the fearsome abstraction of Fichte's 1794 *Wissenschaftslehre,* but we have also noted that right from the outset, the direction of his thinking was one that precisely pulled against that force of abstraction: rather, his is a thinking that moves ineluctably toward the dispersion and dissolution of this kind of process. Far from a drive toward a "contentless" abstraction, Novalis's work represents a persistent and fierce push against the opposition of abstract and concrete, insisting relentlessly on the irreducibility of the latter, and on the intertwinement of both registers. Indeed, rather than a move toward "contentlessness," Novalis pushes precisely toward a fusion of form and content, a mode in which the content does not merely exemplify the formal process, but actuates its own formal specificity.

The text of Novalis that Blanchot has in mind when he insists on this apparent "contentlessness" is the short text entitled "Monologue" that was also of crucial concern to Heidegger. This text certainly appears to lend a playful weight to the thought of a withdrawal from "content." The opening is well known:

> There really is something foolish about speaking and writing; proper conversation is merely a word game. The laughable error that people make is only to be wondered at—that they mean to speak about things. The real peculiarity of language, that it is preoccupied purely with itself, is known to no one. (*W*II: 438/PW: 83)

Blanchot cites this opening, and also the close of the text, which doubles back upon itself in a movement which performs that very self-referentiality, neutralizing the gesture and intention of the "Monologue" itself:

> Even if in saying this I believe I have described the essence and function of poetry in the clearest possible way, at the same time I know that no one can understand it, and I have said something quite silly because I wanted to say it.

The apparent exposure in this text of the self-referentiality and primary contentlessness of language is misleading, however; despite appearances, the text should be considered otherwise than as a gesture toward a "contentlessness," in the sense that Blanchot would like. Instead, the sense of the play of language is quite different than the "contentless" self-referentiality toward which the opening and close of the "Monologue" appear to point. The decisive moment of the text, in fact, will be its center—a center carefully avoided by Blanchot's reading. At this center, and operating still within the models of music (and also of mathematics) that we have already discussed, Novalis indeed reiterates that words, like these models, "play only with themselves, express nothing but their own marvelous nature." But then he adds the following, in a crucial and unexpected move:

> Even thus do they mirror in themselves the strange relation-play of things [*Eben darum spiegelt sich in ihnen das seltsame Verhältnißspiel der Dinge*].

Thought from out of this center, then, what emerges is a quite different sense of play, one that does not align itself so easily with the notion of the "contentless." Instead, what is at work in language is a "mirroring": not a withdrawal from "content" but a very particular reflection of it, a reflecting that engages it in its relational play, its *Verhältnißspiel.* What is essential to understand in this text *is* this curious mirroring, and the play whose strange mutuality seems to drive and orient both word and thing. If, then, we are to engage the question of system, and the matter of fragmentation, interruption and opening which addresses itself so firmly to that question, it will not be in withdrawing or abstracting to a plane of "contentless" writing, but rather in pursuit of what Novalis calls the *Verhältnißspiel der Dinge,* the "relation-play of things." Once again, in this thought of relation-play, we are asked to engage the question of the between: here, specifically, the between-space of relation, of connection. To the extent that the question of system and fragment engages in particular ways the question of completion, it will certainly be operative in the background of Novalis's thinking. But it is necessary to insist that the sense of break, of the opening that the fragment brings in its wake, is shifted in Novalis's writing toward a thinking of the between as a force of gathering. The lacunae of completion are addressed, in Novalis's work, not primarily through the question of the cut, but rather through the question of jointure and of joining, of combination, juxtaposition, and connection: a *Verhältnißspiel.* And it is this question of connection, the question of relationality, which will prove to be a more productive avenue of investigation than that of the fragment.

The Play of Relation: *Das Allgemeine Brouillon*

How, though, does Novalis understand connection, or relation? How would a *Combinationslehre* such as he envisages repeatedly in the notebooks unfold? What is the logic of the "in-between" that would guide the space of connection between one encyclopedic thought and another? How will the rhythm of this connective interchange be made apparent? And most importantly, what determines the field of exchange, the reciprocity between thought and world in which the "relational play" of both are to mirror one another? In relation to these questions, we discover in the notebooks of *Das Allgemeine Brouillon* the following:

> The arbitrary, wonder, and accident, relate [*zusammenhängen*] to the world indirectly, etc. Matter = an Ideal/. The study of one thing—the study of all things—flows in the end into one—where all properly belong together [*zusammengehören*]. / On the Fichtean problem—how things cohere [*zusammenhängen*] with representations. / The binding of the wonderful and the natural world. The wonderful should take place according to rules—natural effects *not according to rules*—Wonder and the natural world will become one. (*Rule* and *Unrule*). Unrule is the rule of fantasy. Arbitrary rule—accident—rule of wonder. (*W* II: 649/*AB* 135)

Dense and cryptic as this note is, it is quoted at length here to indicate the constellations and gatherings of words and ideas that seem to be at work in its wanderings. Novalis, we note, is still drawn back to the Fichtean model that first sustained his thinking. But what inaugurates that recapitulation is the question of the *Zusammen-hang*, of the belonging-together that the note voices at its opening. The between-space of togetherness courses through the note: the thought is present of the gathering of a totality, in which "all study flows into one"; but the question is the question of "binding," of *Verbindung*, of the joins or seams of this togetherness. To a certain extent, Novalis has by now substituted for the central oppositions of Fichte's text a new variant: instead of the opposition of ideal and real, whose particular modes of belonging and of parting we have already explored, we now have a structure in which the constellation of the "wonderful"—which includes the arbitrary, the fantastical, and the accidental—is brought into opposition with the "natural world." But here, too, the question of their opposition is construed in terms of the question of their binding-together: they are "to become one," but only across a between-space that gathers together the contradictory force of "rule and unrule." What seems to be envisioned, in this strange thought of "oneness," is a totality that is subject to both rule and unrule: the ideality of fantasy, of wonder, will be subject to rule to the extent that the natural world will be exposed to "unrule"; the relationship, then, in which they belong together will be subject to an endless unworking, a process in which that which gathers into the ordering of "rule" will be exposed to an energy of decomposition.

The question of rule and unrule, of the passage between, and of their uneasy belonging-together, finds important expression throughout the notebooks in terms of a particular—and sometimes surprising—fascination that Novalis evinces for classificatory systems, methods of organization that occur in this context as modes of encountering the natural world. In what follows, we will review one such classificatory model—a model that catches Novalis's attention for biographical reasons. We will try to gauge what, for Novalis, constitutes its promise, its possibility, and its disappointment. It is through exploring these versions of order and of ordering, and Novalis's reflections upon them, that we can best address the problematic of the "Encyclopaedia" project as a whole.

Orders of Thought: Werner and the Classificatory Impulse

The first notes or sketches for Novalis's "Encyclopaedia" project date from September 1798. At the end of the previous year, he had enrolled—perhaps in response to the traumatic events of that period (the death of his beloved Sophie and that of his brother)—at the Mining Academy in Freiberg. It is there that the thought of the "Encyclopaedia" project originates, generating with it a new and extraordinary enthusiasm that spills over into letters to Caroline and Friedrich Schlegel in Jena. Thus, if the project owes its genesis to the extravagantly synthetic thought patterns of Novalis's early thinking, it is equally true that its motivation derives in a quite concrete sense from his experience at the Mining Academy. This is in no small part due to the influential presence of Abraham Gottlob Werner, who was professor of mineralogy at Freiberg at the time of Novalis's studentship. Now, the most significant aspect of this influence lies in the nature of the important contributions that Werner had already made to the science of mineralogy, contributions for which he was already well known at the time Novalis began his studies. Werner's best-known achievement at that time lay in the establishment of a taxonomic system for the classification of minerals. This classificatory endeavor had been laid out in a publication from 1774 entitled *On the External Characteristics of Minerals*.[9] This work builds upon the hugely influential taxonomic endeavors of Linnaeus earlier in the century, and seeks to rectify what Werner saw as the inadequacies of Linnaeus's approach and that of his followers with regard to geological and mineral formations.[10] There are clearly elements of Werner's approach that fascinate Novalis, indeed to such an extent that he begins to borrow significantly from Werner's vocabulary as soon as his thoughts turn to the possibility of an "Encyclopaedia" project, in particular to the dilemmas of classification and comprehensiveness. What becomes equally apparent, though, are the ways in which both his embrace of and resistance to Werner's endeavor come to be the foil against which he attempts to secure his own project's footing.[11]

The classificatory principles that guide Werner are evident even in the title and opening of his treatise: his endeavor, which explicitly aims at a "comprehensive" and "perfect" ordering of the natural objects that belong to the domain of mineralogical investigation,[12] will arrive at its goal by considering what he calls their "external characters." Werner comes to the determination of these parameters by contrasting his own method with three other modes of considering minerals. These three modes are (a) "internal characters," by which he means a way of classification according to the chemical properties of each mineral; (b) "physical characters," by which he wishes to indicate properties that are "observed in the reaction that minerals display in the presence of other given substances"—their reactive qualities, in other words; and (c) "empirical characters," by which he means what can be ascertained from the mineral's place of discovery. What is significant here is that Werner understands the perfectibility of his classificatory system to be possible only on the basis of very particular exclusions: at core, the domain of ordering is determined by withdrawing the objects of inquiry, in the first place, from the domain of chemical reactivity; secondarily from their geographical situatedness, and thirdly from their geological/historical contexts. As Novalis develops his own very particular interpretation of the "chemical," it is this first mode of exclusion that will prove most vulnerable. But the second and third modes, too, will prove problematic to the extent that both involve patterns of relation, and involve engaging the material object across a field that stretches beyond its immediate sensible components: the field of time (in respect of its historical or geological emergence) and the field of the event of its spatial occurrence (its geographical context). Werner will insist that his approach, for which he coined the term "oryctognosy,"[13] in fact "forms the foundation of the other two subdivisions: geognosy and mineralogical geography." To this end, the project upon which he embarks will take the form of a rigorous and exhaustive descriptive categorization of all that pertains to the sensible experience of mineral formations. The stakes of this approach are high:

> If the idea of the external appearance is *complete*, expressed by us *intelligibly* and in a *proper* order, our description will be *perfect*.[14]

In fact, the descriptions that unfold from out of this insistent push toward the exhaustive display, despite the rigidity of their framework, considerable versatility and resourcefulness of descriptive detail. Thus, categorizing the color of minerals, nine different kinds of yellow are defined and described in exotic detail (e.g., "Isabella yellow," "bell-metal yellow"), ten kinds of red. And a seemingly impossible multitude of different kinds of tactile solidity are defined, and dutifully described, each in turn: "dentiform, filiform, capilliform, veinose, reticulated, arboriform, stalactitiform, coralliform, reniform, globular," and so on: the list is quite extensive.

Michel Foucault has beautifully analyzed the mechanics and significance of the ambition at work in this classificatory process with regard to the work of Linnaeus earlier in the century. He writes:

> By limiting and filtering the visible, structure enables it to be transcribed into language. It permits the visibility of the animal or plant to pass over in its entirety into the discourse that receives it.[15]

Thus, in Foucault's analysis of Linnaean taxonomy, the possibility of a classificatory order depends in the first instance on a drawing of limits, the isolation of domains of exclusion and proscription, within which a zone of "visible objects" becomes available for description. In the case of Werner, too, we can see that the array of descriptive detail flourishes by virtue of its being first placed within a framework which is marked by rigid points of exclusion. Without those points of exclusion, the descriptive array—far from moving toward satisfying the demand for "completion"—would risk scattering and dispersing, deferring indefinitely that completion by mounting increasingly elaborate descriptions, the differences between which would appear in an increasingly fragile series of distinctions.

In respect, again, of the procedures of Linnaeus, Foucault continues:

> By means of structure, what representation provides in a confused and simultaneous form is analysed and thereby rendered suitable to the linear unwinding of language. In effect, description is to the object one looks at what the proposition is to the representation it expresses: its arrangement in a series, elements succeeding elements.[16]

Along these lines, then, one would have to say that what Werner refers to as the "natural order" of description involves the coordination of a series of sensible traits with a certain kind of linguistic ordering, the progressive unfolding of the propositional series that Foucault describes as the "linear unwinding of language." If that is so, then we can see how an intervention that disrupts the limits drawn around the domain of classification would necessarily, and simultaneously, disrupt precisely that same "linear unwinding." To bring into question the limits of the classificatory system, to suggest a breaching of those limits, is equally to disrupt the ordering of the language that coordinates its description. The possibility might arise, under such a pressure, of the emergence of an entirely other kind of ordering, one not so aligned with the rigid demarcation of categories, more willing to play within their interstices, to flourish in their between-spaces. Perhaps, to borrow the title of Foucault's book, such a disruption to classificatory limits might begin to issue in an entirely different relation between "Words and Things."[17]

In effect, this double disruption (of language and of its ordering) is what will take place in the working out of Novalis's notes toward his "Encyclopaedia" project. The mechanisms of that disruption will arrive—once again, as so often in Novalis—as a question about relation, about connection, and will take the form of an insertion of the very field that Werner had been most keen to keep apart from his manner of investigative description; namely chemistry, or the domain of chemical reactivity. We will investigate the nature of this chemical intervention in the next chapter; and this will mean trying to grasp from a historical and theoretical point of view the kinds of tension and difficulty that the idea of the chemical poses for the construction of a system of "natural order." Before that, though, it is necessary to explore further the pressures that Novalis's own brand of thinking places upon Werner's work.

Stone and Time: The Pressures of the Chemical

In the first place, it is important to observe that Novalis is by no means dismissive of Werner's project, and still less is he primarily intent on its dismantling. More than once, in *Das Allgemeine Brouillon*, he refers to Werner's project as the model for his own: "I will practice classifying and defining, etc., using Werner's system," he writes, setting as his goal the "rectification" of Werner's project: "revision of Werner's system and the critique of my undertaking is *my first task*," he insists (*W* II: 595/*AB* 95). His task, then, will be to broaden the scope of Werner's classificatory endeavor, adopting its methods, but deploying its vocabulary in ways that reach entirely beyond its operation in Werner's text:

> Whoever researches in all the sciences . . . and in a philosophical mineralistics that is accompanied by a philosophical, all-embracing system of

> classification, would also organize all these related sciences under the grand science and art of the mineral kingdom. (*W* II: 575/*AB* 81)

The mineral, in this new project, will come to be emblematic of broader investments; and in these reinvestments, the idea of the mineral—of its encounter, its manner of formation, its retrieval and composition—will be filtered through a sensibility forged in entirely other fires than Werner's. For this reason, as Novalis ruminates upon his own methodology and seeks to draw the lines and limits that would enable his "Encyclopaedia" project to unfold, he experiences at the same time a resistance to Werner's strategy, asking:

> Where is his principle of necessity—and where is his principle of completeness? (*W* II: 595/*AB* 95)

Tugging against the limits within which Werner constrains his mechanisms of ordering, Novalis begins to insist on what he calls a "historical oryctognosy," an observational method that would take into account the mineral not merely in terms of its sensible qualities, but equally in the process of its emergence. Clearly, too, we witness the appropriation of Werner's methodology as it is subjected to the force of a sensibility forged in the wake of the critical project. Thus, in the notebooks devoted to studies of Werner's treatise, we encounter the following array of classifications, in which the ordering of "stone" is exposed to possibilities that leave behind entirely the elements of Werner's procedure. "This [Werner's] classification is extremely defective," writes Novalis, as

> a stone can be considered: 1) in relation to its subjective origin—or its determination in our faculty of representation. (In the past, at present, and in the future). 2) In relation to its objective origin or formation . . . 3) In relation to the time of the planets . . . 4) In relation to the space of our earthly body . . . 5) In relation to its connections with other natural bodies or its political nature. (*W* II: 462/*AB* 210)

It is clear, here, that Werner's classificatory structures are being opened up to two central questions: the question of time, and the question of relation or connection. We recall that Werner's purely dogmatic approach insisted rigorously on the restriction of the classificatory system to purely sensory qualities, and that these were to be determined by excluding considerations of history, of context and of relation. Novalis indicates these exclusions through the force of this extravagant iteration of possibilities, as if to challenge directly the principle of completeness or "perfection" that Werner had made his own, and to install in its place classificatory principles of such an explosive breadth as to challenge the very idea of completion.

Above all, though, as Novalis attempts to take up the classificatory task that his encyclopaedia project sets before him, it is a thinking of chemistry that will introduce a kind of disorder into the regular unfolding of ordered determination. A preoccupation with the chemical is explicit in the Werner studies, where Novalis challenges the former's resistance to a classificatory endeavor based on chemical effects. In his treatise, Novalis writes, Werner has ignored

> the possibility of a symptomatics that can be applied to chemistry—a question that is surely of the greatest importance, because the critique of a new, higher science that embraces the two of them begins with this very science. (*W* II: 462/*AB* 210)

It seems, then, that what Novalis is envisaging is an approach to natural phenomena such that chemical transactions and processes are no longer refused entrance into a systematics based on the observation of mineral formations; it is this inclusion of the chemical, Novalis says, which will be the core of an altogether other, "higher" science. In respect of this disruptive possibility, Novalis writes, in a note taken again from the studies on Werner:

> He [Werner] completely fails to discern the possible transition—from the external characters to the inner constituents, or from symptomatics to chemistry, and yet this is the main approach for solving this problem. (*W* II: 462/*AB* 210)

This note suggests that the chemical is emblematic of a kind of interiority, the workings of an inner process that would thus be in direct opposition to the pure externality of Werner's method. This in turn raises the suspicion that Novalis is thinking this opposition far beyond questions of natural scientific methodology, a suspicion confirmed by his insistence that Werner's refusal to countenance the chemical renders him "wholly dogmatic." Novalis continues:

> Opposed to him stands the idealist . . . the magical knower, the prophet. Their unification [*Vereinigung*] / Their crossing over [*Übergang*]. (W II: 463/*AB* 211)

It would seem that Novalis is thinking the chemical very much in relation to the processes of interpenetration and mutual infusion of real and ideal that stretch back to the work of the *Fichte Studies.* Just as in those first explorations, so, here too, his critique of Werner will hinge upon questions of interwinement, of a movement-between, of transitions and the passage between interior and exterior. Chemistry comes to seem the principle of change, of connectivity and alteration—the image of the operation by which the material is invested and transformed by the ideality of thought, and vice versa.

Taking this one step further, we can observe that, for Novalis, it is chemical transformation that introduces into materiality the element of time: time, he writes, is "the co-principal of the chemical" (*W*II: 576/*AB* 81). It is on account of this linkage with the question of time that it becomes possible to see how chemistry becomes the cornerstone for the entire array of classificatory variants that Novalis deploys to restructure Werner's project: the question of time, of emergence and decay, of relation, of contexts of interaction, begin to be governed by this insistence on the primacy of the chemical. To expose the mineral—by which is understood a naturally occurring solid-state object of homogeneous composition—to the work of the chemical is, for Novalis, to subject its consistency and solidity to forces of decomposition, liquefaction, solution, dissolution, and reconfiguration, all of which are to be considered temporal movements. More broadly still, we can see that in exposing the solidity of stone to the ongoing transformative work of these processes, the stone itself—that which emerges and greets us as solid object—becomes merely the momentary fixation, the halting of the rhythms of alteration and growth.

Words of Crystal

It is in this context that a central image takes root in Novalis's thought—that of *crystal:*

> Should crystal[lization] be the truly synthetic, harmonious relation of solid and liquid, and thus crystal truly substantial, an extraordinary being? (*W*II: 463/*AB* 214)

Crystal emerges in Novalis's thinking as the locus of an encounter, as the moment of exchange between movements of liquefaction and solidification. In so doing, it becomes the paradigmatic figure of the between: the unstable convergence, the gathering point in which the object becomes fixed, determined. Crystal, thus, is always a becoming-crystal, a "*kristallisieren*," only emerging into materiality as the nexus (*Verknüpfung*) of processes of alteration and transfiguration. It is this provisional quality, the natural object in its emergence and dissolution, which becomes central to Novalis's attempts to give an account of the materiality of the natural world. The emergence of the object becomes a matter of a "fixing," the temporary coagulation of fluidic processes of connection, combination, solution, and dissolution: "All fixing occurs through a combining [*Verknüpfung*]" (*W* II: 665/*AB* 145).

If Novalis's thinking is beyond all else a thinking of the trans-fusion of the material and ideational, an exploration of the between-space in which they at once conjoin and pull apart, then we might see, here too, the same operation of a between in the emergence of crystal as the nexus of dynamic processes of liquefaction and coagulation. Crystal is, for Novalis, the paradigmatic natural object, the very image of the natural world—not merely as aggregate of sense data, but as fully exposed to the formations and deformations of time, of context, of relation. In this same way the mobile nexus of real and ideal, the between-point of their exchange and intertwining, equally begins to adapt to the language of crystal: "Bodies are precipitated and crystallized thoughts in space."

Just as the movements of formation and deformation in the chemical process will disorder the givenness of the material upon which it operates, so too will the intrusion of these fluidic processes change and disturb the process of their classification. No longer able to define, maintain, and delimit the objects of its inquiry, the "Encyclopaedia" project will equally surrender to the processes of liquefaction and dissolution. And in this dynamic, as the domains of experience become inaccessible to the "linear unfolding" of language, the *word*, too, ceases to be the index of an ordered exposition, and takes on instead a much more fragile character, the mode of an in-between. The word itself, indeed, becomes—like crystal—the point of coalescence, a between-space or mark of concretion amid the fluid rhythms of gathering and dissolution. And if this transfiguration of the word is operative and visible in the notes for Novalis's "Encyclopaedia" project, it is nonetheless in an altogether different text that we find its boldest and most transparent formulation: this text is one to which Novalis turned his attention following the period of *Das Allgemeine Brouillon* and his studies in Freiberg, and thus in the closing years of his working life: the novella *Die Lehrlinge von Saïs.*

Before venturing into the precincts of that particular temple, though, it is necessary to contextualize broadly the question of the chemical, in order to arrive at a clearer sense of the experience out of which

Novalis's' sense of "crystallization" emerges. What follows, then, is a brief exploration of the problem of the chemical as it enters into the field of Kant's vision, and the complex of exclusions and limitations within which it makes its entrance into the *Metaphysical Foundations of Natural Science.* In contrast to Kant's cautious resistance, it will be possible to see in certain elements of Schelling's endeavors to articulate a philosophy of nature an embrace of the domain of the chemical, such that it becomes the center of a systematic enterprise. What we will find, in fact, in Schelling's *First Outline of a System of the Philosophy of Nature,* is an exposition that is in remarkable parallel to Novalis's endeavors. The *First Outline* was indeed composed at exactly the same time that Novalis was most fully at work on *Die Lehrlinge von Saïs,* and it is from the vantage point which Schelling gives us that we will best be able to address that text.[18]

4

The Alchemy of the Word

Chemistry of the Infinite: Schelling with Kant

For the Schelling of the *First Outline,* the challenge that a "philosophy of nature" represents is that of resisting a pull toward a conception of nature that insists on understanding it, explicitly or not, as "the sum total of existence," as a merely inert and passive accumulation. Instead, the endeavor must be to grasp nature entirely from the standpoint of activity—"the action *in its acting*" (*EE* 13/14)—without falling back into a dichotomy of action and effect. The peculiarity of this approach is the reversal upon which it insists: rather than commencing with effect, with the "product" of an action and from thence proceeding to construe the activity of production, a philosophy of nature such as Schelling conceives it will consist in the effort to remain steadfastly within the activity itself, qua activity. From such a perspective, what will be required is an entirely different understanding of the "individual being," of the empirical object. In other words, what is in question is not the nature of the existent, per se, whose speculative "sum total" might "add up," implicitly at least, to a totality that might make possible a conception of Nature. Rather, the question will be one of conceiving the possibility of an individual existent from *within* an infinite activity: how, and why, will an "object"—a "product," as Schelling calls it—emerge at all from within this infinite unfolding? What will be demanded, then, is to "observe what an *object* is in its *first origin,*" to grasp the existent *as* the activity of its emergence. The notion of infinite activity necessarily pushes toward an infinite dispersal; it resists the cohering-together of anything that might inhibit its indefinite expansion, refusing the stability of the individual existent in such a way as to drive toward dissolution. Thought in this way, the empirical existent becomes the necessary condition of an infinity that, as an activity of pure dispersion, can be grasped only by engaging a concept of resistance: without such a moment of resistance, an activity of pure dispersive unfolding would not be graspable as anything at all, least of all could it issue in a "philosophy of nature." Absolute activity—as we saw in the context of Fichte's exploration of the movement of the "I"—can be expressed and articulated only on the basis of that which retards, inhibits, or interrupts its progress. The individual existent will *be* this retardation, this inhibition, interrupting the dispersive unfolding of the infinite activity that Nature is.

Schelling's *Outline* can be seen as an attempt to reconfigure a conception of nature in terms of the operation of certain kinds of force. Specifically, what he has in mind is a reworking of Kant's construction of nature as the product of the interaction of opposing forces, expressed in the *Metaphysical Foundations of Natural Science.* Kant claims, in the preface to that work, that "the fundamental determination of something that is to be an object of the senses must be motion," and that he will attempt to articulate the foundations of empirical experience in precisely those terms. This decision entails, from the outset, that Kant determine matter not as the mere occupation of space, but as its active and dynamic filling: "matter fills its space by moving force and not by its mere existence" (*MA* 497/42). This expansive force must necessarily be exposed to its opposite, otherwise the object would know neither limit nor cohesion. Thus, the object is determined in a play of expansion and resistance that Kant aligns with what he claims are "the only two moving forces which can be thought of," namely, the forces of repulsion and attraction. These two forces are both, independently, necessary conditions for matter, but they are also reciprocally intertwined, such that matter is inconceivable without this intertwinement. The attractive, limiting force must be posited because "an essential moving force by which parts of matter recede from one another cannot . . . be limited by itself, because matter is impelled by such force to continuously expand the space that it occupies" (*MA* 508/56). Reciprocally, "by mere attraction, without repulsion, no matter is possible" (*MA* 510/59) because, exposed to an unchecked force of pure attraction, all matter "would coalesce in a mathematical point" void of space. For Kant, then, these two forces are the determinants that make possible the experience of empirical objects. But they are "fundamental" forces, says Kant, because they cannot be conceived as being derived from others. They are the necessary conditions of the empirical, but are nonetheless fundamentally ungraspable in themselves: our empirical experience entails the positing of these forces as metaphysical ground.

In one sense, then, Kant appears to initiate the possibilities that Schelling will take up more fully, of conceiving matter as determining itself in and through its activity: the motion of Kant's repulsive and attractive forces will be intrinsic to this process of determination. However—and this is where Schelling will sense the limit of Kant's conception—the motion of matter cannot, in Kant's account, avoid a decisive separation between "force" and that upon which it acts: to posit the operation of "fundamental," if, per se, inconceivable forces as the condition of empirical experience is to maintain rigorously a distinction between the two:

as Schelling expresses it, Kant's "force" is one that "is applied merely to the construction of individual products—and exhausts itself in them" (*EE* 20/19).

And indeed, despite Kant's insistence on matter as determined in and by the movement of force, he cannot ultimately avoid recursion to a dependence on a conception of matter as fundamentally inert, "lifeless," the neutral repository of effect: "the inertia of matter signifies nothing but its lifelessness, as matter in itself," he writes. Life is determined here as an internal principle of movement, the "capacity of a substance to determine itself to change" (*MA* 544/105)—a capacity whose sole index is a force of "desire" unknowable to empirical representation: "therefore, all matter as such is lifeless . . . The opposite of this, and *therefore the death of all natural philosophy,* would be hylozoism" (*MA* 544/105, emphasis added). Indeed, the very possibility of systematic enterprise, as Kant conceives it, rests upon this disjunction between active and inert, production and product, force and passive receptacle, cause and effect. This is because, for Kant, "system" as such is a "whole of cognition ordered according to principles," and this ordering can rise to the level of "rational science" only on condition that "the connection of cognition in this system is a *coherence of grounds and consequents*" (*MA* 468/4, emphasis added). Such a coherence would depend upon a clear separation between the two: to abandon this coherence, to elide the distinction between ground and consequent, to step beyond a structure determined by an opposition of cause and effect, would be to threaten the entire possibility of a systematic enterprise. And it is precisely this threat that will oblige Kant to exclude *chemical* process from the pure systematicity of "rational science," banishing it to the margins, to a limit-space from whence Schelling will draw it once again, placing its reinscription at the very center of his enterprise. For this reason we need to explore briefly the sense of the chemical that emerges in Kant, that will be transformed by Schelling, but also by Novalis.

In the *Metaphysical Foundations,* then, we find Kant defining the chemical as "the action of matters at rest insofar as they change the combination of their parts reciprocally through their own force." Now, this is already perilously close to the definition of life as "the internal principle of change," awakening the spectre of an inert matter—"matter at rest"—that is yet drawn into change through an activity of "combination" that belongs to its own inner principle. Chemical process—solution and analysis, the operations of merging and separation of different materials in contact—will thus work against a strict division between activity and product, tending toward a dangerous fusion of cause and effect. But it will make equally problematic the pure determinacy of matter itself, upon which the edifice of systematic "rational science" is to be built. Indeed, for Kant, what is problematic about the concept of chemical solution is that it does not easily permit of limit, of bounds. The notion of chemical process appears, in and of itself, to require the thought of an infinite dissolution, the absolute absorption and penetration of one matter within another that Kant's conception of matter struggles to resist:

> The solution of specifically different matters in one another in which no part of one matter is not united with a part of the other matter . . . is absolute solution, and may also be called chemical penetration . . . Here the question is only whether such a solution can be thought of. (*MA* 530/87)

A metal dissolving in acid, to use Kant's example (*MA* 531/88), offers an image of absolute "chemical penetration" of one matter in another that operates in such a way as to threaten the determinacy of that matter, and with it the boundaries upon which the opposition between active and inert, between cause and effect, must rest. What the possibility of "chemical penetration" suggests, to reiterate, is an absolute *dissolution* within which the distinction between determinate matter and the "force" of its activity can no longer be maintained. It is this thought, that at once belongs to the dynamic conception of matter that Kant is striving for, while threatening the bounds which make that conception possible, that obliges Kant to push the chemical to the margins of the system, to a marginal role in which it maintains the restricted status of "systematic art, rather than science." We must return to Schelling to grasp the potential of a reinscription of just this chemical process, in such a way as to allow its effect, and its threat, to reach into the heart of the system.

It is in relation to this reinscription that Schelling will attempt to unfold a systematic enterprise that involves, indeed entails, the dismantling of the dichotomy of cause and effect that, for Kant, marked out rigorously the very possibility of system. Schelling's effort to grasp the emergence of the object from *within* the activity of its production will retain the fundamental sense of an irreducible opposition of forces such as Kant describes, but will attempt to radicalize the notion of activity to such an extent as to render impossible the distinction between action and product, and neutralize any residue of the notion of a force conceived as *outside* that upon which it works. Schelling will attempt to replace Kant's distinction between a metaphysically conceived force and the "dead" matter upon which it operates with a model that enables this opposition to operate within the unfolding of an infinite activity. To "exhibit the infinite in the finite," to seize hold of the existent in its activity as coming-to-be—in its "first origin," as Schelling says—will entail approaching the finite from the perspective of the infinite, comprehending the emergence of the limited from out of the unlimited. As Schelling himself expresses it: "empiricism extended *to include unconditionedness* is precisely philosophy of nature."

The existent, for Schelling—the "product"—is to be glimpsed only as the "inhibition" (*Hemmung*) of absolute activity, as the limited and temporary concretion of a process that would seek always and at every moment to explode it. Nature, thus, will emerge as a kind of drive toward the formless, whose temporary arrest, whose inhibition, forms the basis of "the drama of a struggle between form and the formless." Form, then, is the self-limiting activity of a fundamental de-formation, one that depends upon its limitation, its inhibition in order to express its infinite expansion. If, "in Nature, there is a continual determination of figure from crystal to leaf, from leaf to human form" (*EE* 30/26), such figuration is a coincident expression, a "seeming" (*EE* 18/18) that belongs to the infinite dispersive activity of production. It is in relation to this concept of figure that Schelling develops a description of the de-formative drive of Nature as fluidic, as liquid. The fluidic here is understood as the intrinsically shapeless, figureless—the formless—but thought not as the pure negation of form, but rather as "that which is *receptive to every form*, formless (ἄμορφον) for just this reason" (*EE* 30/27). What will be sought, then, in pursuit of the unconditionedness of Nature is "the concept of the absolutely fluidic." Nature, in its absolute activity, grasped as pure production, is a drive toward liquefaction, toward the dissolution of form that the fluidic brings. The fundamental "force," then, for Schelling, will be that which "works against nonfluidity (solidity) and continually endeavors to *liquefy* everything in Nature." Schelling writes:

> A stream flows in a straight line forward as long as it encounters no resistance. Where there is resistance, a whirlpool forms. Every original product of nature is such a whirlpool, every organism. (*EE* 18/18)

The whirlpool, itself non-static, in motion, belonging fundamentally to the force of the fluidic energy it resists, in transient defiance of the infinite liquid outpouring of Nature: such is Schelling's beautiful image of the fragility of the concrete.

If the activity of Nature is to be thought of as striving toward a unity, this is possible only as a unity of absolute dissolution: "Nature contests the Individual," writes Schelling (*EE* 43/35), and is seeking always to de-compose the figure, to reabsorb the product into its endless activity. The striving toward the unity of the absolutely fluidic will entail the work of bringing together the disparate: merging difference, compelling the dissolution of the determinate. This is why, for Schelling, what is at stake in the absolute activity of Nature is a "*universal compulsion toward combination*" (Schelling's emphasis) that knows no limit, no end. Equally, though, just as this process can be thought only as unbounded, without limit—dissolving limits—it also cannot be thought in terms of a finite beginning. It is not as if we can begin with raw, "primitive" matter, and then think the processes of combination as supervening upon this primitivity. Rather, the movement of combination is itself originary, groundless, anarchic—a *harmonia*, in the Heraclitean sense.

It is this foundationless, an-archic movement toward the absolutely fluidic, which "reveals itself in no other way than through de-composition" (*EE* 35/29), that Schelling will place at the very core of his system. In so doing, he is excising any residue of a conception of matter that would allow the system to unfold in the way Kant determines it—as "a coherence of ground and consequent"—precisely by installing the very notion of absolute dissolution that Kant had tried to limit to the domain of the chemical. In its stead, Schelling is offering us the possibility of a thinking that, refusing submission to the dichotomy of cause and effect, attempts to stay within the activity of emergence, the exigency of the observation of "the object in its *first origin*."

If Schelling's system still reaches for a totality, still drives toward a unity that would recognize in nature "the sum total of existence," it will do so only within a logic of dispersion, a rhythm of dissolution that opens onto the unconditioned precisely by precluding the very completion it implies. Such a unity, then, must be understood not as the unity *of* a multiplicity, but as the paradoxical figure of a unity *in* multiplicity, a completion deferred. This unity of dispersion will recognize the natural object only as the momentary inhibition of an indefinite process of dissolution. The "system of nature" that Schelling is projecting and outlining expresses itself in a play of the singular and multiple, describing the moments of gathering, splitting-apart, coalescence, and diffusion that would mark out the rhythm of that play.

The question we have to ask is: what *kind* of thinking can respond to this exigency? Or, more precisely, how can we conceive the unfolding of the movement of thought within such an exigency? And further, what kind of language would engage, what kind of writing would a response to this question initiate? It is here, in attempting to respond to these questions, that we can encounter Novalis once again.

We have already seen how Novalis's thinking, in the notes that focus on the natural world and on the language that would address it, is oriented around processes of dispersal and gathering, cohering and dissolving. It is in these notes that the figure of crystallization takes shape in a way that is, as we can now see, close to Schelling's thinking. What we will try to explore, as we turn back to Novalis, is the unfolding of the possibility of an address to the natural world, the possibility of a "system of nature" in Schelling's sense, which develops and extends the consequences of the latter's engagement of "absolute fluidity" as the dissolvent and dispersive center of his systematic enterprise. It is in one of his last beginnings, the unfinished novella *Die Lehrlinge von Saïs*, that we will find Novalis presenting a perspective strikingly close to that of Schelling, yet pointing still further, pointing to the possibility of an enactment of Schelling's intertwinement of fluidity and inhibition at the level of language, at the level of the word, at the level of writing.

In the Precincts of the Temple: *The Novices of Saïs*

In a letter to Tieck from February 1800 describing his projects and ambitions, Novalis tells his correspondent that he has lately become immersed in the work of Jacob Boehme, speaking glowingly of what he calls "a genuine chaos, full of dark longing and astonishing lives" (*WI*: 732). Such a description might be equally apposite to the work into which he had been pouring much of his energies in the previous months, the unfinished novella *The Novices of Saïs* (*Die Lehrlinge von Saïs*). The letter to Tieck speaks of a complete transformation that this project was to undergo. But the work was abandoned: Novalis died the following year, leaving this transformation—however it was to have taken place—unrealized. What we have of the *Novices* is an unpolished torso, an unfinished statue: its contradictions, overlappings, and uncertainties speak of a larger ambition, but one that remains necessarily occluded. Nonetheless, as with the unfinished statue, or even the ruined monument, its interruptions and hesitations, its lacunae and its insufficiencies are themselves expressive; not merely of the project as a whole, but in their own right, as indications of an energy more evident in its failing than in its achievement.

In a certain way, it is this "failing" that brings the work closest to realizing the vision of the novella that the title suggests: the "novices of Saïs" are those that gather at the temple of the elusive goddess whose veiled and dangerous inaccessibility provided a focal point for so much discursive energy surrounding the question of nature in Jena and elsewhere at the time of Novalis's apprenticeship. At the heart of this question, insofar as it is engaged by the image of the temple, lies the well-known passage from Plutarch in which is described a veiled statue:

> In Saïs the statue of Athena, whom they believe to be Isis, bore the inscription: "I am all that has been, and is, and shall be; no mortal has lifted my veil."

It is this passage that provides the framework within which a complex array of reflection and philosophical meditation will occur in the last decades of the eighteenth century.[1] Challenge or warning, incitement or threat, the ambiguity of this inscription will help to crystallize a felt anxiety in relation to Nature, or more specifically around our mode of access to Nature. Inviolable mystery, temptation, seduction, danger—a complex and feverish set of discourses evolves at the end of the eighteenth century around this statue, or rather around its veil. These have been explored and investigated in many important ways, most recently by Pierre Hadot, and this is not the place to follow his fascinating itinerary. In relation to Novalis's own reflections on nature and natural processes, however, we can assert that the image of "the veiled goddess" operates as a gathering point, a force of cohesion that draws the events of the natural world toward one another and sustains them in their difference. In this sense, the goddess represents the "inviolable secret" (*WI*: 203/*NS* 15), the pull toward completion that we have seen as the driving force of the notes of Novalis's "Encyclopaedia" project, and in this sense she functions as an image of the tensional forces of gathering and dispersion that coalesce in the sense that we have been tracing. Thus we might see the "failing" of *The Novices of Saïs*—its incompletion, its merely provisional coherence—not merely as embodying the dynamic of the fragment that we have already explored, but as reflecting and enacting the very inaccessibility of the whole that the veiled goddess represents. The very narrative structure of the novella, too, can be said to express such a dynamic of gathering and dispersion: the shifting and uncertain array of characters that wander in and out of the narrative; the layering of the voices, often of uncertain provenance, that speak of parting, and of return; the leave-takings of the novices themselves; and the shadowy presence of the "teacher" which weaves in and out of the text. All of these suggest the thought of a multiplicity that expresses itself in relation to a whole which yet remains unachieved. It is this, for Novalis, that the image of the "inviolable goddess" expresses.

At a purely descriptive level, the entire text of *The Novices* greets us as a multileveled structure of overlapping voices, a structure which enacts the irreducible multiplicity that the opening sentence invokes: "Manifold are the ways of men" (*Mannigfache Wege gehen die Menschen*). The voices intersect and exchange positions, from time to time (but only rarely) crystallizing into something like a consistent presence. Indeed, the only voice that can claim the status of protagonist—that of the novice—is a shadowy and unstable presence, oscillating in the text between first and third person. At the outset, this novice expresses a "strange bewilderment" (*Verwirrung*) in relation to the multiplicity of voices to which he is exposed, those voices whose indeterminate "criss-crossing" fills him with "dread." It is against the anxious pressure of this bewilderment, this dread, that the novice will attempt to "inscribe his own figure" (*Auch Ich will also meine Figur beschreiben*), reaching for a ground, a solidity, within an unstable and fluid medium: already, in this anxious desire, we begin to see the dynamic of Schelling's fluidity and inhibition taking on a new shape. Thus Novalis writes, in a voice that may or may not be his own, that "it is as if an alkahest had been poured over the senses of man. . . . Only at moments do their desires and thoughts appear to solidify . . . but after a short time everything again begins to swim before their eyes" (*WI*: 201/*NS* 3). The strange and difficult movements of coalescence that are expressed in relation to this array of voices, though, will give way to a broader claim about the natural world itself, which will equally be seen to be caught up in this peculiar dynamic of emergence and dissolution. In the midst of this movement, it is the "inscribing"—of figure, of word—that will allow the kind of provisional and temporary *Hemmung* that Schelling envisages, a "mark" within the tidal pull of gathering and dispersal.

From a structural point of view, we can discover the motivations of this writing in the notebooks of *Das Allgemeine Brouillon*, at the point at which Novalis addresses himself to the form of the *Märchen*. Novalis describes the work of the "genuine tale" to be one in which all is turned toward "the wondrous—the mysterious and disconnected" (*wunderbar—geheimnißvoll und unzusammenhängend*) (*W* II: 514/*AB* 34). A drive toward the disconnected might indeed seem a curious approach to the structuring of a narrative, but from a certain point of view, it is this process that can be seen at work in the collapsing and indeterminate rhythms of *The Novices*. However, and in intimate relation with the tensional structure we continue to explore, what takes place in this novella is that this process—this drive toward the disconnected—enters into a zone of contention with what Novalis terms the "retardant" force of the poetic word.[2] In this field of play it is ultimately the written word that will be seen to act as the "between," the energy that gathers together the dispersive and disconnective energies that make up the scene of this strife.

At the opening of the novella, the novice appears entranced by the goddess, whose secret lures him onward in his investigations:

> I take delight in the strange accumulations and figures in the halls, but to me it seems as if they were only images [*Bilder*], coverings, ornaments, gathered around a god-like, wondrous image [*Wunderbild*], and this is always in my thoughts . . . It is as though they might show the way to

> where, in deep slumber, lies the maiden for whom my spirit yearns. (*WI*: 203/*NS* 13)

But, importantly, the novice tells us that the teacher—who, presumably, is closest of all to the inner workings of the temple—does not share these intimations of wholeness. Instead, this shadowy teacher, who drifts in and out of the narrative, variously gathering the novices together and dispersing them, and whose voice seems to the novice to "come from afar," appears engaged in his own peculiar project of gathering and connecting. He it is who "understands how to gather [*versammeln*] together the traits [*Züge*] that are scattered [*zerstreut*] everywhere." And above all, it is the objects of the natural world that the teacher is concerned with gathering: "stones, flowers, insects . . . arranging them into rows of multiple kinds." It is of significance that while the teacher's work appears to be that of gathering, the ordering that is consequent to the gathering does not appear to be directed toward a unity, but to involve "multiple kinds" of order. And as we shortly learn, the teacher's preoccupations are far from a drawing of the diverse toward the similar. This is how the novice describes the teacher's process:

> Everywhere, he found the familiar again, only wondrously mixed and coupled, and thus strange things ordered themselves often within him. Soon, he began to mark the connections amid all, the encounters and the coincidings. Now, he began to see nothing more on its own . . . he delighted in bringing together things that were strange to one another. Sometimes the stars were men for him, and sometimes men were stars, sometimes the stones were beasts, the clouds plants. (*WI*: 202/*NS* 10)

These strange gatherings, then, are the occasion of difference and conjoinment, of juxtaposition and of connection. Here, too, is the sense of exchange that we noted in Novalis's work at the outset. Once again, we see how these movements of gathering set into play rhythms of connection and division. And again and again, in this text, it is this rhythm of dispersion and gathering, dissolution and coalescence that will be enacted and insistently marked out. But here, more explicitly than elsewhere in Novalis's writing, it is language—and in particular the written word—which will coordinate that rhythm. Language will come to occupy the between-space of this rhythmic movement of coalescence and dispersion, spacing out the play of exchange, intervening to stimulate the processes of dissolution and re-formation.

In relation to this play of gathering and dissolution, it is of importance that the teacher immediately takes distance from the idea that the multiple rhythms of ordering that his gathering sets in motion have to do primarily with something like a "conceptual understanding" of nature. The gathering, collecting, and ordering of the natural world will in no way aim at grasping, at a conceptual seizing-hold. Indeed, another voice—later in the text—will exclaim: "all striving after truth in speech and dialogue about nature only distances always more from the natural [*Natürlichkeit*]" (*W* I: 207). The rhythms of ordering that emerge in the text speak instead of a kind of involvement that "lets nature dance and copies the lines of its movements in words" (*W* I: 226).

Distancing itself from a language instrumentalized as a vehicle for conceptual grasp, the voice of the teacher is heard to say the following:

> We do not understand language, because language does not understand itself, nor does it wish to: the true Sanskrit would speak in order to speak, because speaking is its pleasure and its essence.

These words recall the opening of Novalis's "Monologue," which thereby offers itself for a reading in close parallel with *The Novices.* In that text too, we recall, Novalis had played with the potentialities of a language understood as "preoccupied purely with itself" (*W* II: 438), though we had sought to step back from an interpretation that would see in this preoccupation a drive toward the merely "contentless." Here, now, thought in tandem with *The Novices,* it is possible to see still more clearly that what is at stake in this address to language is not an emptying-out of semantic content so much as a shift in the mode of engagement that transpires between word and thing. The word, as Novalis writes there, does not "speak *about* things" in the manner of an understanding, but plays in their orbit, in the mode of an exchange, an intertwining: "the book," we recall, "is nature put into strokes (like music) and completed" (*W* II: 348).

The play of gathering and dissolution in which the natural world emerges is, then, a play in which language is always intimately involved, and not as the possibility of its description. Rather, the word, and in particular its material inscription, will be intimate to the process of gathering and dissolution itself. In this process, Novalis tells us, what transpires is the emergence of what he calls a "figure": "Who would pursue [*verfolgt*] and compare [*vergleicht*] would see wonderful figures spring forth." This "figure" operates as a kind of crystallization, a temporary and unstable coalescence, like Schelling's natural object, but seemingly intimately bound up with writing: each figure, emerging from the play of gathering, seems to "belong to that great cipher-script" [*Chiffernschrift*] that we "glimpse" everywhere. This figuration, in which we "intimate the key, the very grammar, of a marvelous writing [*Wunderschrift*]," is decipherable, in turn, from out of an extraordinary array of figurations of the natural world:

> Wings, eggshells, clouds and snow, in crystals and stone formations, on frozen waters, on the inside and outside of mountains, plants, animals, men . . . on scored panes of glass and pitch, in iron filings around a magnet, and in strange accidental conjunctions.

An odd catalogue, this, of an apparent arbitrariness, but governed in fact by differences of viscosity, porosity, and indeterminacy. The random quality of lines scratched upon a glass, or the slow heaving of water into ice, suggest either a kind of proto-legibility, the quasi-inscription of marks across a surface, or an indeterminate movement between liquid and the process of its solidification. The most determinate of the forms here—the wing, the eggshell—are equally those that are exposed to the greatest vulnerability, as if the determinate object could enter into the domain of the *Wunderschrift* of nature only under conditions of extreme fragility. This delicate structure of indeterminacies—the temporary and unstable figuration of the natural world—suggests a kind of proto-language, a possible writing, but one destined to remain indecipherable, recalcitrant. If there is to be language, if the word is to form itself, to gather into name and concept, it will do so only as marked in advance by this strange indecipherability.

Once again, it is this strange coalescing, this odd and unstable figuration, which will bring Novalis's thinking in *The Novices* into close proximity to Schelling's conception of nature in the *First Outline*. There, we had seen how the coherence of Nature is addressed by means of an image of "absolute fluidity," a drive toward liquefaction, dissolution, in the midst of which the object emerges as a temporary and unstable "inhibition." We will explore, as we turn to the second section of the unfinished work, how Novalis's text engages and recovers this same sense of the fluidity of the natural world; and see how, for Novalis, it is the word—the "poetic" word—that emerges as its temporary coalescence. Just as the "figures" of the natural world emerge as a kind of proto-writing, so too will the word itself transpire as a kind of inhibition, a mark that seeks to stem the tide of liquefaction, "like a child drawing lines in the sand."

Words of Water: Liquefaction, Inhibition, and Inscription

If the first chapter of the novella (*Der Lehrling*) has already introduced us to the proto-writing that appears to mark our engagement with the natural world, then the second section of the text (*Die Natur*) will develop this idea. Building upon the sense of an intertwinement of language and the natural world—an intertwinement for which the gestures of writing are paradigmatic—Novalis will explore an account of language in which two sets of images interweave and collide. The first of these sets of images is linked to a myth of origin, and emerges at the very opening of the second chapter. The chapter begins:

> It must have been a long time, before mankind thought to indicate the multiple objects of their senses with one common name, and to place themselves in opposition to them. (*W* I: 205)

Language, we are to conclude from this opening, has come to involve a double movement, an ordering in which a sense-manifold is gathered into a commonality—a concept—and from thence is set in opposition to the sensible subject. But—Novalis tells us, crucially—this is not an originary language, but rather a "practice" that has developed or arisen subsequently. This "development" of the concept is then described by Novalis thus:

> This practice fostered further developments, all of which proceeded like splittings and dismemberings, that might well be compared with the diffraction of a ray of light. (*W* I: 205)

This is strange, because it seems that, for Novalis, what the concept achieves is not a gathering toward a unity—nature—but its dismemberment. Far, then, from gathering toward a wholeness, what emerges from this practice of the concept appears to be its sundering. We can say, then, that to the concept belongs intimately, not merely the sense of a unifying or gathering, but also that of a tearing-apart, a separation. In *The Novices*, indeed, the operation of the concept is with frequency described as a kind of splintering, a splitting (*Zerspaltung*), as if the object is somehow "splintered" in being named or spoken. It is in relation to this splintering of the concept that the most violent movements of the text appear, and with them the darkest possibilities of relation with the natural world. A voice from its midst—anonymous, grave—expresses the thought that the pursuit of this *endlose Zerspaltung* (*W* I: 210/102), the unending work of the name, "becomes in the end a true madness, a profound vertigo over a horrific abyss . . . Is not, indeed, everything that we see," asks the voice, "the rape of heaven, the ruin of former glories, the leftovers of a hideous feast?" (*W* I: 211/*NS* 103).

The question arises, then, of the wholeness that this "practice" has divested and disrupted. How are we to think of this plenitude, how address ourselves to its loss, if the way of conceptual inquiry is barred? How, indeed, are we to think of this wholeness at all if not in terms of a conceptual elaboration? Rather than sustaining the fantasy of an original plenitude that might be discoverable beyond or behind the word, Novalis claims that this wholeness must have involved a language of which "every expression was the true lineament of nature [*Naturzug*], and each idea could not but accord with the surrounding world" (*W* I: 205/*NS* 100) It is, he tells us, in order "to seek out the ruins of this language" (*W* I: 230/*NS* 113) that the travelers, late in the novella, venture into the temple precincts. It would seem that if the word is to achieve something other than this dismemberment, it must move somehow otherwise within the element of nature, must belong to it otherwise.

This myth of origin—the fantasy of original wholeness that permeates the thinking of language in this text—belongs, quite explicitly, to the domain of the *Märchen*, or fairy tale which, by the time of the writing of *The Novices*, had become for Novalis and Tieck alike a crucial form. Once again, then, we can turn in this connection to what Novalis has to say about the fairy tale in the notebooks that make up *Das Allgemeine Brouillon*:

> This age prior to the world issues, as it were, in the scattered lineaments of the *age after the world* . . . The world of fairy tales is the *entirely opposite* world to the world of truth (history)—and for this reason so *entirely similar* to it—as *chaos* is to *completed creation.* (*W* II: 514/*AB* 34)

This strange oppositional belonging to the "world of truth"—to the historical world—suggests an approach to the myth of origin that pervades the text of *The Novices.* Insofar as the tale is to operate on the underside of history, as it were, we should say that its function is not to aim at the description or recovery of the lost unity of the past in a historical sense, but rather the introduction of chaos into the present. If, then, the fantasy of origin in *The Novices of Saïs* appears to speak the dream of a language of absolute co-respondence between naming and named, it is not its reclamation that is being proposed. Rather, it is the "lostness," the sense of a dispersion that has already taken place, which the fantasy introduces. What the sense of a lost plenitude achieves, then, is the introduction of a *longing* (*Sehnsucht*) into the world. Under pressure from this longing, the fairy tale is to divide the present from itself. And it is thus that such a longing becomes constitutive of the human: as the direct result of this longing, and in relation to the separation it introduces, we encounter ourselves, always, as living amid "scattered remnants," endeavoring to discover "traces" or "seeking out the ruins of language.

However, it is not in this separation, or dismemberment, that the core of Novalis's thinking lies. Rather, it is in the shadowy possibility of a restoral that Novalis is most original, most incisive—and for us, most significant. This is a possibility that begins to emerge early on in the second part of the novella when, despairing of the decay into which the practice of a conceptual "separating and dismembering" has taken us, Novalis suggests that what has been lost is "the power to mix again the scattered colors of their spirit and . . . to realize new multiplicities of relation between them" (*WI*: 205/*NS* 19). If restoral is possible, then, it will be in the form of new "mixings," new bindings—new configurations of connectivity: but for this possibility to begin to emerge, an entirely different language will have to be spoken. It is in terms of a disjunct between kinds of language that this new possibility emerges, as Novalis moves (somewhat schematically, it must be admitted) to distinguish between a certain mode of investigative approach into the natural world, one that he identifies with the natural scientist, and a mode that he will now identify as the "poetic":

> If these latter have gently pursued the fluid and fleeting [*das Flüssige und Flüchtige*], the former have sought with sharp knives the inner construction [of nature] and discover the inner relations of its parts. (*WI*: 205/*NS* 19)

We find here, then, crucially reintroduced, a particular sense of the fluidic as the means of a productive and creative engagement with the natural world—the same sense of the fluidic that we had identified in Schelling's account. Thus, Novalis writes of an archaic sensibility that "sought the origin of all things in water . . . a water in which a primal fluidity [*das Urflüssige*] is manifest, as it comes to appearance in liquid metal" (*WI*: 228/*NS* 103). We have understood from Schelling's account how an absolute liquidity becomes the dissolvent image of nature, in which the presence of the solid becomes the temporary inhibition or seizure of this onrush of liquefaction. For Novalis, then, we too are possessed of an "immense longing for dissolution," a longing experienced in intoxication as the "bliss of liquefaction [*Wonne des Flüssigen*]" (*WI*: 228/*NS* 103). We are driven by a longing to lose ourselves in the fluidity of the natural world, in dissolution. But, paradoxically, and in keeping with Schelling's insights, the only mechanism of expression of this longing, the only means of approaching the longed-for dissolution, is the word—utterance or inscription—that interrupts that dissolution. For Novalis, then, the interruption of this process, the possibility of an instant of solidity, however fleeting, is the word that, in its inscription, with its "strokes," echoes and "completes nature." In the process of liquefaction, the word—the very expression of longing for that nullification, and the occasion of a correspondence—becomes equally the mark of a resistance, a solidifying. Words—the poet's words—become, in this event of corresponding, "the fixed point that sets in an infinite fluidity [*unendlichen Flüssigkeit*]" (*W* I: 225/*FS* 93).

It is of this movement of the word, a movement saturated with longing for the liquefaction that would erase it, that Novalis says:

> Thoughts arise, or new kinds of perceptions, which appear to be nothing more than delicate movements of a colored pencil, wondrous contractions and figurations of an elastic liquid. (*W* I: 220/*FS* 95)

Moving within this liquid, elastic element, the word forms the eddy in which the fluidity of the natural world coalesces and gathers, and the medium of the human finds its measure. For, in the end, thoughts

> seem to be nothing but emanations and effects which each I calls forth in that elastic medium, or the breaking apart of the I in that medium or, above all, a strange game that the waves of the ocean play. (*W* I: 220/*NS* 95)

* * *

The world of *The Novices of Saïs* is far from us. Its atmosphere is ethereal, elusive, recondite. In many ways, evidently, this sense of distance is written into the text, a part of its fabric. In its unwillingness to cohere, to gather itself into a linear narrative that might support resolution into the daylight clarity of character, thought, and action, the novella operates in a dusky, penumbral light, a shadowy border zone. In this sense, its "farness" is constitutive, built-in: its world can never have been anything other than far away. And yet it seems inadequate—too easy, too comforting—to address this distance purely in terms of the internal operations of the work itself. Restricting the question in this way does not allow for an acknowledgment of the immense historical gulf that separates our world from the world in which this text became possible, or indeed from that of its author. For this reason, it seems necessary to pull back from this ethereal element, to draw away from the swirling mists of the text, and to ask the question of the resonance that its world, and that of Novalis's thinking in general, might have in our own.

The wanderings of Novalis, across a landscape, and following a route, that we have in some measure tried to follow here, took him from a first flush of excitement generated by the appearance of Fichte upon the scene at Jena, through several years of meditative appropriation of that encounter. We have seen how this appropriation of Fichte pursues and radicalizes the imagination whose productive capacities the latter had in turn drawn from Kant. In Novalis's recasting, the imagination becomes more than the connective link by means of which an "I" experiences its world: for Novalis, the "between" that the imagination represents is the productive field from out of which both I and not-I emerge—that which generates, which gathers together, and which keeps apart. When Novalis, then, is drawn back toward the material, it is in the light of this new generative possibility that his work will unfold. The work of the scientific notebooks, of the encyclopedia project, is not a scientific realism of the empirical sort, but neither is it a whimsical "projection," as the usual misunderstandings of the Romantic continue to maintain. Rather, it is an attempt to bring the human fully into a zone of creativity in which its belonging-to and distance from the non-human are recognized, not merely as accidental contingencies, but as generative necessities. It is in this domain that Fichte's curious claim that "I = Not-I"—Novalis's "highest paradox"—takes on an urgency altogether unprecedented, one far removed from the rarefied environment in which it was first elaborated. This is because this difficult equivalence comes to express a domain both of belonging and of separation, a bondedness that is never simple absorption. In this sense, Novalis's work becomes an exploration, a sustained meditation upon the mode of relation that the human being has or might have with an other, be it human or non-human.

It is in this light that the subsequent movement in Novalis's itinerary needs to be seen—the movement that gives rise to *The Novices of Saïs*, to *Heinrich von Ofterdingen*, these strange works that marry an ambience of childlike fantasy to ruminative speculation, that conjoin the world of the fairy tale to brooding and strange conjecture. It is in these works, above all, that Novalis's elaboration of the domain of relation turns back on itself and comes to reflect upon the word. Word, indeed, comes to be *as* this relation, the fragile and fraught index of a between. To think word as crystal, as crystallization, or as an eddy marking off the tide of liquefaction, is to see the word as intervention, as a coming-into-the-midst (*inter-venire*)—as belonging to and emerging *as* the between of a relation. It is in this sense that we can see Novalis's work as a kind of poetics of materiality: poetry names the word insofar as it emerges from and as a zone of relation between the human and the natural world. Poetry, thought thus, *is* relation. It expresses the fertility of Heraclitean *harmonia*: the between as abyssal nexus of coming-together and pulling-apart, as the interwinement of irreconcilables. The poetic word—like crystal, like a figure inscribed in the sand—marks out and voices the fragile and transitory moment of coalescence and splitting-apart. Neither emanating from the expressive intensities of a subject, nor as a mere gloss upon a calculative determination of the world, the poetic word is rather the generative transformation of the harmonic relation of human and non-human. "We are settled on the earth in relationality," Heidegger will say. The poetic word—in Novalis's sense—lends to us the brief hope that we might, still, remain so.

Part 2

Heidegger: The Pain of the Between

Nobody ever inflicted or endured laceration as much as the daughters of Harmony.

—Roberto Calasso

5

The Darkness of What Is Near

Between World and Thing

In one of Heidegger's reflections on the work of Georg Trakl, we find the following:

> Pain rends [*reißt*]. It is the rent [*Riß*]. But it does not rip apart [*zerreißt*] into fragments experienced apart from one another [*auseinandererfahrende Splitter*]. Pain indeed rips asunder, yet in the way that it at the same time pulls everything to itself, gathers it to itself. Its rending is, as a separating that gathers, at the same time that pulling which, like the sketch or the incision of an outline, indicates and joins what are held apart from one another in separation [*das wie der Vorriß und Aufriß das im Schied Auseinandergehaltene zeichen und fügt*]. Pain is what joins the separated-gathering rending [*das fügende im scheidend-sammelnden reißen*]. Pain is the joining of the rent [*Riß*]. The joining is the threshold. It sustains the between, the middle of the two that are divided in it. (*GA* 12: 24/191)

The central thought here is not one of shattering, of tearing-apart or rending: it is the thought of a holding-together across a separation. Not an arbitrary separation, though, but the tension of a play of belonging such that what is kept apart is joined in that very separation, and what is joined is kept apart in its very joining. The "threshold" sustains because it is both within and without: it is the space of the between. At this threshold, difference is instituted and maintained, but equally, what is differentiated is brought into a belonging-together. The tension of this sustaining, of this belonging is, for Heidegger, the instauration of pain (*Schmerz*): pain is the bearing of the *agon*, the agony of irreducible difference, of a restless belonging.

If we think back to Novalis in light of this tension, a structural similarity emerges immediately, just as soon as we recall Novalis's speculation (one which spoke directly to Heidegger) regarding the possibility of a "highest principle," a "paradox" that

> knows absolutely no peace, that incessantly draws and repels, that incessantly becomes incomprehensible anew, just at the moment one has already understood it. (*W* II: 314)

It would seem, then, that in Heidegger's thinking of pain, we discover once again the figure that guided our investigation of Novalis: the figure of a separative-gathering, of a conjoining that also and simultaneously pulls apart, of a relation whose between-space is to be understood as nothing other than that conjoining and pulling apart.

Despite this reiteration, though, there is clearly a difference: while it is true that a certain pain of longing, even of loss, does certainly pervade Novalis's writing, the generative force of his thinking is always geared toward fertility, toward increase. In this respect, the tensioned between-space that we identified at the core of that thinking is possessed of an entirely different affectivity. If both Heidegger and Novalis are thinking in parallel ways the tension of conjoinment, it is apparent that, for Novalis, words as it were blossom from out of this between, proliferating, germinating, exploding: it is for this reason that we have cast the sense of the between which Novalis discovers as one of fecundity. By contrast, Heidegger appears to pursue this same figure in terms of an agonistics. Appropriating more explicitly than Novalis the tensioned space of Heraclitean *harmonia*, Heidegger will find there not the logic of proliferative increase, but a pull toward silence, toward a *Sprachlosigkeit.* Here, evidently, it is pain that has come to express the tension of the between; and it will be the project of the next chapters to explore the genesis and implications of this shift which—and this is the claim—lies at the heart of Heidegger's thinking. Whether the movement of this shifting reappropriation is a matter of historical exigency, of missed opportunity, or of an opening onto altogether new possibilities of thinking cannot entirely be decided here.

To return, then, to the text on Trakl with which we opened: the occasion for this speculation on the nature of pain is the reading of the Trakl poem "Ein Winterabend," which contains the line:

> Schmerz versteinerte die Schwelle
> (Pain has turned the threshold to stone)

It is from out of this line of Trakl's that Heidegger draws his sense of pain as threshold, as a sustaining in-between of difference, in which what is separated can be thought together in its difference and its belonging. More broadly, in the essay, the tension of gathering and joining that the threshold sustains in pain describes a relation between what Heidegger calls "world and thing." The differing of these two (*Unter-Schied*) is addressed by Heidegger in terms of a reciprocal dynamics of emergence, as "things bear world," and "world bears things." World is understood as what sustains things, the locus of their emergence and persistence; things are understood as what sustains world, what allows for the emergence of something like world. Neither has precedence, neither has priority: they are determined in and as their difference, which both gathers them together and keeps them apart. Heidegger speaks of this tensional dynamic as the "intimacy" (*Innigkeit*) of their separated belonging—and he speaks of this intimate belonging in terms of of pain: "Then would the intimacy of the difference for world and thing be pain? Most certainly" (*GA* 12: 27/205).

The question we are pursuing here is: how does the between-space of this difference come to be expressed as *pain*? In order to approach this question, we can first consider the nature of the between that Heidegger seems to be developing. The sense of a between-space articulated here can be considered a reconfiguration of a passage from two decades earlier that belongs to the essay on "The Origin of the Work of Art." The reconfiguration is striking in that, although the passage does not hold pain at its core, it nonetheless also centers around the sense of a rent. It is this divide or fissure that Heidegger will elaborate in similar terms to that with which he addresses pain in the later essay. The term in question is *Riß*—a rift or rent—and the passage in question is as follows:

> The strife is no rift [*Riß*] in the sense of the tearing open of a simple cleft; rather, the strife is the intimacy of the mutual dependence of the contestants [*Streitenden*]. The rift carries the contestants into the source of their unity [*Einheit*], their common ground. (*GA* 5: 51/63)

The strife in question here is the strife of "world" and "earth." We cannot assume a homology or an interchangeability between these terms and the senses of "world" and "thing" that Heidegger develops in the Trakl essay; but the deep structural similarities in the passage in terms of the configuration of this strange between-space are clear. As we approach this passage in the essay on the origin of the work of art, Heidegger has already addressed the relation of strife as an "intimacy"—*Innigkeit des Streites* is the phrase he uses—and the particular sense of their belonging-together has been engaged. But here the strife (*Streit*) itself is addressed directly, the rift that divides as it conjoins. Developing and elaborating the sense of a "between," Heidegger will go on to describe the *Riß* as being at once *Grundriß* and *Auf-Riß*; and insofar as it also sets the bounds, the measure and limits of the strife, it is also an *Umriß*. Apparent in this strange agglomeration is that the between-space of the elements of strife cannot be contained, narrowed within the frame of a single spatial image: *Riß* both surrounds (*Um-*), rises up and tears apart (*Auf-*), and grounds (*Grund-*). If it evades identification with spatial or geometrical figuration, this is to suggest that the "between" of the *Streit* has in some way stepped out of the bounds that would limit its operation to a strategy of mediation: what surrounds, grounds, rises up and tears apart cannot be simply identified as the mediating third of an oppositional relation. At the same time, this figural polyvalence engages another semantic complex that relates to senses of *Riß, Umriß, Auf-Riß* as sketch, outline, design. What will gather these semantic complexes together is a sense of incision, of a movement that tears open the ground—with pen, with knife, with plow; and this is the sense of *Aufriß* to which Heidegger will return in *Unterwegs zur Sprache* two decades later, when the between-space will have emerged as pain.

Across this span of years, the sense of the simultaneous rending and conjoining that Heidegger associates with the space of the between flows like an undercurrent, surfacing most fully in these essays on Trakl. It will be necessary, then, to ask about the various between-spaces of *Streit* and of *Unter-Schied*—to ask, in other words, about what has happened to this space in the intervening years, the years in-between. Because it would seem as if, in the years that follow "The Origin of the Work of Art," the between-space of *Streit* exposed in the polyvalence of the rift has become occupied: pain has taken up residence in this between. To join up the senses of "rift" across this intervening space will mean in part tracing back the question of pain to the arena of its first emergence, which happens to be in the group of texts known as the *seynsgeschichtlich* (or onto-historical) treatises—texts whose composition follows on chronologically from the years in which "The Origin of the Work of Art" emerges.

The casting of pain as difference in Heidegger's thought is by no means, then, unique to the essay "Die Sprache": there is, in fact, a discourse of pain that runs through Heidegger's thinking—intermittent, to be sure, though striking in each of its appearances. There is obscurity here, in these passages, but it will be possible nonetheless, and without arbitrary conflation, to grasp a kind of consistency by tracing the explicit articulation of pain in the Trakl essay back to earlier instantiations. To that end, we will examine, first of all, its fullest and possibly most explosive appearance, in the *Bremen Lectures,* which were given in 1949, just after the war. From thence we will move backward to the first extensive elaboration of the question of pain, in the volume *Das Ereignis,* of 1940–41.

Intimacy and Inaccessibility

This is how pain emerges in 1949, in the *Bremen Lectures*—a moment that is both central to the series and at the heart of the third lecture, which is entitled "Die Gefahr" ("The Danger"):

> Immeasurable suffering creeps and rages over the earth. The flood of suffering rises ever higher. But the essence of pain is concealed. Pain is the rift [*Riß*] in which the basic sketch [*Grundriß*] of the fourfold is inscribed . . . In the rift of pain, what is granted on high safeguards its enduring. The rift of pain rends the veiled movement of favoring in an unwarranted coming of grace. Everywhere we are assailed by uncountable and immeasurable suffering. But we are without pain, are not brought into the ownership of pain. (*GA* 79: 57/54)

To describe briefly the different moments of this exposition: the claim is that such a suffering rages upon us that we can no longer see its pain. Such, indeed, is the depth of this occlusion, says Heidegger, that we experience ourselves as "without pain" (*Schmerzlos*): the pain is in a certain way inaccessible, even as it rages within us. This is the condition that he describes as not being "brought into the ownership," or "not appropriated [*nicht vereignet*] to the essence of pain." It is not for us, therefore, to own the pain. We are rather to be owned by it. Despite this, we find ourselves paradoxically adrift in painlessness. But this is because, for Heidegger, pain itself has a centrality that what we term suffering somehow occludes. It is here, then—as we approach the "essential being [*Wesen*] of pain"—that Heidegger says, as he will repeat later, that pain is the "rift," or "rent." This *Riß*, he goes on to say, is the *Grundriß*—the fundamental rent—"in which the fourfold is inscribed." It will be necessary to engage the question of "the fourfold" and its inscribing in order to grasp the centrality of this figure, which has become one of pain. But we shall do so only after we have sought a fuller understanding both of the *Grundriß* itself and of the function of this figure in the lecture series as a whole.

There is, in this passage, a good deal more that is said of the "rending" that is pain, and the operation it appears to effect. Three observations present themselves:

1. Heidegger says that it is from the *Grundriß* that "the stature of what is too great for humans receives its greatness." The pain of the "rending" thus exceeds the human; a kind of magnitude is invoked of which the human—however this figure is to be understood—is not the measure.

2. Secondly, Heidegger writes that in the rift of pain "what is granted on high safeguards its perseverance." The German, here—"*wahrt das hoch Gewährte sein Währen*"—is necessary in order to indicate something of the constellation of meanings that revolve around this strange phrase. This constellation, which attaches, we remember, to pain, to the rift, is one that revolves around a sense of protection, of safeguarding—a keeping-safe in the sense of a sustaining, a preserving of something vouchsafed—and is equally a constellation that moves in the same orbit as truth (*Wahrheit*), as the true, the genuine, the proper (*wahr*).

3. Thirdly, addressing now not the properties of the rift but its operation, Heidegger says that what is rent (*reißt*) in the rift is a kind of veiledness that attends this sustaining, one that has to do with a sense of benevolence, of the favoring that attends an arrival—a privileging, a granting of privilege: "the rift of pain rends the veiled procession of grace into an unneeded arrival of favor."

We are being asked, then, to understand this rift as something that in a sense exceeds, something that operates beyond the limits from out of which human being can be construed. And from out of that exceeding, there is an arrival—a beneficence, a bestowal—which is held, sustained in the rending that pain performs. Although it is not possible to pursue this here, it is important to insist that this strange language of "granting" and "bestowal" is not to be understood in the sense of an activity of which the human might be the recipient. "Granting" must rather be understood here as a kind of "opening," in which the differential structure that Heidegger calls "the fourfold" emerges as such: the "rift" of pain is, then, the sustaining and drawing-together of this differential structure.

So, then, to summarize the configuration that gathers in this passage: it seems as if to the "immeasurable suffering" around us belongs a kind of pain that is strangely concealed by that suffering, hidden in its essence by the very rage that expresses it. Pain is to be thought, we are told, as what rends, as a rift—a rending or tearing, an opening, a gap—which, in a certain manner, is the locus of drawing together "the fourfold." It is this rift that will bring with it, particularly in relation to the later interpretation of Trakl, a sense of at one and the same time sundering and joining, of keeping-apart and of separating. It is a pain that exceeds the human, one that is in some sense "granted"; one, we can say, that might grant the human a place, a place in which he might find himself inscribed. The difficulty, clearly, is that, through this lens, we seem to be being asked to view the suffering of the world as a function, albeit concealed, of a pain that is somehow central to the possibility of the human. This is a troubling thought. It may indeed be sufficiently troubling to force us to ask Heidegger once again: why "pain"? Why should the rift that gathers and keeps apart, that sunders and conjoins the differential possibilities of world and earth, be a figure of pain?

It is not, then—to return to Heidegger's exposition—that there is no experiencing of the painful: after all, "immeasurable suffering creeps and rages over the earth." But what appears to be the case is that, in a certain way, this suffering offers to us a concealment, an occultation: it is this occultation that, for Heidegger, belongs to what he terms "the danger." Of this "danger" he writes:

> Death, the refuge of beyng, pain, the *Grundriß* of beyng, indigence, the release into the propriety of beyng, are all markings by which the danger lets it be noted that *the* distress remains outstanding in the midst of tremendous distresses, that the danger *is* not as the danger. (*GA* 79: 57/54)

Death belongs together with pain and with indigence—a poverty, an acceptance of abyssal emptiness—in that within them, in their belonging-together, lies concealed a danger which Heidegger claims is not a danger *for* being, but the danger *of* being, a danger that lies at the heart of being itself. It is in death, pain, and indigence that this "danger" might become manifest as such. If the danger lies in a certain form of concealment, then pain—in its belongingness with death and indigence—serves both to mark that concealment and to provide the possibility of its exposure. It would, then, be in the exposure and embrace of the differential "rift" that Heidegger calls pain that the "danger" might instead "turn," instead, into "that which saves," *das Rettende.*

In order to better understand the pivotal nexus that this between-structure of pain expresses, in both the danger of its concealment and the saving of its exposure, we need to see that the figure is central to the thinking not merely of the third lecture, but of the lecture series as a whole. This centrality can be seen if we observe that the obscuration of the productive nexus of pain that suffering effects seems to be the obscuring of a primal "intimacy," the acknowledgment of which is necessary if we are to be "saved" from the "danger" of being. Thus, the question of the saving becomes one of the acknowledging of a hidden proximity, the intimacy of what Heidegger will call "nearness": the rift of pain is closer to us, more intimate, than the suffering which obscures it. Nearness, and its obscuration, is in fact the topic that Heidegger claims as the heart of his lectures, the central issue, address to which might allow, he hopes, "Insight into That Which Is." In the next section, we will explore not just the thematic of nearness but its loss, too, as it finds itself driven into the neutrality of the distanceless (*Abstandlos*). From thence, we can consider the possibility of its reclamation.

Nearness and Loss

The *Bremen Lectures* receive their governing impulse from the opening paragraphs, which were originally composed as the opening of the first lecture, but later separated out and entitled "Point of Reference, or "indication" (*Hinweis*). This directive indicates that the lectures will concern themselves with what Heidegger calls "nearness" (*der Nähe*). Whatever course the lectures will take, then, all therein will in some way concern modes of distance and proximity. It is thus in relation to nearness that we can better understand the figure of the between that Heidegger calls the "rift" of pain, and engage its intimacy.[1]

This thematic of nearness is, in part, a reworking of an earlier thinking of distance in relation to the human that has its roots in §23 of *Being and Time*. There, Dasein is presented in relation to a tension of distance and proximity to world and the modes of its experiencing: "Da-sein," writes Heidegger here, is possessed of "an essential tendency toward nearness [*Nähe*]." This constitutive "nearing" (*Näherung*), termed in *Being and Time* "de-distancing" (*Ent-fernung*), is such that the experience of distance itself is only possible on the basis of this constitutive comportment. "World," in the sense of *Being and Time*, will necessarily be configured, for Dasein, in terms of a play of proximity and distance, closeness and farness. It is not a question, then, of imagining that our way of being somehow "eliminates" distance, but rather of understanding the extent to which we are always caught up in this play of the drawing-close, or "nearing," of the far: "This de-distancing—the farness from itself of what is at hand—is something that Dasein can *never cross over*" (*GA* 2: 108/100)

In *Being and Time*, Heidegger is content to imply that the function of technological modernity is in keeping with this constitutive comporting, though leaving open the question of the implications of this development: "With the radio, for example, Da-sein is bringing about today a de-distancing of the 'world' which is unforeseeable in its meaning for Da-sein" (*GA* 2: 105/98). However, at the opening of the *Bremen Lectures* this linkage—and the assumptions that underlie it—will be decisively challenged. By the time of these lectures, it seems to have become clear to Heidegger that the "de-distancing" that technological modernity performs is not a "nearing" in the sense of a drawing ever closer of spatial and temporal configurations. Rather, what is taking place is a *neutralization* of distance, the nullification of the entire contours of spatial and temporal experience:

> Everything washes together into the uniformly distanceless [*Abstandlos*]. How? Is not this moving together into the distanceless even more uncanny [*unheimlich*] than everything being out of place? (*GA* 79: 4/4)

Starting from this insight, a different perspective on "nearness" (*Nähe*) will be required, one quite other than the effort to redetermine the spatiality of Dasein that motivated the development of the notion of *Ent-fernung* in *Being and Time*. Nearness, now, will become something entirely other than the constitutive mode in which Dasein determines itself as spatial. Instead of being opposed to a sense of the far, nearness is now to be set over against the "distanceless" (*Abstandlos*). Nearness will be what is lacking, what remains absent—inaccessible to the drift toward the distanceless. Here, it becomes possible to see how the thematic of intimacy—its rarity, its difficulty—comes to be of such significance for Heidegger. Nearness will be what beckons from the shadows of the distanceless.

It is in light of the governing directive of nearness that the first two lectures of the Bremen cycle must be read: in contrast to their later manifestations as independent lectures,[2] "Das Ding" and "Das Ge-Stell" must be thought together, two entirely imbricated aspects of "That Which Is," as the title of the lecture series has it. And if the third lecture of the series—"The Danger"—is to engage the belonging-together of the different possibilities opened up in the first two lectures, then the encounter with pain that will take place at the center of that lecture invites us to consider the relation of pain to the overall thematic of the series—to the question of "nearness," of what is closest, most intimate with us. We will consider, first of all, aspects of the second lecture, "Das Ge-Stell," in order to explore both the risk and the possibilities to which "nearness" is exposed, before addressing ourselves to its celebration in the first lecture.

Following the path laid out in the initial directive, then, Heidegger begins the second lecture by reiterating his discovery—that "nearness is not shortness of distance . . . the remote is not at all the cancellation [*Aufhebung*] of nearness" (*GA* 79: 23/23). Withdrawn from the oppositional structures that govern the spatial configuration of near and far, he says rather that, on the contrary, it is only in nearness (*im Nähern der Nähe*) that what is far achieves its farness (*fernt die Ferne*) and retains itself *as* far (*und bleibt als Ferne gewahrt*). Nearness, then, is clearly not to be understood in spatial terms, either measurable or experiential. In this thinking of "nearness," what is primarily challenged is the primacy of the *gegenständlich*, of the "oppositionally objective." It is not simply that what is close or spatially immediate is given priority, but rather that "nearness" is entirely removed or withdrawn from the domain in which the spatial (conceived as *Gegenstand*) could operate. Indeed, says Heidegger, "the dominance of what is oppositionally objective [*gegenständlich*] does not secure distance. Rather, there already lurks in it the imposing [*Andrang*] of the distanceless" (*GA* 79: 25/24). The *Gegenstand* is already caught up in the mechanics of the *Abstandlos*, the distanceless: its emergence is the first deterioration, the first falling-away in a process in which ultimately "even the object crumbles as characteristic of what presences" (*GA* 79: 25/25).

It is in respect of this relation to the oppositionally objective that Heidegger's analysis takes a difficult turn, as he seeks to bring his thinking of "nearness" into relation with senses of *stellen*—of placing, of position. The question will be one of engaging a sense of "positioning" without lapsing into standard forms of object-presentation. The intimacy of the near will not be understood as a refusal of the exteriority of the object, but as a new and entirely other kind of relationality. In this second lecture, then, Heidegger will describe a process of deterioration by means of which "that which is" is to be transformed into *Bestand*, into what "stands in reserve," a mode he calls *Ge-stell.* This transformation into *Bestand*, says Heidegger, occurs on the basis of a particular kind of *stellen*, or positioning, which he proposes to call a *Be-stellen*, a certain kind of ordering (*GA* 79: 26/25).[3] In order to describe, by way of contrast, this deteriorative transformation, Heidegger proposes the following example:

> The carpenter produces a table, but also a coffin. What is produced, set here [*das her-gestellte*], is not tantamount to the already finished. What is here stands [*Das ins Her Gestellte steht*] in the purview of what concernfully approaches us. It is *set here* [her gestellt] *in a nearness.* (*GA* 79: 26/25)

The example, it turns out, is not accidental—the image of the coffin, and of death, will have some centrality in the exposition that follows. What needs to be observed first of all, though, is that "nearness" is being conceived not in opposition to, but rather as a particular form of *stellen*: the coffin is "set here in a nearness." Now, if a sense of "placing" or positioning (*stellen*) lies at the heart of the progression which will pull "that which is" into the realm of *Bestand*, then we might be tempted to assume that "nearness" would be understood as a resistance to that pull. In other words, we might assume that "nearness" would have to be thought otherwise than as a "placing," or a "positioning." But on the contrary, Heidegger tells us that the coffin is "*set forth* [her gestellt] *in a nearness.*" This means that the "nearness" of the coffin must represent a *particular kind* of placing, one in which something like a "nearness" becomes apparent, accessible. So, "nearness," it would seem, is indeed a kind of positioning; if a distinction is to be drawn, it will not be between nearness and the mode of being of placing, or positioning. The distinction between "nearness" and that which drifts toward "standing reserve" is a difference *within stellen* itself, not over against it. But if nearness is to remain caught up in the dynamics of positioning and placement, it must be in some way accessible along the path toward the degradation of oppositional placement.

"Nearness," then, will be that kind of positioning (*stellen*) which offers resistance within the inevitable march toward "standing reserve."

As Heidegger presents this march, the stakes could not be higher, as within a few short paragraphs of his description of the "nearness" of the coffin, he will have traced out a progression that leads from this mode of placement, through a series of examples—the peasant positioning his ox to remove a tree, the positioning of men and women in a labor force—to an invocation of the production (*Fabrikation*) of corpses in an extermination camp (*GA* 79: 27/27).[4] We have, then, a progression, a movement that is bounded or circumscribed by two different modes of death, two different kinds of body. If it is "nearness" that renders this difference, then the key to this turn—the turn in which "nearness" becomes unavailable, absent—is a particular experience of death. It seems that it is in a certain manifestation of death that nearness becomes apparent, and in a certain manifestation that it is evacuated entirely. "Nearness" will have to be understood from within this difference—a difference between a mode that, on the one hand, enables a coffin to be produced in such a way that the death that it embraces is "set forth in nearness," and one in which the body is abandoned to a paroxysm of degradation. These are the stakes of "nearness."

What, then, does Heidegger say about the "nearness" of the coffin, of the death it encloses? He explains:

> The carpenter in the village does not just complete a box for a corpse. The coffin is from the outset placed [*hin-gestellt*] in a privileged spot in the farmhouse where the dead peasant still lingers [*verweilt*]. There, a coffin is still called a "death-tree" [*Totenbaum*]. The death of the deceased flourishes [*gedeiht*] in it. This flourishing [*Gedeihen*] determines [*bestimmt*] the house and farmstead, the ones who dwell there, their kin, and the neighborhood. (*GA* 79: 26/25)

We see, then, that the placing-down (*hin-stellen*) of this coffin is such that the death it encloses is present in a particular way: its placing privileges the absence of the deceased, who lingers (*verweilt*) in that placing. This placing is of such a nature that the absence of the deceased does not merely linger, but *flourishes* (*gedeiht*) in that placing: it is death that flourishes (*gedeihen*—to develop, prosper, grow, increase) here, and in such a way that the human and material environment is gathered and attuned (*bestimmt*) in the flourishing of this loss.[5] We have, then, an indication of what is entailed in the "nearing" that belongs to the positioning of this coffin. It seems that what is effected in this nearing is the determination of a world that gathers itself around an absence: in a sense, the pain of loss that death effects is that which collects the material and human context of that absence and renders it "near" in the mode of a material presence—the coffin—that both holds and withholds what is absent.

It is, then, in a certain presentation of death, a way of manifesting radical absence, that what Heidegger calls "nearness" becomes accessible: death "flourishes" in a mode of placement (*stellen*) in which a coffin presents itself. It is in this mode that the contextual fabric of situatedness that envelops the coffin is determined, attuned, and brought together. The nearness of this fabric is, then, conditioned upon an absence, a loss. It is not that the presence of death or of pain immediately occasions the emergence of nearness. Rather, nearness represents a particular configuration of loss, a mode of its appearance. The reclamation of nearness, then, must involve exposure to this loss, this pain of absence. It is here that a kind of intimacy of pain, such as Heidegger's Trakl readings introduce, begins to show itself, as nearness becomes linked with experiences of loss. But we can understand this intimacy better if we explore elements of the first lecture of the series, entitled "The Thing," as well as the transition into the second lecture, and from thence examine the emergence of this strange nearness, this intimacy of pain.

The Harmony of the Thing

Heidegger's first lecture is an attempt to describe and to give access to entities in their activity of presencing, without recourse to the language of *Gegenstand*, of the "oppositionally objective." In order to evade this language, Heidegger develops a complex and dynamic sense of what he calls a "thing," one that depends on the unfolding of a kind of rhythm of emergence. It is this rhythm that Heidegger calls the "fourfold": deriving a set of terms from Hölderlin, the elements of the fourfold—earth and sky, mortal and divinity—are intended to describe, in their interdependence and indefinite motility, the dynamics of occlusion and transparency, presence and absence that attend and make possible the emergence of a "thing."[6]

The eventuation of a thing, then—Heidegger's oft-cited example is that of a jug—brings about and engages an interdependence, a reciprocity between elements that make possible this eventuation: on the one hand, the elements of earth and sky, which we might think at least provisionally in terms of an occlusive heaviness and the transparence of light; and on the other, the twin poles of mortal and divine, a relation which is to be thought as engaging the full complexities of the intertwinement of visible and invisible. The eventuation of the thing, then—its "thinging," as Heidegger would say, insisting on adapting the referential noun to a processual verbal form in order to remain within this eventuation—happens in that it draws together like a net this fabric of interrelations, all of which exceed anything that could be understood under the aegis of objective presence. To this exceeding, and its difficult gathering, Heidegger gives the name "world." What is remarkable about the figure of world as it appears in this text is the way in which its elements belong and reciprocate, without either collapsing into one another or separating out into independent parts. Instead, the elements of the fourfold are co-constitutive and mutually interdependent—a network or web of shifting and mobile textures, from the dynamic midst of which something emerges and becomes present. Heidegger uses for this figuration a double set of descriptives, which also belong together but without simple equivalence. On the one hand, the elements of the fourfold are described in terms of a kind of abyssal mirroring in which the constitutive elements of world are caught in a web of reciprocal reflection:

> Each of the four in its way mirrors the essence of the remaining others again. Each is thus reflected in its way back into what is its own within the single fold of the four . . . In this appropriating-lighting way, each of the four reflectively plays with each of the remaining others. (*GA* 79: 18/17)

On the other hand, the four are conceived in terms of the movement of a ring, a figure which gathers together different elements without allowing them to touch one another. Both of these figurations converge in a way that displaces any purely conceptual apparatus by enacting at the level of verbal rhythm the fluidity and inconstancy of the figures themselves. One example might be the following: "*Das Spiegel-Spiel von Welt ist das Reigen des Ereignens.*" This phrase, like many others in the text, is untranslatable to the extent that it depends both on the rhythmic movement and on the internal aural resonances of the two pairs of terms on either side of the "*ist*" which is to make them equivalent. These rhythms and resonances are not merely decorative, but belong to the semantic experience of the terms themselves: *Spiegel-Spiel* enacts a kind of playful mirroring, just as *Reigen des Ereigens* enacts a kind of aural circularity bordering on, but not absorbed into, tautology.

The figuration of the fourfold is being conceived here in terms of what Reiner Schürmann calls "henological difference." This is a figure of a oneness that is not resolved, dissolved, or absolved into a unity; a one that is not a totality made up of different parts, but instead constituted *in and as* difference.[7] It is the same dynamic and differential harmony that we have, from the beginning of this study, identified with a figure of the "between": Heidegger's "fourfold" is a distinct crystallization of this fluid and itinerant idea.

Heidegger thus understands the eventuation of the "thing" as the motile and unstable gathering-together of the elements of world: presencing becomes a question of a context in which the elements of the fourfold come to "linger," a gathering in which their belonging-together becomes manifest in its indeterminate wholeness. World and Thing, here, are bound up in one another—not merely in the sense of being interdependent, as separate entities that require one another for their subsistence. Thing and World are bound together in that they are, in a very particular sense, the same—the thing *is* as the gathering of world, world *is* as gathered in the thing: "the thing lets the fourfold abide. The thing things the world." In this context, "nearness"—to come back to the central term of the lecture series—is determined *as* that gathering or drawing-together: Heidegger will again substitute for the substantive "nearness" a processual verbal form to describe this—"this bringing near is nearing. Nearing is the essence of the near" (*GA* 79: 16/16).

Nevertheless a question arises here, in respect of this gathering of the elements of the fourfold, which comes close to the central question of this book: the question of harmony. With regard to Heidegger's "fourfold," the question is specifically whether it is possible to sustain, on the one hand, a sense of agonistic difference between the elements of the fourfold as they gather, or whether this difference will necessarily become absorbed into a concordance.[8] In other words, how are we to understand the belongingness of the different elements of the fourfold, their sympathetic intertwinement, without in some measure implying the collapse of their difference?

The question often presents itself most clearly at a linguistic level, because it is here, in the ludic or ludicrous domain of Heidegger's writing, that these figures of intertwinement become evident. By way of example we can consider the following formulation, which occurs at the playful heart of Heidegger's lecture. The formulation is as follows: "*Aus dem Spiegel-Spiel des Gerings des Ringen ereignet sich das Dingen des Dinges.*" Andrew Mitchell's English translation gives us the following version: "From out of the mirror-play of the circling of the nimble there takes place the thinging of the thing." In other words, Heidegger appears to be saying, once again, that the "thing" eventuates from out of the reciprocal mirror-play and rotational exchange of the elements that together constitute "world." But beyond this basic, and translatable, semantic structure lies the sentence itself, with its immeasurably obscure conjunctions of word-forms whose operation has been defined purely immanently in the essay. *Gering des Ringes*, for instance, along with *Spiegel-Spiel*, is meaningfully resonant because Heidegger has elaborated an immanent context for their operation. Still more striking, though, is the way in which *Gering des Ringes* operates in an almost pure melodic consonance with *Dingen des Dinges.* This is the ludic aspect of Heidegger's writing, an aspect that, at least here, is not incidental, but belongs entirely to the sense of the ecstatic harmony of the thing. The question, then, will be about this belonging-together, this consonance, and about the ways in which it appears to dissolve the differential structures that put it in place.

Heidegger's formulation, then, brings the two semantic complexes that describe the presencing of world and thing into an aural consonance with one another. World and thing thus appear as sounding out a kind of harmony that echoes their conceptual belonging-together. To that extent, their consonance is not just a rhetorical performance: *Gering des Ringes* and *Dingen des Dinges* operate in consonance because the rhythm of their sounding articulates the belonging-together of world and thing, as Heidegger is describing it here. His terms therefore gather together around a syllabic repetition that allows them, as it were, to ring in consonance. The ringing-together of this consonance is a sounding that pushes toward a unison, an *Einklang* that gathers toward a fusion. Operative, clearly, in this *Einklang* is a particular notion of the harmonious: harmony thought as concordance, as concord.

This is precisely the movement in which the sense of *harmonia* shifts and falls away from the tensional, differential sense operative in Heraclitus. In the introduction, we saw how the tensional sense of *harmonia* that clearly underpins the Heraclitean experience tends to move away from the agonistic sense of a gathering-together of the dispersive, and toward one of pure sympathetic resonance: concord, *Einklang.* Now, what is striking here is the extent to which Heidegger appears to be adopting and embracing, in his formulation of the interweaving domains of world and thing, not the Heraclitean sense of a *harmonia* of difference—which time and again has been the dominant model that undergirds his thinking—but a sense of harmony as *concordia,* one that drives toward the submergence of difference, an envelopment that pushes toward an absorption in the folds of unanimity. The difficulty—the central difficulty which Heidegger will face as his lecture closes—is that this conception of harmony will drive, always, toward the elimination of difference: "thing" and "world" will tend to be drawn into a kind of play which dissolves any sense in which they might pull against one another, any sense of a *Streit* which might sustain their difference. Instead, difference will tend to be sacrificed in favor of an interaction that absolves both world and thing in a gathering of concordance: this it is, indeed, that explains the strangely celebratory, almost ecstatic tone of these passages.

This sense of concordant gathering, of pure consonance, appears to work against the movement of the lecture series as a whole, which, far from offering a celebration of the fulfillment of "nearness" in the consonant ringing of world and thing, wishes to show its desiccation, its emptying-out. But the ecstatic concordance of world and thing does not allow for an easy passage into the second lecture, dependent as it is on the sense of absence and lack, on pain and the loss of "nearness." In part, this accounts for the way in which these first two lectures of the series drift apart in the years that follow their first delivery, both in content and context. Far from developing a closer bond upon their repeated delivery, these texts develop in ways that draw them apart from one another, surfacing some years later as separate essays. More significant than this separation, though, is the appendix that Heidegger attached to the published text of the *Bremen Lectures*. This is because in these brief notes, written some time shortly after the delivery of the lectures,[9] we see Heidegger addressing precisely the question we have posed: namely, the question of how the exposition of the concordance of world and thing in the first lecture will allow for a passage to the collapse of "nearness" that guides the work of the second lecture. It is this between-space of the two lectures that will bring us back to the centrality of pain that is given voice, as we have seen, in the third lecture of the series.

Between Concordance and Dissonance

The notes that make up the appendix of the first lecture effect a reclamation of the question of difference. Here, difference is expressed—as it will be later, only more fully, in the essay "Die Sprache"—as *Unter-Schied*: "Thing and world referred to differentiation [*Unter-Schied*]" (*GA* 79: 22/21), notes Heidegger at the beginning of the appendix. The hyphenation of *Unter-Schied* serves to delineate a figure that both gathers and holds apart—the same figure that we saw Heidegger appropriating from Trakl in terms of a "threshold." In other words, Heidegger, at the opening of his self-reflection, is reinscribing a figure of irreducible difference precisely at the point at which it appears to have been forgotten: at the juncture, the join between world and thing. Indeed, asks Heidegger, "from this to the *forgetting* of beyng: how to think this?" (*GA* 79: 22/21). This forgetting, the desiccation of nearness, will be what is crucial now, and Heidegger is pondering how to think the connection between the ecstatic consonance of the first lecture and the agonistic difference of the second. What is decisive to this transition, Heidegger appears to think, is that world and thing are to be considered in the way in which they hold themselves toward one another, in the difference of their relation: "*Das Ver-Hältnis für Welt zu Ding und Ding aus Welt.*"

To reinscribe difference, then, is to force apart the *concordia* of world and thing, to reconfigure their belonging-together in terms of a *harmonia* that does not absolve their apartness. What is crucial now, in respect of this reinscribing, is not the *intertwining* of world in thing and thing in world, but rather the question of their joining:

> The differentiation [*Unter-Schied*]
> From this as the *jointure of beyng* [*Fuge der Seyns*]—all joining of the saying [*Fügung der Sage*]—all rigor of the joining. (*GA* 79: 22/21)

More than anything, it is this move, in the strange between-space of the notes conjoining the two lectures—that connects the *Bremen Lectures* both to the work of the *seynsgeschichtlich* treatises, for which the manifold senses of joining are decisive, and to the lectures on Heraclitus that emerge in the wake of that series, and in which the question of the join, of *Fügung*, is explicitly expressed in terms of *harmonia*:

> The Greek word for the joining [*Fügung*] sounds as *harmonia*. In this word we think right away of the joining of tones, and grasp "harmony" as concord [*Ein-klang*]. Only, what is essential in *harmonia* is not the domain of ringing or of tones, but rather *harmos*, that whereby one fits to another, the join in which both are joined, so that the joining *is*. (*GA* 55: 141)

What transpires, then, in the between-space of these two lectures is the recovery of the irreducibility of the join of world and thing, the reclamation of the *harmonia* of their difference. Once again, the reclamation of difference is fundamental for Heidegger because, in the second lecture, it is as a forgetting of difference that the nearness of the thing slips into the *Abstandlos*, that the gathering in which death flourishes in the pain of loss can give way to the sordid betrayal of the body as just so much inert resource, as *Bestand*. Now, we have noted that the discourse of the first lecture celebrates the nearness of the thing, gives voice to the possibility of nearness that obtains in the *Einklang* that gathers the thing from out of world. But equally, we saw that the cost of this celebration, the consequence of its articulation, is a kind of elision of difference; and that it is only the retrieval of that difference which might save us from the slippage in which the intimacy of the thing falls into the desiccation of the object. If this is so, then the celebration of the concordant nearness of the thing, in that it forgets the irreducible difference of *harmonia*, might also indeed *be* the forgetting of what makes that nearness possible at all. And if that were the case, then we would have to consider the paradoxical possibility that the fulfillment of nearness in the rapt engagement of thing in world is the very thing which makes that nearness impossible. If the elision of difference is the occasion for the falling-away of nearness, for the drift into *Abstandlosigkeit,* then the originating point of this drift would be the moment in which that nearness is most completely celebrated.

If nearness is lost in its celebration, it will be pain that will institute its recovery, pain that will enable the restoral of the question of the belongingness of world and thing, pain that allows for the retrieval of the risk, the danger that attends the collapse of that question. Pain, then, is the emergence of loss, the loss of the ecstatic convergence of world and thing, of its celebratory articulation. Pain is the confounding of the *concordia* in which the fourfold articulates its gathering—it is the incision of a rift, the gap whose difficult sustaining disallows the collapse of difference. This is how the passage with which the inquiry into these Bremen lectures opened acquires its centrality: "Pain is the rift [*Riß*] in which the basic sketch [*Grundriß*] of the fourfold is inscribed."

* * *

At the opening of this chapter we saw Heidegger reflecting on Trakl, addressing himself to the relation of world and thing, and asking, and answering, the same question we have posed: "Then would the intimacy of the difference for world and thing be pain? Most certainly," he exclaims.

If it is in its language, in its mode of articulation, that the celebration of the thing engages a *concordia* that occludes difference, then it would be another kind of language that would enable the recovery of that same difference. And if pain is the insistent reinscription of difference, then this other language, this other mode of articulation, will be one that makes apparent its intimacy with pain. What will be needed, then, is a language *of* pain, in the double genitive sense, a language that both considers pain and makes it manifest. And this is what we will find if we look back toward the *seynsgeschichtlich* treatises, where the first emergence of that language is to be marked, and where the thematics we have been trying to trace out make their fullest appearance.

6

The Pain of Belonging

> Bewilder'd in the Maze of Life, and blind.
> —John Dryden

In between the first and the second lectures of the Bremen series, it is the retrieval—unsettling, disquieting—of an original *harmonia* of difference beyond pure concordance that draws the sense of closeness, of the near, into the orbit of pain. But Heidegger will also insist, in this between-space of the first two lectures, that what needs to be recovered is not just the question of originary difference, but the question of forgetting. He asks, as we noted above: "From this to the *forgetting* of beyng: how to think this?" (*GA* 79: 22/21). The introduction of this question implies that the elision of original difference is linked, somehow, to a primal forgetting. If this is so, then the recovery and restoral of that difference will be linked to the question of remembrance and recollection. This is why Heidegger continues as follows:

> The thinking that retrieves is commemorative thinking; to retrieve—to take into nearness [*Nach-holendes Denken ist das Andenken: nach-holen—in die Nähe holen*]. (*GA* 79: 23/22)

The purpose of the hyphenation here seems to be to emphasize the sense of retrieval (*nachholen*) as a drawing *after* (*nach*), which would suggest the presence, in commemoration, of something lost, of a pastness. Important, then, for the links we are trying to establish, is that Heidegger is clearly pointing to an etymology that would link the sense of *nach*, as a "coming-after," with a sense of the near—*die Nähe.* As Gerhard Richter has elaborated at length, these etymological considerations link the two words with the common Old German root *Nâh*, and the Old English *Neah.*[1] Thought in this way, the near is brought into the orbit of what follows-on, what comes after. How is this possible? How are *nach* and *die Nähe*, what comes after and what is close, to be thought together?

We have seen in the last chapter that, to the deep nearness of the thing (as expressed in the first lecture) there belongs an elision of the difference of world and thing. If we say this, then we can also say that there is a quality of forgottenness that belongs intrinsically to nearness: originary difference is forgotten in the way in which the thing draws near. This would indicate, in turn, that in the near, there lies always the sense of having missed what is in need of retrieval. What is near comes after what is lost: it is in this sense that the two belong together. It may be this that gives the occasion for Heidegger's central example—the coffin—which we considered above: the loss that death eventuates is the site of the particular nearness that the coffin appears to represent. So, then: to the gathering into nearness there would belong, always, something lost, something past—an "afterness," in Richter's telling coinage. What draws toward us most fully in nearness, is also what comes after: in the intimacy (*Innigkeit*) of the near, there is a quality of the forgotten, of the lost.

It is this sense of loss—of the already absent residing at the core of the deepest intimacy of the near—that speaks to us in the reflections that comprise the volume *Das Ereignis* of 1941–42; and it is among these reflections, too, that we find the clearest signs of the development of the vocabulary that is of such critical importance to the texts from the decade of the 1950s. It is here, in fact, that the question of a language of pain first comes clearly to the fore. In what follows we shall try to draw together some of the threads of that vocabulary, to track its origin and observe its consequences, in order to arrive once again, as we shall see, at the beginning.

The Configuring of the Between

Heidegger initiates the text of *Das Ereignis* by quoting from the opening scene of *Oedipus at Colonus.* Here the blind Oedipus, led by his daughter to rest in the grove of the Eumenides, is addressed by a stranger, who asks of Oedipus: "What is to be asked of one who cannot see?" Oedipus responds, in Heidegger's translation: "*Was wir auch sagen mögen, Alles sagend sehen wir*" ("Whatever we might say, we see in what we say") (*GA* 71: 3/xxiii). The text, thus, commences in an acknowledgment of blindness, but an acknowledgment that opens nonetheless on to another kind of seeing, one that is tied to words, tied to utterance. "This seeing," Heidegger comments, "is the sight of the pain of experience" (*GA* 71: 3/xxiii). Right at the opening, then, a relation is established between a kind of saying, between words that will emerge upon the withdrawal of sight, and a kind of pain. Whatever else may transpire in the text, then, it is clear that what will be said will speak of and from pain. Commenting on the mode of writing upon which he plans to embark, Heidegger remarks that "everything since *Contributions* . . . to be transformed in this saying" (*GA* 71: 3/xxiii), indicating elsewhere that the transformation is occasioned by the limits that *Contributions* (*Beiträge zur Philosophie*) runs up against, and that there arises now the need for a speaking-beyond, a reaching over those limitations.

If, then, it seems to be in some way a saying of pain that will induce this transformation, it is not surprising that, among the principal developments that the text of *Das Ereignis* undertakes is an exploration of a configuration of terms intimately connected with pain, and not developed in the *Beiträge*: a configuration revolving around *Schmerz*, *Austrag*, and *Abschied*. In this chapter we will observe the movements of this configuration; observing, too, the relations that obtain between the terms. This will enable us to deepen our understanding of the expressions of pain that we noted in later texts by returning to their source.

As a guide, we can take up a moment right in the midst of Heidegger's text, a moment that surprises, even in a text as open and itinerant as this. It comes in the section of the text entitled "Das Da-Seyn," when Heidegger is considering the history of the word *Dasein*, its eighteenth-century sense and its development. He addresses the *Da* of *Dasein*, iterating a series of words that revolve around manifold inflections of the sense of "there" as presence. But then, and quite unexpectedly, Heidegger quotes Goethe, from a letter to Bettina von Arnim, in which the *Da* becomes, not the index of a simple "being present," but a moving sign of loss, an index of pain:

> And if I (Goethe) now come into the theater and look toward his (Schiller's) place and realize that he is no longer present [*da*] in this world, that those eyes will no longer seek for me, then I find life vexing and would prefer not to be present [*da*] any longer. (*GA* 71: 208/178)

Thought in relation to the opening of the text, for which the possibility of a certain kind of saying was attendant upon a blindness, we can say that, here, what is at stake is the writing of another kind of unseeing, the unseeing of what is lost, the lack of the eyes that look for mine, the *da*—the "there"—as at one and the same time an expression of presence, and one of irrecoverable loss.

We have indicated that a configuration of terms revolving around *Schmerz*, *Abschied*, and *Austrag* belongs intimately to the movement that takes place in the wake of the *Beiträge*, the movement that Heidegger describes as "transformative." The word "configuration" here intends to invoke the question of relation—a constellation of elements whose coordinates appear determined in relation to one another. Configuration, too, intends a kind of motility, a sense of transience, a resistance to the hypostatization of the definition. The term is not accidental, but is specifically deployed here because the questions the term raises—of relation, of motility, and of instability—belong absolutely to the kinds of language and of thought initiated in the *Beiträge*. The opening of that text, indeed, speaks mysteriously of what is to follow as "the straight edge of a configuration" (*GA* 65: xiii/1), implying that what will unfold in its wake will require the orientation of an edge as a guide in a less stable landscape. Just as with the configuration of terms from *Das Ereignis* that we are to explore, so too the description of the *seynsgeschichtlich* texts as a whole as a "configuration" is intended to bring into focus the question of relation, and with it the question of a "between": it is precisely the indefinite and motile quality of the idea of a configuration that draws attention to the question of relation. The instability, or inadequacy of expression that attends the writing and the deciphering of these texts can be understood as an indication of a particular attention that is being paid, not just to the coordinates of the configuration, but to the space opened up between them. This instability in the between-space of configuration can, in fact, be understood as the central structural axis around which the text of the *Beiträge* unfolds; this possibility will be addressed later. In this chapter, though, what will be addressed is the operation of pain (*Schmerz*), that of an enduring or sustaining (*Austrag*), and that of a partedness, or departing (*Abschied*). It will be seen that this configuration elaborates a between-space consonant with the understanding of *harmonia* that resonates down into later texts. To begin to address this configuration of terms, though, we must first consider the sense of the *Da* around which they can be seen to revolve.

"*Dasein*," Heidegger had written in the *Beiträge*, "is the crisis between first and other beginnings" (*GA* 65: 295/233).[2] In chapter 7 we will contend with the question of beginning, with its first-ness and its otherness; but here, what needs to be addressed is the between-ness of this determination of *Dasein*, the sense of a constitutive instability that attends the condition of the between: the sense of "crisis." This latter is clearly intended in the Greek sense of the term, indicating a separation, a division: in terms of this description, it would thus be utterly inadequate to understand *Dasein* as subject to the experience of a separation as a matter of mere historical contingency. This would be to suggest that the uncertainty that attends this in-between might—in due course, given the working out of certain historical trajectories—resolve itself. What is said here is something entirely different. What is said, here, is that *Dasein* *is* as this between, *is* as the drama of this separation.

It belongs to the process of the *Beiträge* to exploit insistently a multiple sense of the between in order both to disorient and to establish resistance to the pull toward static, substantive determinations that would, for Heidegger, merely reassert the claims of a moribund metaphysics. This thought of the between, then, is consistently withdrawn from subordination to the polarities that it would separate. Now, it is certain that, to the extent that the history of metaphysics unfolds in terms of patterns of opposition and their attendant hierarchies of value, the "between"—its difficulty, its necessity—would belong to the passageway between elements. To negotiate the passage, for example, from sensible to intelligible, must allow for the imagining of a between. But, in terms of this history, it is a between that, however multifarious and complex, remains subordinate to the poles it conjoins. The sense of the between that Heidegger is attempting to explore in the *seynsgeschichtlich* texts requires a reorientation. No longer will the between be understood as the connecting thread of a structure whose elements it would both conjoin and keep apart, thereby fixing and reinforcing their complementarity. Now, the between will start to be given a kind of priority, to speak in a voice that does not defer to the complexes it separates. Constitutively unable to free itself from those complexes (how could it, after all, and still remain a between?), in danger always of becoming subject to its own strange kind of reification, the weakness of the between will express itself by claiming the space of an empty and abyssal ground. The voice with which this between speaks is one that embraces its frailty, not failing to remain attached to its coordinates, but pulling at them, deflating and dislodging their dominance. It is thus that one can read the following articulation of the "there," the *da* of Dasein:

> The "there": the open, clearing-concealing "between" [in relation] to [*zu*] earth and world, the center of their strife and thereby the site of the most intimate belonging-to [*zu-gehörigkeit*], and so the ground of the to-itself [*zu-sich*], of the self, and of selfhood. (*GA* 65: 322/254)

The "there"-ness of *Da-sein* is here directly expressed in terms of a between: the *Da* is, as Blanchot might say, *ne uter*, neither one nor the other. But the strategy of this formulation expressly resists the ossification of place: the *Da* is not the locus *of* a between, but is the between itself, and is so as a movement *toward*: the "there" is the midst of division, strife, conflict insofar as it is the between that is in motion *toward* (*zu*) earth and world, in the direction of a belonging-*to* (*zu*-gehörigkeit) that of which it is the between, the grounding movement (*Er-gründung*) toward self (*zu*-sich). The insistence on the *there* as movement-toward forestalls the reinscription of a static presence, insisting on the locus of a between which is affected with transience. It is within this indefinite transience of a between that “selfhood” (*Selbstheit*) itself can be restored, but now no longer as the foundational ground-point of the movement of consciousness, but as an unstable oscillation, fragile and evanescent: “Selfhood is the trembling of the countering of the strife in the fissuring” (*GA* 65: 322/254). Da-sein, we read elsewhere, is “the self-opening center of the counterplay between call and belonging [*Zuruf und Zugehörigkeit*],” torn between response, between responsive listening, and attachment, at once conditioning and conditioned. Displaced, massively, from identification with the “human,” “Da-sein is the between”; not a between that “simply results from the relation of gods to humans; rather, one that first grounds the time-space for such a relation” (*GA* 65: 311/247).

Thought in the space of this between, Da-sein will occur as a “splitting apart” (*Ausfälligkeit*) and will belong intimately to the “fissuring” *(Erklüftung*) that, time and time again, is mobilized to articulate Heidegger's sense of “event.” Pulled apart across this fissuring, Da-sein is the restless and fragile occasion, the *Zwischenfalls*, the incidence of the between “into which the human must be dis-lodged [*ver-rückt*]” (*GA* 65: 371/251). It is this essential dis-lodging, the restless displacement of the between, that can bring us closer to the textual environment of *Das Ereignis,* where the fragile, restless instability of this between is explicitly articulated as pain:

> The between and the pain. Here in the in-between, especially the “between” between beyng and beginning, between beingness and beyng, between beyng and the human being. (*GA* 71: 209/179)

The connection, then, between the hovering dislodgement of a between, and some sense of pain is evident here. But what must be inquired into is the derivation and scope of this notion of pain: what, for instance, does Heidegger mean by insisting that the question is one not of the “experience of pain,” but of the “pain of experience”? What is pain, here? What the painful, its reach, its domain? And what is its relation with the configurations of pain that we encounter later on in Heidegger's work and that we have already considered?

The Dark God Returns: Jünger with Nietzsche

The insistence on the inversion—from “the experience of pain” to “the pain of experience”—is of particular significance in that it serves to deflect an association that might lend itself to too facile an assimilation, namely with Ernst Jünger's essay "Über den Schmerz" ("On Pain") of 1934. Heidegger's interest in, and friendship with Jünger necessitates brief remarks on this association; although it will be in resistance to the implications of this text that the emergence of a thematic of pain in Heidegger's work of this period will be best understood. Jünger's text—radical and fascinating, disturbing and prescient to an alarming degree—was written to complement the thesis of his widely read work *Der Arbeiter* of 1932. As that work attempts a radical reenvisioning of the individual in relation to the new operations of power and technicity of which Jünger possessed a clear vision, so too the essay "On Pain" tries to develop an understanding of this new "formation" (*Gestalt*) on the basis of a certain ubiquity of pain. But the very opening of Jünger's text, its central if obscured position, immediately—and in ways that Heidegger will clearly see—limits the scope of his endeavor. This is because Jünger insists on the "relation" of the figure of man to pain: "Tell me your relation to pain and I will tell you who you are!" he begins, and later:

> Man's relation to pain is in no way set; rather, it eludes our consciousness . . . since we have a novel and particular relation to pain, in that our life finds itself without binding norms.[3]

This insistence on a "relation" to pain draws Jünger toward a kind of reification of pain: what is at stake in the treatise is precisely the "experience of pain," an experience to which "we"—"man," "mankind" "humanity" (with however much depth and originality these figures may be conceived)—are subject. Because of this, Jünger is prevented from interrogating either the subject of this experience, or the nature of pain as such. The latter indeed appears to be conceived on the basis of a dominant model of physical pain, although the spectrum of experience indicated in the text is broad and far-reaching.

Now, among Heidegger's significant body of reflections on Jünger's work (*GA* 90) are annotations and marginal notes from his copy of the latter's *Blätter und Steine*, in which the essay "On Pain" is to be found. Despite his ongoing curiosity regarding Jünger's conception of "the worker" as a thinking of the domain of the human beyond the constrictions of the metaphysical subject, Heidegger is unequivocally critical of Jünger's essay:

> A treatise "On Pain" which nowhere and in no way treats of pain itself; does not ask after its essence; nor takes any account of the questionworthiness of the question. (*GA* 90: 436)

Heidegger's address, not to "the experience of pain," but to "the pain of experience," takes shape precisely as a resistance to the metaphysical underpinnings of Jünger's treatise: in Heidegger's reformulation, it will not be man who is determined or who determines himself in relation to an experience of pain. Rather, it will be pain that is constitutive of *Da-sein*, constitutive of the *Da*, in ways that defer the identification of pain with feeling—with *Gefühl*—in any sense that may be aligned with a history of the subject. ("Pain must not be misinterpreted as 'disposition' [*Stimmung*] in the ordinary sense of 'feeling' [*Gefühl*]," writes Heidegger [*GA* 71: 219/188]).

However, there is another direction that emerges from Heidegger's reflections on Jünger, one that presents the possibility of a more positive reception of the account of pain, and that brings us close to the sense of pain that we encounter in *Das Ereignis*. In notes on Jünger that date from 1939/40 (*GA* 90: 245–46) in the midst of the composition of the *seynsgeschichtlich* series, Heidegger writes that "in his thoughts on pain Jünger has not simply reached Nietzsche's fundamental insights, but has genuinely grasped them." He proceeds to quote from the end of Jünger's treatise: "the question thus arises whether we are witnessing the opening act of the spectacle to come, in which life appears as the will to power, and nothing else?"[4] and then juxtaposes this with a fragment of Nietzsche's from 1885, which begins:

> And do you know what "the world" is to me? Shall I show it to you in my mirror? This world: a monster of energy, without beginning, without end; a firm, iron magnitude of force that does not grow bigger or smaller, that does not expend itself but only transforms itself; as a whole, of unalterable size, a household without expenses or losses, but likewise without increase or income; enclosed by "nothingness" as by a boundary; not something blurry or wasted, not something endlessly extended, but set in a definite space as a definite force, and not a sphere that might be "empty" here or there, but rather as force throughout, as a play of forces and waves of forces. (*KGW* VII—3: 338)[5]

For Heidegger, Jünger has appropriated profoundly this Nietzschean vision, has seized hold of the "monster of energy" and found, in a radical rethinking of the relations of power and subjectivity, a paradigmatic exploration of the implications of a "world" conceived "as force throughout, as a play of forces and waves of forces."

There are, though, in the fragment that Heidegger cites in its entirety, indications that point in the direction of an understanding of pain that would operate in a different register. This other possibility would certainly allow Heidegger to think pain in a way that is still drawn from the folds of Nietzsche's thinking, but beyond the constriction of Jünger's articulation. This new mode, though, involves a thought that points toward an aspect of Nietzsche's thinking to which Heidegger, at least ostensibly, does not appear to have been especially open.[6] This thought is the thought of Dionysus. Here is how the same fragment intimates this figure:

> Out of the play of contradictions [*Spiel der Widersprüche*] back to the joy of harmony [*Einklang*], still affirming itself in this sameness of its courses and its years, blessing itself as that which must return eternally, as a becoming that knows no satiety, no disgust, no weariness: this, my Dionysian world of the eternally self-creating, the eternally self-destroying, this mystery world of the twofold voluptuous delight. (*KGW* VII—3: 338)

It is not merely the Dionysian that this passage invokes, as emblem of intoxication, but the figure of Dionysus himself, in a way that draws the fragment quite specifically back toward *The Birth of Tragedy*. It is there that the sense of a "play of contradictions" attains force, that the "eternally self-creating, eternally self-destroying" god shows his affinity with the thought of pain that absorbs Heidegger throughout the text of *Das Ereignis*. To bring home the affinity, let us juxtapose two passages. The first is from this latter text, and appears in a paragraph entitled "Der Schmerz des Austrags" ("The Pain of the Enduring"). It reads:

> Pain is the forbearance that, outstanding, has originally gathered together the terror [*Schrecken*] of what threatens [*Drohenden*] and the bliss [*Wonne*] of what entices [*des Lockenden*]. (*GA* 71: 234/202)

And here, from *The Birth of Tragedy*, at a moment when the excess that belongs to the Dionysian is shown to belong, equally constitutively, to the Apollonian:

> Excess unveiled itself as truth. Contradiction, the bliss [*Wonne*] born of pain, spoke out from the heart of nature. (*GT* 126/46–47)

The thoughts that are drawn together here clearly involve a confluence of vocabulary, the gathering of pain and bliss in an environment in which threat (*Drohen*) and terror (*Schreck*) are always apparent. The question that arises, therefore, is how far the sense of pain that develops in Heidegger's work owes its articulation to the figure of Dionysus as it unfolds in Nietzsche's work. This is the sense of the Dionysian that "embodies the primordial contradiction [*Urwiderspruch*] and the primordial pain [*Urschmerz*], together with the primordial pleasure [*Urlust*] of what appears [*des Scheines*]" (*GT* 129/49), the sense of the figure whose "dismemberment, the properly Dionysian suffering, is like a transformation into air, water, earth and fire . . . the source and original ground [*Quell und Urgrund*] of all suffering" (*GT* 157/53). If the pain that Heidegger is conceiving, the "pain of experience" that "first unfolds the bliss and the terror" (*GA* 71: 234/201), is drawn from the figure of the dismembered god, it would imply that this figure is being thought far beyond the confines within which Heidegger himself, for the most part, would seem to want to place it.[7]

The sense that would need to be restored to Nietzsche's Dionysus in order to effect the translation into the ambience of the *seynsgeschichtlich* treatises is one that would place *Urwiderspruch*, and the *Urschmerz* that belongs to it, beyond the reach of dialectical resolution; it would place the tension of dismemberment and restoral, the belonging-together of the "tears of man" and the "smile" of the gods (*GT* 157/75), in a domain in which the intimacy, the *Innigkeit*, of this togetherness precludes their absorption into one another. Thought in this way, the "intimation of a newly restored oneness" (*GT* 157/75) that art is to represent would be equally the intimation of a dismemberment, a dispersal. Oneness will be thought as inherently fractured, a gathering that is always, and in an irreducible sense, subject to a force of dispersion. *Urwiderspruch*, then, would be the figure that challenges assimilation, that moves beyond the mediation of opposites, invoking an unstable arena in which the between-space of an opposedness is never allowed to ossify into the narrow structure of a mediation. As John Sallis, who has meticulously unfolded precisely such a reading of the figure of the Dionysian, writes: "it is a contradiction in which the opposites are held in their opposition rather than cancelling one another, and it is a contradiction that is not simply unsaid in being said but that is spoken out from the heart of nature."[8]

It is this tense play of gathering and separation that enables us to place the figure of Dionysus within the orbit of the Heraclitean *harmonia* whose movements we are attempting to trace, and of which the figure of pain becomes, in Heidegger, the central marker. The underground operation of this figure can be understood well in relation to the stated task of the Nietzsche lectures, in respect of which Heidegger speaks of attempting to move "in an orderly fashion through the entire labyrinth of Nietzsche's thought, mastering that labyrinth as we proceed." It seems as if the thought of Dionysus, or for that matter of a Heraclitean *harmonia*, cannot find a home in such an orderly proceeding; that Ariadne, whose thread must lead us through the labyrinth, cannot quite be abandoned to the ecstatic dissolution of the dismembered god. However, if it is in the text of *Das Ereignis* that this Dionysian thought makes itself most properly felt, it is also true that there are moments in the lecture series on Nietzsche that do point clearly toward this reading. If there are traces of this figuring to be found in the undercurrent of the lectures, they occur often in relation to lines of filiation that Heidegger indicates between Nietzsche and Hölderlin. But they make themselves felt equally in relation to a term which Heidegger appropriates from Nietzsche, and whose complexity and ambivalence he explores. The term is *Zwiespalt*—conflict, discordance, literally "two-splittedness." Nietzsche uses the term in connection with the relation between Art and Truth, and Heidegger cites a fragment which speaks of a "horror" in the face of the conflict of these two, a "raging discordance [*Zwiespalt*]" (*GA* 6-I: 143/142). Following a line of thought developed from an exploration of the Platonic senses of this relation, Heidegger will suggest that the discordance, in respect of the Plato of the *Phaedrus*, was in fact a "felicitous" (*beglückenden*) one. Given, then, the overturning of Platonism that Nietzsche wishes to undertake, Heidegger claims that this overturning will involve a shift, a movement in relation to this conflict, from a sense of gladdening, a felicity (*beglücken*), to a sense of horror (*entsetzen*). This, then, is to be thought as an alteration in the nature of the *Zwiespalt*, which pushes Heidegger to question the term itself: "what does discordance [*Zwiespalt*] mean?" he asks. And answers: "Discordance is the opening of a gap between two that are severed" (*Der Zwiespalt ist das Auseinanderklaffen von Zweien, die entzweit sind*) (*GA* 6-I: 191/189). But for Heidegger, as we have seen, what operates as an *Entzweiung* or "severance" functions not as a separation, but at the same time as a belonging: "precisely by being apart they enter into the supreme way of belonging together." Thought thus, then, "*Zwiespalt* is ambiguous"—it is *Zweideutig*, as Heidegger says, and in that sense can be said to speak its matter quite precisely. *Zwiespalt* will operate in relation to a double pull—a movement that simultaneously gathers and draws toward and tears apart.

In the midst of this movement, then, a between-space will open up, a tentative and fragile space, subject always to the tensions of its opening. It is of no small significance that Heidegger names this tension *Einklang*, "harmony": "Harmony [*Einklang*] too, requires, longs for [*verlangt*] the twofoldness of severance [*Zweiheit der Entzweiung*]" (*GA* 6-I: 192/189). Most importantly for this undertaking, Heidegger connects this thinking of *Entzweiung*, of the fundamental movement of discord in harmony, back to the *Republic* (607b) where, he says, "Plato speaks . . . in a shadowy and suggestive way" of the *diaphora* between philosophy and poetry. It is precisely as *Entzweiung*, as "severance," that Heidegger translates the term *diaphora*, thus connecting it closely to his own analysis of the operation of *Zwiespalt*, or discordance. So the question would be whether or not the *diaphora* between philosophy and poetry, which is so central to the text of *Das Ereignis*, is being thought in terms of a tense separative belonging, of an agonistic and Heraclitean harmony of difference. Is there a way in which this figure can be deployed to grasp a new sense of the relation between philosophy and poetry? We will be able to explore these questions by tracing out lines of filiation between the Dionysus that we discover in Nietzsche and aspects of Hölderlin's work—aspects, though, that are little addressed by Heidegger in his extensive encounter with the latter. But in order to understand the significance of these lines of filiation, it will be necessary, first, to investigate more fully the question of pain as it emerges in the text of *Das Ereignis*.

The *Stimmung* of Pain

Pain, in the text of *Das Ereignis*, is, then, clearly associated with a betweenness. It might even be better to say, avoiding the pitfalls of Jünger's account, that pain is not merely associated with the between, but is identified with it. If this is so, then the fragment we quoted earlier, entitled "Pain and the Between," can be understood, in some measure, as a claim of identity:

> The between and the pain. Here in the in-between, especially the "between" between beyng and beginning, between beingness and beyng, between beyng and the human being. (*GA* 71: 210/179)

It is from out of this identity that the continuation of the fragment must be understood:

> Only for Da-sein as the *Between* does the pain of experience accord with the disposition [*Stimmung*], which remains attuned [*gestimmt*] to the voice [*Stimme*] of beyng in its twisting free [*als verwundener*]. (*GA* 71: 210/179)

The possibility of a "there" is tied, then, to the emergence of an unstable, motile, and agonistic between-space. And here it appears that it is as a *Stimmung* that this something like a "pain of experience" is to appear. In and as the between, there will be for Da-sein a kind of attunement, a listening-responding that stems from its primary dislocation in beyng. What this "being-there" will be attuned to is the sound of this dislocation, in the form of a voice that calls or intimates from beyond it. The *Stimmung* (attunement) that is open to the *Stimme* (voice) is one that hears the pain of its dislocation, and thus "accords" with that pain. That *Stimmung* is to be understood from out of the originary pain of the between is clear from the following:

> Everything concerning "dispositions" [*Stimmungen*] must be thought from out of the experience of beyng and its question-worthiness; i.e., must be thought from the pain of the history of beyng [*seynsgeschichtlichen Schmerz*]. (*GA* 71: 218/187)

In the text of *Das Ereignis, Stimmung* is clearly thought in relation to its development in *Being and Time.* Here, too, *Stimmung* is presented within the orbit of *Befindlichkeit* (*GA* 2: 134/126), and here, also, the cautionary apophasis of *Being and Time* will be repeated—the insistence that *Befindlichkeit* not be considered as merely descriptive of the "psychological situation" of the human. In *Das Ereignis, Befindlichkeit* is considered to be the "ecstatic self-situatedness [*Sich-be-finden*] in the 'there' as the locus of the estranging temporal realm [*unheimischen Zeit-tums*] of *Da-sein*" (*GA* 71: 217/187). It is this ecstatic estrangement of the "there" which is to be understood as pain, a pain that comes to the fore as it listens to the siren call of a beyond of metaphysical polarities. *Stimmung* is an attunement to the voice of the unmooring of these polarities, an intimation of the fundamental instability of the between.

The absolute centrality of the foregrounding of *Stimmung* in the unmooring of metaphysical polarities can be understood from the following:

> Because the thinking of beyng cannot lay claim to "the sensible," one might believe that it must furnish itself with a kind of "sensibilization" of concepts. But the origin of "concepts" is disposition [*Stimmung*]—the dispositional [*das Stimmende*] is that by which thinking does not need the sensible and images. The imagelessness of disposition is never complete. But the remnants of the imagistic are also never supports of a missing and all too missing sensibilization. (*GA* 71: 220/189)

What is claimed here is that the movement that is to open up a beyond of metaphysics cannot in any way be construed as a return to the sensible, or indeed as any kind of a renewed or reclaimed dominance of sensible experience—a "sensibilization" (*Versinnlichung*). The "twisting free" of metaphysics is not at all a refusal of the intelligible in favor of some invigorated tactility or emancipated hearing. Rather, what is at stake is a reconfiguration of the between-space of these two, such that the intelligibility of the concept no longer mediates the sensible: no longer is the passage from sensible to intelligible to be governed by and subordinated to its destination, or understood in terms of a mimetic ordering. Now, the concept will be thought, in its origin (*Ursprung*), in terms of *Stimmung*, whose operation is precisely that of a displacing: *Stimmung* is that which renders unneeded (*unbedürftig*) the sensible, leaves behind its vicissitudes, taking up its remnants (*Reste*) not as the expression of a lack, but as a plenitude of a different order. It is this between, this *Stimmung*, which is the primary site of *Da-sein*, a "there" that is constituted neither in sensible immediacy nor in conceptual understanding, but in the uncertain and painful space of their destabilization.

How, then, is the *Stimmung* of this between to be grasped or described, without recourse to a language either of sensible immediacy or of discursive conceptual elaboration? The answer lies, for Heidegger, in a language of contradiction, a language that refuses to settle, to allow itself to be appropriated into familiar patterns. It is in this regard that Heidegger has recourse to the vocabulary borrowed or appropriated from Nietzsche that we saw deployed in conjuring the complexity of the figure of Dionysus. It is here, indeed, that the sense of Nietzsche's "bliss born of pain" resonates most completely in Heidegger's texts; here that the sense of an *Urwiderspruch*, a primal contradiction, is fully taken up. It is this appropriation that we need to explore.

Stimmung, Heidegger has told us, must be "thought from out of . . . pain." Pain is the pain of a between, which we understand as the unmooring of the stable poles of metaphysical opposition. There is, then, a complex of relations that associate *Da-sein*, and more specifically the *Da*, the "there," with the pain of a pulling-apart, a pulling-away from the stable orderings of sensible and intelligible and into the unstable domain of a between. This pulling-away, this unsettlement in the between, is what Heidegger knows as the "pain of experience." The pain of the between is not manifest as one or another "feeling," in a sense that could be subject to analysis, and thus to entrapment in the hierarchies of the history of metaphysics. Pain as *Stimmung* is not subject to conceptual analysis because it is the source and origin of the concept, the trace that marks the leaving behind of the sensible, the opening of a space, the partedness of the between. As we shall see, Heidegger will call this partedness of metaphysical destabilization *Abschied*.

Now, Heidegger marshals the full power of his proscriptive anger against the temptation of aligning this thinking of *Stimmung* with what he claims is the history of "feeling," or *Gefühl*. This history, he insists, is inseparable from a kind of determination of the human that sees itself as a "living thing endowed with faculties" (of which a faculty of feeling would be one among many). This determination, in turn, becomes wrapped up in the hierarchization of those faculties, and feeling is thus subordinated to will, to calculative reason, and so on. However, what becomes apparent in these *seynsgeschichtlich* texts is that this proscriptive anger is not aimed at the affective domain as such, but rather at the reduction that belongs so intimately to the history of metaphysics. If, then, Heidegger insists upon a distance between the *Stimmung* he is addressing and a discourse of "feeling," it is not because of a desire to downgrade the domain of affectivity. Rather, it is the opposite: the history of the discourse of "feeling" is precisely that which has, for Heidegger, only been able to think of itself in a relation of subordination to domains of knowing and willing. The operations of the *Stimmung* that belong to the between, that accord with pain, will disassemble those relations, will open a space in which the affective can no longer be delineated in contrast to the rational: in this new configuration, affectivity will begin to occupy an entirely new space. It is, too, in a sense very close to Heidegger's that Novalis understands *Gefühl* as the domain of the in-between, the between-space that binds the movements of real and ideal, intertwining and conjoining them—a mode of thought that entirely presages Heidegger's foregrounding of *Stimmung*.

This new order of experience, which posits pain as the wellspring of the "there," will fight for its space as a between which is not merely "accompanied" by the affective, the way a "feeling" might be said to accompany a conceptual elaboration. Instead, when Heidegger writes of "*die Schrecken des Abgrundes*," or of "*die Wonne des Abschieds*" (*GA* 71: 68/55), these terms must be understood in ways that bind them to their affect: *Abgrund* and *Abschied* become, in the fullest sense, affective words, words generated in the between-space of *Stimmung*; and it is only in entering this strange and unfamiliar between-space that their import and resonance can be measured. What is necessary to the articulation and opening-up of this between-space is an insistent effort to think together complexes of affect, to refuse to allow these moments to slip into an itemization, to fall into the serial: the space of the between, its *Stimmung*, is the space in which bliss and terror, joy (*Freude*) and sorrow (*Trauer*) are held together in contradiction: the pain of the between is the pain in which these affective complexes both gather and pull apart, the place of *Urwiderspruch*, of *Urschmerz* in Nietzsche's sense. Thus Heidegger:

> Inceptual pain is the originary oneness of terror and bliss; not a compound of both. (*GA* 71: 219/188)

This is the pain of a between that cannot be sublated, one whose internal fracture resists the blandishments of unity, but which at the same time cannot be thought other than as a oneness:

> In metaphysics, the horror of the abyss and the bliss of eventual appropriation [*Er-eignung*], the twofold-unitary pain of separating [*Abschied*] is unknown and inaccessible. (*GA* 71: 219/188)

The "pain of inceptual separation" (*Geschiedenheit*) is the pain of a oneness, a gathering that is pulled apart *in* its very gathering—separated, fractured, and riven in its wholeness: the pain of the dismembered god, whose suffering emerges here in the space of the between, in the dislocated and unsettling space that origins the "there" and underscores its estrangement; for "from the smile of this Dionysus sprang the Olympian gods, from his tears sprang man" (*GT* 157/75).

This, then, is what separates the "pain of experience" from the "experience of pain": the former articulates the restless unsettling of a between that does not allow itself to be drawn into the secure space of a mediation—a between that is both fragile and motile enough to resist the pull of oppositional structures, but that will find itself again and again incessantly torn apart by that pull. This is the between-space of the "there," of *Da-Sein*, which recovers itself, recognizes, knows itself—if dimly—in that pain: "catching-itself in the hovering of the in-between" (*das Sichfangen in die Schwebe des Inzwischens*) (*GA* 70: 18). This it is, too, that links our first glimpse of pain in the lecture "Die Sprache" to the elaborations that precede it in *Das Ereignis*: the sense of *Unter-Schied* that develops in the later text, the sense of the inhabiting of difference, of abiding in its rent, unfolds from out of these *seynsgeschichtlich* texts.

If the unsettlement of the in-between is to be thought in terms of pain, then equally, what needs to be addressed is the way in which the difference that is the pain of the between is sustained, or held together. This sustaining, the enduring of the pain of the "there," Heidegger refers to as *Austrag*, crucially emphasizing the "bearing" or "carrying" of the verb *tragen* over against the more usual sense of "issuance" or "result." When Heidegger, in this context, speaks of the "sustaining of difference [*Der Austrag des Unterschieds*]" (*GA* 71: 237/204) and of "the pain of the sustaining [*Der Schmerz des Austrags*]" (*GA* 71: 237/205), he is forging close ties with Nietzsche's Dionysus. But the sense of this sustaining, this enduring, takes Heidegger beyond Nietzsche's metaphorical configuration. What is to be endured, what sustained, is a thinking that can no longer ground itself in metaphysical oppositions, experiencing these oppositions as pure difference: abyssal, without ground. The insistence of and in difference is the displacing or removal (*verrückung*) of the support structure by which a self-understanding might unfold on the ground of a relation to beings. When Heidegger claims that "the enduring [*Austrag*] of the difference is the noticing/marking [*Aufmerken*] of the abyss" (*GA* 71: 237/205), it is this attentive marking that belongs to an order of experience connected with the fragility of the between.

We have seen that the elaboration of this between-space, the pain of its irreducible unsettlement, is to be grasped from out of *Stimmung*: *Stimmung* is the locus of this unsettlement, the first home of the pain of its conflict. As such, the *Stimmung* of the between is itself divided, torn in separating ways: and in *Das Ereignis*, it is above all the terms *Schreck* and *Wonne*, terror and exaltation, that carry the burden of this pain. In sustaining that burden, they open onto the possibility of an experience no longer established on the self-evident basis of beings, one that is accessible only as a kind of vulnerability, a raw exposure to groundlessness. This is why Heidegger says that

> experience is the pain of the separating [*Abschied*], a pain which corresponds to the twisting free [*Verwindung*] of beyng, and as a twisting free first unfolds as exaltation [*Wonne*] and as terror [*Schreck*]. (*GA* 71: 233/202)

In this stepping-beyond, in the glimpsing of a between that is no longer the mediating space of being and beings but the thought of difference in itself, it is the abyssal quality of thought that is experienced as terror, even as a kind of horror: the phrase "*Der Schrecken des Abgrundes*" courses through the text.[9] But it is not in this *Schrecken* that pain lies, but rather in the tensional pull between this recoil and a kind of exaltation, a bliss (*Wonne*) that seems to accompany it. This Heidegger describes as the bliss of separating (parting)—*die Wonne des Abschieds*, an exaltation invariably thought together with abyssal terror. And if, in respect of pain, it seemed that it was the figure of Dionysus that loomed most immediately, then now, in this sense of exaltation, in the ecstasy of leave-taking, it is the figure of Zarathustra who steps forward:

> Tearing to pieces the God in man / No less than the sheep in man / and *laughing* while tearing—*this, this* is your bliss [*Seligkeit*]. (*KGW* 4: 300; *GA* 6-I: 756)

* * *

So far, we have considered the question of pain in *Das Ereignis* from out of a transfiguration of elements of Nietzschean thought. But the affectivity of *Abschied* in its exaltation suggests also a different context and orientation. It is at this point, then, that we can take up the lines of filiation, proposed earlier, between Nietzsche and Hölderlin. The vocabulary of

Abschied—the sense of a moment of separation, of leave-taking, of anguish thought as exaltation (*Wonne*)—suggests indeed a deep link with the latter. However, this link remains for the most part no more than an undercurrent in the commentaries on Hölderlin collected in *Erläuterungen zu Hölderlin's Dichtung* and in the full-length lecture courses.[10] It is therefore necessary to look a little beyond the bounds of Heidegger's own inquiry and address ourselves, as in the case of Nietzsche, to textual moments that fall outside the main current of his thinking. That Heidegger remains fully in touch with the link between Nietzsche's Dionysus and elements of Hölderlin's poetics is evident from his remark, in the Nietzsche lectures, that "even though since his youth he [Nietzsche] knew more clearly than his contemporaries who Hölderlin was," he could not have known "that Hölderlin had seen and conceived of the opposition in an even more lofty and profound manner" (*GA* 6-I: 104/104). Later, too, Heidegger will repeat that "as a secondary school student, Nietzsche especially venerated the poet Hölderlin, whose *Hyperion* exulted in Heraclitean thoughts" (*GA* 6-I: 498/III-30). What is to be be gained, then, from following the threads that connect Nietzsche with Hölderlin, and thus with the orbit of Novalis's thinking, is an intimation of the thinking that finds its voice in the writing of pain that courses through *Das Ereignis*. We are in pursuit, then, of a thought, not an influence. This is the thought that seems to flow as a deep undercurrent through the *seynsgeschichtlich* treatises: our purpose is to make clear its tidal pull. The central address, here, will be to central motifs in Hölderlin's epistolary novel *Hyperion*, and to certain aspects of the immensely demanding essays that he developed in relation to his Empedocles project.

The Song of Pain: Hölderlin with Trakl

Here, then, to begin, and in a register that Heidegger's vocabulary in *Das Ereignis* will appropriate wholesale, is Hölderlin's eponymous hero Hyperion:

> Oh Earth! My cradle! All bliss [*Wonne*] and all pain [*Schmerz*] is in our leave-taking [*Abschied*] from you! (*H* 53/100)

This exclamation belongs to a letter to Diotima that expressly addresses her absence. All letters, evidently, are written thus, to address an absence, but the essential absence of the epistolary is marked, here in a very particular way, in that the letter speaks of her silence: "I have hoped anxiously for a word of parting [*Abschiedswort*] from your heart, but you are silent," the letter begins (*H* 52/100).

The complex narrative structure in which this epistolary novel unfolds allows the whole to be construed as a kind of extended *Abschiedswort*, a complex, interweaving play of leave-taking and return, enfolded in a figure of absence. It is enough to recall the basic outlines of the narrative: the novel consists in a series of letters written by Hyperion to his friend Bellarmin following their separation and Hyperion's return to Greece. In a narrative, then, opened up by a leave-taking and a return, Hyperion relates retrospectively the events and movements that led to his sojourn in Germany and his return to his homeland. Within this structure, the letters between Diotima and Hyperion are copied and sent to Bellarmin retrospectively: "I was in a lovely dream as I copied out for you the letters I once exchanged" (*H* 59/102). In this gesture of sending on, the complex movements of parting and togetherness that form the history of Hyperion and Diotima's relationship are reenacted, played out once again, but beneath the sign both of the absence that occasions the act of copying and sending, and the more decisive absence of Diotima herself: she is dead before the commencement of the book, and the restaging of the coming-together and parting of Hyperion and Diotima takes place beneath the shadow of this loss—"distant and dead are my loved ones, and no voice brings me news of them anymore" (*H* 9/3), writes Hyperion at the opening of an early letter to Bellarmin.

Within the folds of this structure of reminiscence, the reenactment of Hyperion's love and loss holds a central place. And within that center, within the reenactment itself, the moments of parting between Diotima and Hyperion occupy a very particular space: the center of the center. It is at this center—in relation to the figure of parting and absence as it is experienced, envisaged, and described by Diotima and Hyperion—that we encounter the very poignant gathering of *Schmerz, Abschied*, and *Wonne* that finds its way into Heidegger's thinking in *Das Ereignis*. Elsewhere—indeed, precisely as he narrates to Bellarmin a moment of first parting from his beloved, Hyperion will write of this leave-taking (*Abschied*) in terms that conjure, quite precisely, a sense of abyssal disorientation that Heidegger will see it as his task to rediscover:

> I had killed everything around me; I was alone, and I reeled before the boundless silence in which my seething life had no hold. (*H* 18/83)

In connection with the gathering-together of affective contradiction, it is necessary to observe that this experience is by no means unique to Hölderlin's poetics. To engage a broader context, we can cite the following passage, in which Hyperion is writing to Bellarmin, recalling his happiness with Diotima, and intimating at the same time the collapse of "this mortal bliss of my remembrance" (*H* 123/56). He writes:

> Oh, it is so to be desired to drink the joy [*Wonne*] of the world from *one* cup with the beloved! . . . But when the life of the earth was kindled again by the rays of morning, I looked up and sought for the dreams of the night. I looked up, and they had vanished, and only the bliss of grief [*Wonne der Wehmut*] bore witness to them in my soul. (*H* 126/57)

The phrase *Wonne der Wehmut*, the "bliss of grief," reveals the extent to which Hölderlin's thinking is embedded in the literary environment within which it emerges. This phrase, which will go on to to become a central trope of a developing Romanticism, is in fact the title of a poem by Goethe—of sufficiently broad currency to be set later to music by, among others, Schubert and Beethoven.[11] Here, too, the ecstasy of sadness is conceived in relation to absence, in a way that is echoed repeatedly throughout Goethe's poetry. The following, from the poem "Willkommen und Abschied," of 1771/85, will need to suffice to indicate the intimacy of leave-taking and an ecstasy of suffering in Goethe's poetic discourse:

> Doch ach, schon mit der Morgensonne
> Verengt der Abschied mir der Herz:
> In deinen Küssen welche Wonne!
> In deinem Auge welcher Schmerz!
>
> (But Oh, already with the morning sun
> Parting wrings my heart:
> In your kisses what bliss!
> In your eyes what pain!)

Evidently, then, the drawing-together of *Schmerz, Abschied,* and *Wonne* does not in itself belong uniquely to a Hölderlinian poetics. Indeed, this trope, already as familiar to Schiller as it was to Goethe,[12] operates along a fairly consistent continuum through the decades that follow, opening onto a late flowering in the work of Eichendorff and Lenau, among others. If Heidegger, then, can be said to be drawing—implicitly or explicitly—on this trope in his understanding of pain, it will be in a sense that is not merely driven by a preoccupation with Hölderlin, but is connected with a deep core of German Romantic literature.

In the passage above, the reminiscence of joy, of togetherness, is pointedly enclosed within the experience of its loss: joy, Hyperion tells Bellarmin at the opening of the letter, "falls upon my soul like a sword-stroke" (*H* 122/56), the very movement of memory instituting a vertiginous fear. Cast within this ecstasy of pain, the thought of "drinking the bliss of the world from *one* cup"—the thought of oneness—emerges as from the night, as dream. Sunrise, the raw emergence of light and warmth—of life ("but when the life of the earth was kindled again by the rays of morning")—brings with it loss, the resolution of the chthonic fantasy of oneness into separation. The sign of this resolution is the melancholic pain of grief-joy. In a fictional and poignantly affective register, then, the passage articulates a drama of unification and separation that is decisive in Hölderlin's development, and which is manifest both in his essays and in the different versions of his Empedocles project, where the distinctive directions of his thinking become more apparent. It is this difficult drama of apartness, so intimately a part of Hölderlin's thinking, which will manifest itself in Heidegger's text as the pain that belongs to the between-space of Da-sein.

Hölderlin's essay "The Ground of Empedocles" begins with the vision of a kind of harmony, one that transpires, says Hölderlin, "when life is pure." In this domain of purity, "nature and art are opposed merely harmoniously [*nur harmonisch entgegengesezt*]."[13] This is a harmony of reciprocity, of reciprocal completion and balance—one, though, says Hölderlin, that is accessible only to "feeling" (*Gefühl*), and not available to a knowing. In order, then, that it know itself—that it recognize itself *as* harmonious—its purity must suffer a kind of interference, a disruption. This movement—the movement within itself of the pure harmony of the one—is described by Hölderlin in terms of a pull of reciprocal forces that he terms "*organisch*" and "*aorgisch*."[14] We have noted already how, in *Hyperion*, harmony was expressed as a oneness of affective mutuality that was subject to separation, to division. In this process, a nocturnal unity ("drinking the joy of life from *one* cup") is made subject to the pressure of light, the awakening of a knowing. Under this pressure, the oneness of a pure harmony is shown to have been already divided from itself, already subject to separation. Similarly, here too, in the Empedocles essay, a "pure" harmony is shown to have belonged to a mythical "before," becoming a harmony whose recognition involves the acknowledgment of its loss.

If it is to be knowable, then, the harmony (of nature and art) must "separate itself off from itself," a separation that Hölderlin says occurs in an "excess [*Übermaß*] of intimacy [*Innigkeit*]." In the movement that is initiated from this excess is generated a process in which the belonging-together of nature and art—the pure harmony of their reciprocity—comes to be measured, increasingly, in terms of strife (*Streit*). Pure harmony then, comes to be revealed as an immeasurably complex and incessant dynamic of individuation and reunification, a tension of pulling-apart and gathering: "in this birth of supreme enmity," writes Hölderlin, "supreme reconciliation appears to be actual." The individual, in this movement, becomes the expression of "the highest strife," the function of an incessant dynamic of dissolution and a restoral that is occasioned only by loss. For the figure caught in the "celestial fire" of this between, all is

> more infinitely interlaced, that is, in such a way that everything is more infinitely permeated touched implicated in pain and in joy, in strife and at peace, in motion and at rest, in configuration and disfiguration.[15]

It is in terms of a reinvigoration of these Hölderlinian motifs that the thought of *Abschied,* or parting, must be understood when we encounter it in Heidegger's work of the late 1930s. At a linguistic level, Heidegger is thinking *Abschied* from out of *Unterschied* (as a cognate of the verb *scheiden,* "to separate"), and thus in relation to terms that express difference. But beyond the play of these various cognates, it is of more importance to emphasize the way the word plays in an affective domain, a domain in which the differing of separation is also loss, and in which the partedness that comes with separation belongs to a sense of the bereft. In Heidegger's writing, the decisive term for this complex of solitude and lack will be *Abgeschiedenheit* (or "partedness"), a word which Heidegger will later take up in relation to Trakl's poetry (*GA* 12: 48–73). When Heidegger writes, in the text on Trakl, that the locus (*Ort*) of Trakl's work is *Abgeschiedenheit,* "because the poetizing of this poet is gathered in the song of the *Abgeschieden*" (*GA* 12: 48), he is thinking this word in a register that belongs at once to the thinking of difference, of *Unterschied,* and to an affective domain of loss that is opened up in Hölderlin's work. Heidegger's readings of Trakl are the occasion of an emergence of *Abgeschiedenheit* in a different register of thought, but one nonetheless deeply correlated with the sense of *Abschied* that we have begun to address.

We have been concerned here principally with understanding the emergence and strategic operation of a notion of pain in Heidegger's thinking. In following this line, we have traced this figure back to a particular moment in Heidegger's itinerary, that of the volume *Das Ereignis,* written in the wake of the *Beiträge,* but claiming for itself a place beyond it (*GA* 71: 4/xxiv). The overall sense of the movement that is guided by the thought of pain has to do with a sense of the between, a between-space that never lapses into the static and subordinate position of mere connection, but which is rather constituted in an utterly primary movement of pulling-apart and gathering-together. There belongs to this motility a sense of conflict, of unrest, which brings into the gathering of every unity, the belonging of every harmony, the force of dislocation, of disruption. *Dasein* it is, then, that endures, that *is as* this between-space of pain, and that carries the burden of this dislocation. In beginning to trace the lineaments of this movement, we discovered, in the confluence of words that gather around pain in the text of *Das Ereignis,* shadows of a thinking in which Hölderlin and Nietzsche find a home, but one whose address reaches somewhat outside the main thrust of Heidegger's ostensible concerns.

It seems now, though, that in engaging the term *Abgeschiedenheit,* we have arrived at the verge of Heidegger's Trakl readings, and have thus come full circle. We began our investigation with a moment in which Trakl's "Ein Winterabend" speaks to Heidegger—a moment in which Trakl comes to assist in giving voice to pain. If, though, in reading Trakl, and a decade after the work of the *seynsgeschichtlich,* Heidegger once more encounters pain, and encounters it in a way which is entirely correlate with its operation in earlier texts, the context of this encounter is now circumscribed by the inquiry into language, the matter of *Unterwegs zur Sprache.* It becomes necessary, then, following along the path already opened, to ask the question: what, fundamentally, is the relation of pain and language? It is from out of the full history of his thinking of pain, and out of the same semantic complexes that we explored in the earlier texts, that we can hear the Heidegger of the essays on Trakl: "How can partedness bring a saying and a singing to the way?" (*Wie kann die Abgeschiedenheit ein Sagen und Singen auf den Weg bringen?*) (*GA* 12: 63)

The question, then, will be whether it is possible to hear in language the same tension of gathering and pulling apart, the same primal movement of a one always differentiated in itself that seemed to mark out the space of pain in Heidegger's discourse. To suggest this is to suggest that the gathering that is the *logos* is always attended by a movement that places that gathering in tension with itself. Furthermore, it is to suggest that this tension does not merely describe pain, does not merely operate in a parallel way to the conceptualization of pain in Heidegger's thinking, but that language, word, *is* a kind of pain. From such a vantage point, it might be possible to understand what Heidegger intends in the following: addressing the line from Trakl that runs "And gently stirs an ancient stone:" (*Und leise rührt dich ein alte Stein:*), he writes:

> The ancient stone is pain itself, in such as it looks toward mortals. The colon after the word "stone" signifies that now *the stone* is speaking. Pain itself has the word. (*GA* 12: 59)

If we are to address this question, it will first be necessary to follow the same path back into the *seynsgeschichtlich* treatises, into the crucible of pain, and begin to think about the operation of language in those texts. There we encounter a mode of utterance entirely distinct from other moments of Heidegger's itinerary, a discourse set apart, indeed, from the main currents of philosophical writing. Language there becomes fragile, becomes frail, fragmentary—prone to silence and to interruption. But it is there, too, in this difficult discourse, that we can locate and unfold the relations we seek. Indeed, it is in one of the later texts of this series that we encounter the claim that "*die Sprache entstammt dem Abschied,*" "language arises from the parting," an idea that in itself warrants this trajectory. It may be that it is in the very frailty of language which those texts expose and which—as Heidegger says—is also the frailty of questioning, that the question of language and its relation with a thinking of pain can best be seen:

> The frailty of questioning must itself be endured [*ausgetragen*] in the sustaining [*Austrag*] of the pain [*Schmerz*] of the parting [*Abschied*]. (*GA* 71: 238/205)

The following chapter will move in that direction, but will attempt to approach the question from out of the broader context of the *seynsgeschichtlich* project. Here, it will be seen that the sense of the between that comes to light in Heidegger's address to the question of pain is central to the operations of that project. The chapter will address the question of beginning, of inception (*Anfang*), which, it will be argued, is never far from the question of difference, of the pain of difference. Our effort will be directed toward the discovery of difference at the heart of inception, and the operations of a between-space in the very thought of origin. From thence, in chapter 8, we will be able to address directly the question of the language of the *seynsgeschichtlich* treatises, and thereby to understand the intimate relation which the question of language sustains with the fragile experience of the between of which we are in pursuit.

7

Between Beginnings

In the last chapter, we explored the sense in which the "there-ness" of Da-sein is understood by Heidegger as an agonistic between-space. The "there," for Heidegger, expresses a tension of gathering and pulling-apart which is articulated—inheriting a vocabulary from Hölderlin and a metaphorical apparatus from Nietzsche—in terms of an affective complex that revolves around the figure of pain. But the *seynsgeschichtlich* treatises also offer another way to think the between-ness of the "there"—a way that is clearly expressed in a formulation we have already cited: "Dasein is the crisis between first and other beginnings." What the following pages will address, then, is this multiplicity of beginnings (inceptions, *Anfänge*), and in particular the sense of the between whose crisis we have already understood in terms of pain. In exploring this question, it will be necessary to look beyond the apparent linear chronology that the terms "first" and "other" appear to imply, and to try to uncover a sense of beginning, or inception, which is not mere historical occasion, but a way of thinking about being itself. In this speculative realm, the agonistic "there" of Da-sein can be thought of as caught between the chronological specificity of a historical inception and the ontological sense of being *as* event, *as* inception.

In order to indicate the direction this inquiry will take, we call upon the following, from the text of *Das Ereignis*:

> Of the first inception and of the other inception—*which are not two separate inceptions but rather one and the same in their incessant inceptuality*—we are equally lacking experience, or are perhaps even entirely without experience. For we do not know difference [*Unterschied*] and we have no inkling of the parting [*Abschied*]. (*GA* 71: 235/219, emphasis added)

What needs to be explored, then, is the strange sameness of these beginnings. The passage claims that this sameness remains obscure to us precisely because we lack an understanding of difference. The sameness of the inceptions appears thus to be a sameness *in* difference: "first and other"—a particular *kind* of multiplicity, this—are gathered together in their difference in that they are "one and the same in their incessant inceptuality." The guiding idea of what follows, then, is that the thinking of pain that we have undertaken thus far allows for an understanding of precisely this figure of sameness in difference. It is Heidegger's thinking of pain that allows for the keeping open of the unresolved tension of difference, and for leaving unsettled and unhealed the fracture that attends the thought of unity. The investigation will take the following path: first, the double sense of "inception" will be addressed, in order to see beyond the sense of linear historical narrative ("Spectral Narratives"). Then (in "Repetition") we will consider how these multiplicities are to be thought together. Following this, the third and fourth sections will deal with the questions of how to understand difference in relation to the sameness of these beginnings ("Confrontation") and then how to think their oneness across the divide of difference ("Belonging").

Spectral Narratives

The *Beiträge zur Philosophie* speaks in a mode of impermanence, in a mode of transition: what is articulated, unfolded, is an in-between, an interstice. This between-space is expressed in relation to two poles—two extremes, two limits, within which and from out of which the play of this "between" emerges and becomes manifest. These poles, or limits, are *both* described as inceptions: in other words, the kind of transition we are considering cannot be pictured as moving between a beginning and an ending. Instead, to think the "crisis between first and other beginnings" is to think the between as occurring somehow in the midst of beginning, an inception that is doubled, subject to repetition.

If, though, these two poles present themselves in the text as a "first inception" (*erste Anfang*) and an "other inception" (*andere Anfang*), we must say that what is at stake is not just repetition, but reciprocity too. A between becomes articulate in the gap that is expressed by the "firstness" and the "otherness" of these two inceptions. It is this difference, too, that allows for the emergence of a linear narrative of inception: first one, and then the other. The text will play, insistently, within the shadow of this narrative arc. Never coalescing explicitly, the narrative will nonetheless be always operative as a kind of spectral background against which emerges an entirely other vision, a vision of inception as originary multiplicity, of the event character of being thought most purely as inception, of the "there" of Da-sein as plunged into the midst of this incipience. In order, though, to glimpse this wholly other possibility, we need first to engage the linear narrative against whose background it will make its presence felt.

In itself, the narrative outline of the *Beiträge* can be described and presented quite simply. It is reducible as follows: a chronologically identifiable beginning (*erste Anfang*), the story goes, has given way, in its exhaustion, to a period of transition (*Übergang*). Operating within this transitional moment, given the exhaustion of the resources of the "first beginning," our obligation is to await a "new beginning" (*andere Anfang*), attending the "future ones" who will emerge to supply such a possibility. In the meantime—while we wait, as it were—we must occupy ourselves with "preparation" for this reinvigoration. Expressed thus, this narrative is quite familiar, even banal: it is a tale of decline and the possibility of renewal that is far from unfamiliar in the cultural environment within which it was composed. Indeed, given the historical moment of its composition (1936–38), and the kinds of "new beginnings" that were being envisioned and worked through at that time in a political milieu, one might with legitimacy be alarmed by the risks that such a narrative runs.

Given the reductive simplicity of this outline, then, it is clear that what is necessary to a reading of these *Contributions* cannot be merely a consideration of the merits of this spectral narrative.[1] Rather, what is required is a confrontation with, and an exposure of possibilities of thought that occur within its shadow, in its interstices, and that are opened up by the differential movement that the narrative introduces. Such a reading, in fact, is suggested by Heidegger himself, who opens the *Beiträge* with an exhortation to precisely such a double reading, one that looks beyond the obviousness of the terms to be deployed, even that of the title itself:

> The official title must now sound dull, ordinary and empty and will make it seem that at issue are "scholarly" "contributions" . . . (*GA* 65: 3/5)

This exordium, then, sets up a double reading, a reading in which words measure out a distance from themselves, one that can be roughly expressed in terms of a difference between public and private, between the self-evident and the hermetic, the open and the concealed. The *Beiträge*, then, is to be the "*Beiträge*"—a text that is already distanced from itself, at odds with its own movement; a text that risks being lost in an endless abyss of "inverted commas," "on account of the exhaustion of every basic word" (*GA* 65: 3/5). Thus, it will be a work, but only in the sense that it will "keep its distance from every false claim to be a 'work' in the previous style" (*GA* 65: 3/5).

But why this doubling—this double writing? What necessitates the play of distance and engagement that such a doubling allows? Heidegger tells us: such a doubling becomes necessary on account of the "destruction of the genuine relation with the word." It would be of some importance to try to understand what is meant here by both "destruction" (*Zerstörung*) and by "genuine relation" (*echte Bezug*): what is a "relation to words," such that its "genuineness" can be thus fragile, exposed to such a vulnerability? And what is to be understood by the threat of its dissolution? Without sidestepping these questions, however, what confronts us more immediately in engaging these "*Contributions*" is a question of the possibilities for thinking that the doubling of the text might expose. The question, then, is as follows: what kind of thought of beginning, of inception (*Anfang*), is made possible by the spectral historiographic narrative that Heidegger articulates, and by the distance that he takes from it? Beyond the linear, historiographic narrative of "progression," then, the central terms of the narrative—"first beginning," "other beginning," "transition/crossing"—must be seen to break out of the constraints that a chronology would impose on them. This is the thought that Heidegger describes as an attempt at a "speaking of" and "from" event, "*vom Er-eignis*" (*GA* 65: 4/6). In other words, what is at stake can never be a "description," or an analytic account of some sort, one that stands outside the matter it desires to express, but rather a "speaking from" that owns its emergence and does not presume to leave it behind.

It is in one of the later texts of the *seynsgeschichtlich* series—*Über den Anfang* (*On Inception*)—that Heidegger makes this direction of thought explicit, claiming both that "event *is* inception" (*GA* 70: 47) and that "inception is *beyng itself* as event." To the extent that this text forms part of the "configuration" of which the *Contributions* is "the straight edge," then we can conclude that these equivalences—of event, inception, and beyng—belong to Heidegger's "attempt at a thinking which would arise out of a more originary basic position." In the historiographic domain, to which the linear narrative sketched above clearly belongs, the concept of "event" is reduced to that of some kind of "significant occurrence" within "beyng." In that sense, the statement "*das Ereignis ist Anfang*" (event is inception) becomes merely platitudinous, merely proclaiming some event-like significance for every historical "beginning." But what if, instead, inception were to be thought not as a determinate moment along a historical continuum, but rather *as being itself* in its irruptive, evental happening? Might we not then see the triple equivalence of beyng–event–inception as delineating the inceptive quality of beyng itself, in a way that lifts the notion of beginning, or inception, beyond the reach of a chronology?

The aim, thus, of the set of equivalences expressed above cannot be a matter of simple identity, merely a question of "different terms for the same." Each word, each term, has its own deep specificity, a history that renders the equivalence purely speculative: suggestion and implication rather than claim and argument. The expression of the equivalence of being–event–inception sets up, rather, a web of correspondences whose aim is to loosen the grip of a thinking of the kind that would subordinate the concepts of event and inception to a dominant notion of being as presence. To be able to think in a new way the confluence of being, event, and inception such that "what is" (being) no longer takes precedence over "what occurs" (event): this is the goal here. A claim is staked for the possibility that the inceptive need no longer be thought as attendant upon an already given ground, a solid bedrock of what is, but might be thought instead as the event of being itself. In this thought-world, event and its inception are no longer to be considered "occasion" or as occasional, but rather as the fullest articulation of being itself. *Sein ist Anfang*: being is inception; it is incipient, it eventuates.

In light of this endeavor, the question of plurality becomes crucial: that there is more than one inception will become the decisive mark of this rethinking. If we are to think beyond a continuum, beyond the lines of the spectral narrative that haunts the text of the *Contributions*, we will have to think entirely differently about the structure of inception: no longer will it mark a moment of archaic instauration (this would be the archaic inception of historiographic description). Instead, we are asked to think an inception that, at its core, is already surrendered to the multiple.

It is this mode of speculative endeavor that Heidegger is indicating when he describes the *Contributions* as an "attempt at a thinking which would arise out of a more originary basic position." We have noted already that the *Contributions* derives much of its dynamic from a movement in which a "first inception"—*erste Anfang*—is counterposed to a second—*andere Anfang*. It will, then, be necessary to try to sketch out a picture of this movement as it might appear beyond the pressures of narrative chronology. The thinking that belongs to this attempt—Heidegger will call it "inceptive thinking"—will be one that attempts to engage inception beyond the constraints of linearity.

Inception, in a certain way, is beyng itself. But if this is so, we must also retain an awareness that this inception is not, and cannot be, a unitary concept: the insistence on multiplicity, on "first" and "other," suggests that inception must be considered as subject to refraction, repetition, that it is turned against itself in some manner. We might, then, think that this doubling of the moment of inception forces within it a division, a split: as if it is only in its fracturing that inception is to be accomplished. "Inceptive thinking" will be the thinking that *sustains* the doubling, that holds together the inception across and through its fracture: "a confrontation between the first inception, which is still to be won back, and the other inception, which is to be unfolded." The "history of beyng" that emerges in this thinking will be a way of marking the joins, of experiencing the fracture lines—the leaps, the resonances, the interplay—that emerge through and are discovered in the "there" of *Da-sein.* In respect of the thinking of this new kind of "history," whose articulation is described in the different sections that make up the *Contributions,* Heidegger writes as follows:

> Inceptual thinking is the original carrying out [*Vollzug*] of resonating, interplay, leap, and grounding in their unity. "Carrying out" here means that these—resonating, interplay, leap, and grounding in their unity—are taken up in their unity and borne only in the human way and that they themselves are essentially other and pertain [*gehören*] to the occurrence of *Da-sein.* (*GA* 65: 64/51)

We will, in chapter 8, address the different moments of this history: its echoing, its intertwining, and its leaping-forth—the multiple gestures and movements of difference. But for now, we will focus on their "unity," on the gathering-together in which the thinking of inception is to be "carried out." To "carry out," to enact and fulfill the thought that arises from the idea of inception as originary multiplicity, is to sustain this unity across its fractures of difference. What appears to be at work here, then, is a thinking of the "there"—the "crisis between first and other beginnings"—as a holding-together of the irreducibly multiple, prior to its lapse into the historiographic domain of chronological itineraries. And it is in this sustaining of difference that we encounter again the figure of the between that has accompanied this investigation throughout—a *harmonia* of difference, a convergent-separation.

The sustaining of such a thought—the "carrying out" of inceptive thinking—will, though, necessarily be subject to the vicissitudes of discursivity: the pressure of the linear, of the continuous, that belongs to the environment of expository writing. If, then, the writing of the fissure of difference will be subject to the demands of iteration, the sense of a continuum, then it will—of necessity—fail in its endeavor, and the burden of the thought of self-differing will be forgotten:

> The word fails, not as incidental occurrence . . . but originarily. This failing is the inceptual condition for the self-unfolding possibility of an originary—poetic—naming of beyng. (*GA* 65: 35/30)

The thinking of the belonging-together of inception and being—the thinking of being as inception—is, then, conditioned upon a failing, a misdirecting (*Verschlagung*) of the word. Subjected to the pressure of a discursive unfolding, the thought of inception will always fall away, will always decay. This is why this complex and paradoxical figure of double inception—a whole divided in itself, complete *and* sundered, fissured *and* intact—will tend, will almost *need*, in its unfolding, to move toward the historiographic: the sheer weight, the extreme difficulty of sustaining the holding-together of a split inception will be lessened if one inceptive moment is allowed to precede, or to give way to another. If the first beginning is allowed a determinate chronological moment, if the second beginning is cast in the discourse of a "possible future," then the energy and intensity of the thought of double inception will begin to dissipate. And this it is that occasions the "double-writing" that belongs so intimately to the structure of the *Contributions*: a writing that performs the linear, the chronological, the narrative—even as it breaks away from such continuity. It will be this, too, which will be the occasion of the strange language of the *seynsgeschichtlich* treatises—their interruptions, hiatuses, ellipses, and fragmentations—that we will come to address in the following chapter.

It would be possible, here, to construct an analogy with Nietzsche's figure of eternal recurrence, of which this thought of double inception is a near relative. For this figure, too, chronological succession will always be on hand to come to the rescue of the "abyssal thought." For Nietzsche, if Zarathustra's dwarf can "murmur contemptuously . . . 'all that is straight lies . . . all truth is crooked; time itself is a circle,'" this is because the abyssal thought of eternal recurrence crosses so smoothly and effortlessly into the thought of mere endless circularity. In like fashion, then, Heidegger's thinking of double inception operates in the orbit of a similar falling-away, in which a rhetoric of decline and reclamation will always tend to step in to support a thinking that falters before this abyssal holding-together. It seems, now, indeed painfully clear that Heidegger was himself lured by such a rhetoric, that the "overcoming of metaphysics" and the futurity of a second beginning slipped into the dark historiographic schematics of the time. We will, though, not dwell upon this falling-away, which continues to be the subject of much productive inquiry, and focus instead on the other, difficult and tentative, but positive possibilities that the density of Heidegger's thinking and writing can be seen to contain.

What needs to be thought, in this difficult and dynamic realm, is the unity of a wholeness fractured at core; and the thinking that will respond to this need is, for Heidegger, the thinking of the "in-between"—*das Inzwischen*—and the corresponding and concomitant vocabulary of "transition" or "crossing" between inceptions. If, as we have seen, *Dasein* is to be thought as "the crisis between first and other beginnings," then this crisis of the between will be understood, in the *Contributions*, in terms of a movement of transition (*Übergang*). Here, too, the double writing—and double thinking—of the text is fully operative, as *Übergang* works well within the structure of chronological narrative, in which sense it might indicate a temporary unease, the disquiet of a passageway toward the renewal of another beginning. But beyond the chronological, in the more difficult space of inceptive thinking, it seems we are to think instead of a constitutive withstanding—of *Austrag*—not as a resolving but as an enduring or sustaining. Thought inceptively, then, in terms of a tension of inception, the between is no longer that of a chronological mediation—the passage from out of one historiographic beginning to its renewal, or to the institution of another. Rather, the complex of terms that circulate around the thought of the "in-between" indicates the sustaining, the holding-together, of the fractured unity of double inception. It is this sustaining of the "in-between" that Heidegger calls *Inständigkeit*—an insistence in the "there."

To progress further toward an understanding of the strange transitional between-space of the "there," in respect of the figure of inception we are trying to draw out, we reiterate that a kind of doubling attends the thought of inception: this is because, if inception is to be thought as event, and event as being itself, then the singularity of "the" inception must be given over to an original multiplicity. This means that, in the "uniqueness of its incipience," the inception is fractured, sundered. The sense of this fracturing, in Heidegger's thought, is of a confrontation within this multiplicity of inceptions. In this self-difference, this confrontation of dividedness, inception can be said to turn against itself. Inceptive thinking—the thinking of, and therefore *in* inception—can be construed, then, as a kind of questioning, one which puts into play this dividedness or, as Heidegger will term it, this "turning in the event":

> That the questioning rests on the ground means that it finds its way into the extreme domain of oscillation [*Schwingungsbereich*], into the belonging to the most extreme occurrence [*Geschehen*], which is the *turning in the event.* (*GA* 65: 57/46)

Expressing itself as a figure of *absolute instability* (and embracing the paradox of this formulation), inception finds its own proper thinking in moving across and between this turning. Thinking will be the questioning that sustains itself in the divide. In this way, thinking itself might be said to occupy a transitional space, a space of crossing-over (*Übergang*). Decisive, here, as always, will be our capacity to resist the drift which would insist that "transition" must be subordinate to the poles it traverses, or that a journey is rendered meaningful only by its destination. Instead, we will have to think inception as sustained in and by the between-space of the transitional. Thus it is that "transitional thinking," a phrase hereby rendered pleonastic because all thinking is transitional, is imagined as a bridge, "but a bridge which soars out [*ausschwingt*] toward a shore that must first be decided" (*GA* 65: 165/139). The project, then, of the "there"—of *Dasein* thought as crisis—is, as Heidegger expresses it elsewhere, "*auf der Brücke zum bleiben*": "living on the bridge" (*GA* 71: 48).

What we have yet to consider, though, from the vantage point of the between-space of the transitional, is the mode of relation that inception has in its dividedness: how, and in what ways, are first and other beginnings opposed to one another? How do they confront, belong, and correspond? We will approach this matter from three different perspectives, which broadly gather around the following ideas: the thought of repetition, the thought of confrontation, and the thought of belonging. In each of these three modes, what will become apparent are ways of thinking the between, ways of articulating the between-space that Heidegger's inceptive thinking seeks to bring out. We begin, then, with the question of repetition.

Repetition

Heidegger writes:

> Because every inception is unsurpassable [*unüberholbar*], it must constantly recur [*wiederholt*], set through confrontation into the uniqueness [*Einzigkeit*] of its incipience [*Anfänglichkeit*] and of its ineluctable reaching ahead [*Vorgreifens*]. This confrontation is original when it itself is inceptive, but this necessarily is *another* inception. (*GA* 65: 55/44)

This passage appears to say something about the way in which the poles of the fissured inception confront and oppose one another—how they are different, in effect. It is worth examining some of its implications. In the first place, then, we can note that "inception"—all inception, inception as such—has the quality of being "unsurpassable": it cannot be overtaken, in the literal sense that it cannot be "stepped over." This indicates that "inception" marks a kind of limit. Indeed, one can say that inception, in a sense, *is* the institution of limit, the cut whose constitutive singularity is beyond the possibility of transgression because *it is itself* the instituting of the line that would be transgressed. However, we can also say that inception—irrupting unwonted into the fabric of what is—is already itself a kind of transgression. It is in this sense, also, "unsurpassable": it cannot be overreached, but not just because it determines what proceeds from it, and still less because it somehow "cannot be improved upon" (as the historiographic narrative might be taken to suggest). Inception is unsurpassable because its instituting represents the rupture that first articulates the frame within which the thought of a surpassing first becomes possible. This is what is meant by the claim, in the *Beiträge*, that "inception is what is self-grounding": it is self-grounding in that it cannot be thought as unfolding from the pre-given, from out of a preexistent structure, but is itself the very instituting of that structure.

However, such a description of a pure instituting, of the event-like occurrence of the inceptive, does run the risk of a kind of enshrinement of origin, of establishing "the inception" as a kind of absolute, not merely unsurpassable, but "unreachable," and thus subject to a mythology of genesis. It is precisely here, however, that the peculiar densities of Heidegger's text move forward to forestall such a resolution. Heidegger says that *because* the beginning is "unsurpassable," it must therefore constantly recur, must be subject to a continuous reiteration, to a reenactment. How so? Are we to understand this repetition merely as the ever-weakening reverberation of some chronologically distant occurrence? Such an understanding would certainly appeal to the spectral linear narrative that we identified as informing the writing of the *Contributions*; but it would fall short of the complex weave of Heidegger's thinking here. He says, "*because* every inception is unsurpassable, it must constantly be repeated." So, repetition occurs *because* of the constitutive unsurpassability of the inception. Its irruptive and singular force is *itself* the occasion of its continuous recurrence.

One way to understand this sense of constitutive recurrence is by considering further the question of limit—the rupture or marking of the inception. Limit measures out what occurs within its bounds: it takes place as a setting of measure, as a measuring out of what lies in its wake. Insofar as it sets the measure, then, the inception can be said to "reach forward" (*vorgreifen*). In a sense, indeed, inception *is* such a reaching-forward—it articulates itself precisely in and as this irruptive reaching. This is why Heidegger calls inception *das Sichgründende Vorausgreifende*—"that which grounds itself in reaching ahead": the rupture of inception, the institution of limit, occurs *as* a stretching beyond itself. This means not merely that inception cannot be conceived without its repetition: more properly, it means that inception takes place *in and as* its repetition. The beginning constitutes itself *as* repetition, *as* recurrence.

It is in this structure of repetition that inception, in a seeming paradox, becomes unique. This is why Heidegger says that, in repetition, inception is "placed through confrontation [*Auseinandersetzung*] into the uniqueness of its incipience." Inception thus can be said to *become* singular in its repetition: it is singular precisely as divided from itself, refracted through a multiplicity. "*Solely what occurs only once stands in the need of repetition,*" writes Heidegger (*GA* 65: 55/45). In that it becomes unique only in and through its division, we can say that inception is the event of this tension of singularity and multiplicity, the *agon* of an event that becomes whole only in its sundering.

As its own repetition, then, beginning confronts itself, entering into its singularity as fractured, as an incipience whose uniqueness is always already multiple: "indeed the beginning can never be apprehended as the *same,* since it reaches ahead and thus encroaches differently each time on that which it itself initiates" (*GA* 65: 55/44). As this insistent self-differing, inception occurs in confrontation, in being placed over against itself. It is in this confrontation of itself with itself, in the opening of its self-differing, that inception eventuates. Inception comes to be thought in and as its otherness: it is in this sense that a "first beginning" finds itself thought over against "another beginning"—the latter manifesting itself as both repetition *and* rupture.

Confrontation

We have already seen that Heidegger understands the self-differing of inception as a "confrontation" (*Auseinandersetzung*) of the first inception with its other. But what is to be understood here by "confrontation"? How can the moments of self-difference in inception be understood as "confrontation"? In claiming that one inception confronts another, Heidegger is saying, in effect, that there belongs to this difference a "turning-against" one another. What is the "against" of this difference? It appears that Heidegger is introducing into his thinking of the originary multiplicity of inception the quality of negation, a moment of the negative. It will be important to understand the negation, because it is here that Heidegger can be seen to address himself, and confrontationally, most particularly to Hegel, whose ghost so clearly haunts the thinking of the *Contributions,* both in its speculative dimension and in relation to the linear narrative that appears to underpin that speculation. For Heidegger, then, Hegel's is a presence that can only be addressed by maintaining it in the closest proximity. If a confrontation with Hegel is to be possible and necessary, it will only ever be one that occurs in awakening possibilities "that must lie hidden *within* Hegel's philosophy, yet as its inaccessible and indifferent ground" (*GA* 70: 4). It is only by stepping *within* its folds, by inhabiting it that the limits of this thinking might be sensed. However, the question of limit, here, is not at all generated by a desire to take distance from Hegel's thought, by a reserve, or by some kind of "disagreement." To proclaim a limit in this sense is to assert some kind of inadequacy: but this is not at all the tenor of Heidegger's confrontation with Hegel. On the contrary, he writes, in a text on Hegel contemporaneous with the *Contributions*: "The '*limits*' of a thoughtful thinking are never a . . . lack, but rather the out-soaring and hidden indecision/undifferentiatedness [*Unentschiedenheit*] as the necessity of new decision [*Entschiedenheit*]" (*GA* 68: 34). In other words, what lurks explosively within the folds of Hegel's thinking are possibilities that reach beyond and rupture the structure in which they first emerge, and which would seem to contain them. It is the unlocking of these possibilities that requires the energy of confrontation in order to free them into their full operative capacities. It is for this reason that Hegel's thought is kept so close here: not in order to disagree, but to unlock its full potential.

The axis of this confrontation with Hegel will be the question of the negative—the negation that is encountered in the confrontation, in the turning against one another of inceptions. The negative, Heidegger tells us, is the *Grundbestimmung* (*GA* 68: 6), the "grounding-direction" of Hegel's thinking. If that is so, then it is here, in the negative, that is to be found the "inaccessible and indifferent ground," that which lies hidden—not in the sense of an unspoken assumption, but in the sense that it remains unexposed, unquestioned (*GA* 68: 39). These new possibilities of thinking with Hegel are to be found in opening up the question of the negative, and it will be for this reason that Heidegger must enter into such dangerous proximity to the movement of that thinking. Indeed, in thinking the difference of inception as confrontation, as negation, Heidegger is working quite close to the possibility of absorption into the dynamics of Hegel's thinking, which has its own way of thinking the gathering-together of what is sundered. If, then, in addressing difference in terms of negation, Heidegger is coming close to the possibility of such an absorption, how will it be possible to resist this pull and thereby, as Heidegger suggests, "bring Hegel's systematics within the predominant view but to think it quite oppositionally" (*GA* 68: 39)?

It will be a matter, as Michel Haar saw clearly, of the difficulty of thinking difference—which means, here, thinking the fracturing of the inceptive—as a "non-dialectical immediacy."[2] In other words, it means thinking the togetherness, the binding of what is fractured, in a mode that cannot be withdrawn into the separate "moments" of a dialectic. Heidegger writes, of Hegel, that "negativity is that which is conditioned neither by the one, nor through the other of the one, nor yet through the other of the other, but rather is that which, uncoupled from both, *binds* them in their reciprocal belonging" (*GA* 68: 39). Such a logic of binding can be equally be seen to govern his own thinking, provided only (and this is the decisive shift) that the binding of the negative is not allowed to sediment into the figure of an opposition. The negative will *belong* in a way that is entirely other than the mode of opposition. It is to belong in such a way, as Heidegger says, as to be "the abyss of beyng itself"—it must saturate, seep through the field of the event in a way that cannot be circumscribed within the boundary of an opposition.

If the negative is to be construed other than oppositionally—if the binding of the fracture, its holding-together, is to be something other than the absorption of difference—then confrontation, too, must be thought of as something other than an "opposing." This is why Heidegger writes that "the other inception is not a counter-direction to the first; rather as something *utterly different* it stands outside of the 'counter-' and outside of all immediate comparison" (*GA* 65: 147/187), and again that "beyond counter-forces, counter-drives, and counter-arrangements, something wholly different must commence" (*GA* 65: 146/186). What will be needed, then, in order that the difference that is articulated in the turning of confrontation be beyond opposition, beyond the logic of "comparison," is that the "belonging" of the negative must no longer be thought in terms of containment or exclusion, but rather as a belonging that broaches the distinction between these two, the distinction between inside and out, a belonging that exceeds, that answers to the demands of a within-ness by transgressing its borders. If we can think such a figure—even if the "utterly different" nature of that figure will, indeed must, present itself as resistant to the very processes of thinking—then we might have a way of thinking confrontation without resorting to a vocabulary of "countering"—without engaging, in other words, the structure of an opposition. This is how Heidegger is able to claim that "the confrontation is . . . not an opposition, in the sense of a rejection nor by way of a sublation of the first in the other." With the displacement of the figure of difference from a structure of opposition into something like a figure of broken belonging, the negative of confrontation is also displaced. If confrontation can be said to occur as a belonging that exceeds, then the negative of difference, the "moment" of the turn, will no longer stand outside the "moments" of the confrontation, but will course through them, wrapped up in their belonging as much as in their "reciprocal overstepping" (*GA* 65: 230/181).

The "confrontation" of a "first inception" and an "other inception," as Heidegger's narrative presentation expresses it, means the placing of one kind of thought against another, allowing them to engage a project of mutual reinscription, mutual rearticulation, without resolving into opposition. Here, in this play, the fluid figures of exceeding, of falling-short, of displacing and of porosity will dominate, rather than the resolution of a dialectical mechanics. It is this play of different movements, at once constituting and disfiguring a whole, which Heidegger will call "joinings" (*Fügungen*). These will become the object of consideration in the next chapter. But before that, a problem has to be addressed which relates directly to the kind of belonging-together that the confrontation of inception expresses, and that we have tried to describe. The problem has to do, not with the way in which inception comes to confront itself, but with the way in which the fractured singularity belongs together. It emerges in the way that Heidegger describes "first" and "other" inceptions as being "assigned" to one another: how are we to understand the belonging that this "assignation" of difference expresses?

Belonging

At the outset of the *Contributions*, we read the following:

> The other inception of thinking is so named, not just because it is formed otherwise than any other former philosophy, but rather because it *must be* the only other in relation to the one and only first inception. From this assignedness to each other of the one and of the other beginning, the character of thoughtful meditation in the transition is determined. (*GA* 65: 5/7)

In its general outline, this passage can be understood in terms of the thinking of inception that has thus far been attempted: the thinking of an inception whose singular completeness occurs in and as its own displacement, a wholeness whose integrity is dependent upon its fracturing. But here, in addition, there are kinds of formulations that present a rather different problem. This is because we find, alongside the play of figures of uniqueness and multiplicity that indeed supports the sense of the originary diffraction of the inceptive, a mode of thinking that appears to threaten that diffraction. We indeed encounter again the reciprocal belonging of beginnings, the intertwinement of inception with its otherness, and thinking as the mode of "transition" that eventuates in that difference. Equally, we find here once again the "uniqueness" of inception set into play with its refraction: the "one and only first beginning" is again confronted with a repetition in the form of an otherness that will both disrupt and confirm its uniqueness.

The new difficulty that arises here quite specifically, though, has to do with what Heidegger calls the "assignment" of one inception to the other. Inception, we are told, is "assigned" or "allotted" (*zugewiesen*) to its other. The sense of this assignment seems to be that of an ineluctable and necessary gathering: Heidegger says indeed that the "other inception" "*must be the only other*" in relation to the uniqueness of the first beginning. It will not, apparently, be adequate to conceive of just any kind of otherness or differing to which the first beginning might be subject: instead, a kind of exclusivity obtains in this relation of difference. Of course, we could water down the problem by claiming that all Heidegger means is that the force of gathering indicates a certain appositeness in the strife of difference, an intimacy of belonging which one might call an "assignment" of one to the other, an allotment. But this seems inadequate: does not this insistence on the specificity of allotment, on the uniqueness of *this particular* belonging, drive Heidegger to start to abandon the hard-won territory of the diffraction? Heidegger says that the other beginning "must be the only other" in relation to the first: thus, we might say that to the uniqueness of the first beginning is appended an otherness that is equally a singularity, a uniqueness. But why this retreat from the multiple? Why should the uniqueness of incipience have an otherness that is purely one, purely singular? What determines that restriction? Furthermore, and more pressing still: given the mutual reciprocity of inceptions, the ineluctable irreducibility of their intertwinement, how is one to understand the "firstness" of the first inception? In other words, how is the hierarchical relation of first and its other to be understood, from within the frame of a thinking that clearly wishes to avoid simply lapsing into the historiographic? Is such an avoidance possible?

We can see this question emerging quite clearly in the section of the *Contributions* that is entitled "Zuspiel," or "Interplay," in a passage that revolves around the possibility of the encounter or confrontation between inceptions. The passage opens:

> The confrontation with the necessity [*Notwendigkeit*] of the other inception, out of the originary positing of the first inception.
>
> The guiding disposition: pleasure in the interrogative and reciprocal surpassing of the inceptions. (*GA* 65: 169/133)

Confrontation, in the form of an interplay, is to take place as an encounter, not merely between inceptions, but with *necessity*, with the necessity of that "other inception." The question we are asking emerges immediately here: how are we to think the "necessity" of this confrontation (one whose *Stimmung* is, he tells us—oddly—to be a kind of pleasure[3]); and what governs the priority of the first inception, presuming such a priority is to be maintained? Heidegger insists on the reciprocity of first and other inceptions—a sense that the experience of beginning is intertwined with its other in such a way that the beginnings complete, but also exceed one another. In this sense, when we read of "a confrontation between the first beginning, which is still to be won back, and the other beginning, which is to be unfolded," we hear a bindedness in the space of confrontation, but also a kind of mutual inaccessibility.

We have insisted here that inception must be understood, in these texts, as the uniqueness of event always already differing from itself, made whole through the fracture of that self-difference. From such a perspective, the firstness and otherness of inception belong together as a difference that cannot be resolved into the unicity of a whole, but yet cannot be withdrawn from the fracture that binds them: "uniqueness fissures itself in inception and only thus obtains the simplicity of the inceptive" (*GA* 70: 12). From this perspective, it is in the fissuring of the inception that a oneness is achieved. But given this insistence on the constitutive fracture, how is it possible to maintain the priority of the first inception? And without that firstness, is the thought of inception possible at all?

At the opening of *Das Ereignis*, of 1941–42, as we have already noted, Heidegger reflects upon the project of the *Contributions*, finding it wanting in certain key respects. Among the issues he submits to question is that of inception. Heidegger suggests, here, that in the *Contributions*, inception remains an "accomplishment of thought" and is still not conceived from out of its "essential unity with event." It would seem, then, in this later re-visioning of inception that a kind of limit is marked, an inadequacy. There would be a kind of failing that attends the thinking of inception in the earlier text. However, it would surely be a significant error to fall too easily, on the basis of this self-questioning, into a narrative of "progress," as if *Das Ereignis* were to represent a work that in Heidegger's estimation "improves" upon the thinking of the *Contributions*. In the context of the thinking that takes place in and around the *seynsgeschichtlich* writings, it is not clear that the tangential and exploratory nature of the text(s) lends itself to a developmental interpretation, in which one text might be said to "supersede" that which preceded it. Such a narrative would imply the kind of containment—the reduction to "philosophical statement"—that the writing of these texts is designed to forestall. If so, then the relations between the texts of the *seynsgeschichtlich* period would demand to be thought through on an entirely other basis—one that belongs more fully to the interruptive and fragmentary energies of the discourse itself. From this perspective, we can wonder whether, in interrogating the sense of "assignment," and the priority of the first in this discourse, it is not that we just run up against a "weakness" a "flaw in argumentation." Rather, might it not be that what comes to expression in the text at this moment concerns the very limits of a thinking of the belonging of difference? The question will be, in other words, whether such a thinking does not necessarily open onto a kind of frailty, such that the movement of tension in self-difference must lapse from a difficult *harmonia* of difference into an easier and smoother concordance.

We can ask, then, whether the aspect of "failure" under which Heidegger addresses the *Beiträge* at the opening of *Das Ereignis* is not one that belongs intrinsically to the project of thinking that Heidegger is undertaking here. If that is so, we can say that the attempt to rethink inception in the subsequent texts must be understood not as an attempt to reach beyond that failure, but rather as a way of making explicit, or thematizing that failing. In this respect, we can consider the following, from the text that is specifically devoted to the question of inception (*Über den Anfang*):

> The word "inception" retains a multiplicity of senses and must retain this multiplicity, because it is thus that it keeps open the incipience of inception in the inceptive and never allows inception to be explained and thus come to an "end." (*GA* 70: 37)

Does this "keeping-open" of inception imply an energy of dispersion that renders impossible its unambiguous articulation? Is it only thus that inception can be addressed? The fractured unity of inception; the abyssal difference that attends event thought as inception; the thought of the belonging-together of first and other inceptions in their difference: in the face of these, perhaps words themselves halt, reaching a kind of limit, a breaking-point in which a silence, a *Sprachlosigkeit* will come to dominance.

8

Fragmentation, System, and Silence

Early on in the *Contributions*, we find a description of the relation of first and other inceptions that is cast in terms other than those we have so far encountered:

> In the first inception: wonder.
> In the other inception: foreboding. (*GA* 65: 21/18)

These, then, are the *Grundstimmungen*, the "fundamental attunements" of inception—energetic and affective complexes that make possible the thinking that takes shape in their wake. In the previous chapter, we tried to see that the "first" and "other" inceptions are not to be thought in terms of linear chronology, but rather as differential and fissured aspects of inception, thought now as event, as being itself. If we are to follow that same line of interpretation with regard to this new formulation, we must surmise that we are being called upon to think these *Grundstimmungen* otherwise than as chronological coordinates in a linear narrative—first one ("wonder") and then the other ("foreboding")—but to think instead the *Grundstimmung* of inception as the holding-together of these two, the tensional *harmonia* of contradictory impulses. Viewed in this way, we can see inception in the light of other affective contradictions whose generative impact on the *seynsgeschichtlich* treatises we have already explored. The tension of wonder, of astonishment (*Er-staunen*), and foreboding (*Er-ahnen*)—which Heidegger describes in terms of recoil, of shock, of horror—maps closely on to the gathering of terror and bliss (*Schreck und Wonne*) that courses through the later treatises of the period. There, as we saw in chapter 6, their gathering is understood as pain, provided that "gathering" is not understood as either compound or resolution: "Inceptual pain is the originary oneness of terror and bliss, not a compound of both." This pain is the pain of a between, which we identified as the unsettled space of the "there," of *Da-sein* (being-there) as a mode of the in-between. It is this pain of the "there" that Heidegger will later discover in Trakl:

So painful, that which is.

We noted earlier, too, that it is in the Trakl readings that the relation between language and pain comes to the fore: "pain has the word," Heidegger told us. To reiterate, then: what is at stake here is clearly not a writing about pain, nor a predilection for painful words, but a sense of the word itself as pain. And if pain is to be understood, too, as the tensional between-space of *Dasein*, it is evident that language, that word, must also be understood as belonging to this between.

It is, once again, in the *seynsgeschichtlich* treatises that the irruptive pain of the word is to be most clearly felt, in the interruptive and fragmentary discourse that comes explicitly into play there. In that what guides this thinking is a tensional affective complex of wonder and foreboding, it is worth observing that both of these *Grundstimmungen* are modes of silence, arenas in which language fails, falls short. What needs to be explored, then, is the way in which that particular and strange mode of writing develops which, in foregrounding the fragmentary and interruptive, foregrounds also the experience of the word as the mark of the between. The investigation will be in two parts. In the first part, we will discover that the strongest clue to the processes of writing that govern these works lies in the thinking of language that Heidegger develops in his contemporaneous reading of Herder's *Treatise on the Origin of Language* (*GA* 85). The second part will extend the inquiry into the nature of the interruptive writing of the *Contributions* by considering the question of structure. This consideration will take the form of an examination of Heidegger's construal of the notion of *system* as he encounters it in the 1936 reading of Schelling's *Philosophical Investigations into the Essence of Human Freedom.*

Mark, Rupture, and the Event of the Word

We can begin with a claim that is both central to Herder's project and true to the rhetorical drama of his writing: "Now it is in the face of this sort of deep abyss of obscure sensations, forces, and irritations that our bright and clear philosophy is horrified most of all." The enthusiasm of this claim, but also its anxieties, might serve well to describe the ambience of Herder's thinking in general, a thinking that plays always in the space between clarity and obscurity, caught in the pull of both. Nowhere is this truer than in the *Treatise on the Origin of Language,* in which the self-evidence of the sounded word is pulled toward the obscurity of its origin, just as that very origin is wrested toward a clarity that will remain always provisional. Herder's investigation can indeed be read in terms of such a double pull: its most provocative and radical gestures—the reflection on the centrality of listening, the curious notion of the mark-word—seem already to be generated in a between-space: not the between which lingers in a gray dawn on its way, as it were, to the brightness of day, but rather an in-between that is sustained by an active resistance to the inquisitive pressure of the light. In a way, one might say that Herder's insights are generated in an intertwinement of obscurity and illumination: a "listening" that occupies the center ground of a relation to language, but which cannot be clarified in terms of a subjective capacity, remaining necessarily opaque to clear delimitations of the domains of sensibility and understanding. Or, further, a conception of the word as "mark," a "marking" that is neither the externality of sound nor the index of a silent internal registration.

Heidegger's reflections on Herder revolve in and around the orbit of this tension, leaning on the difficulties of the text, forcing open its radical possibilities, and watching, too—sometimes with palpable frustration—its withdrawal, its retreats.[1] The reflections take the form of a series of notes or short fragments composed for a seminar given in the summer of 1939. They are elliptical, fragmentary, and condensed, and thereby hold much in common with the *seynsegeschichtlich* treatises. It is the fact of this sustained endeavor of writing, however strange and uncertain, that enables us to see that, just as the treatises hover between private note and public exposition, between the fragmentary and a systematic unfolding, so too do these reflections on Herder hover in a between-space, neither exactly "lecture notes" nor still expository discourse. Instead, both notes and treatises seem to want to engage a kind of writing of a different nature, one that foregrounds its lacunae, that celebrates incompleteness and embraces uncertainty. The stylistic congruity of notes and treatises clearly suggests, then, that the ruminations on language that Heidegger undertakes in his reading of Herder might be peculiarly germane to an understanding of the writing of the treatises.

Herder's text asks after the "origin" of language. The title of Heidegger's seminar asks after its "essence." A shift is marked, then, a difference. What does this shift imply? The movement from a question of origin to a question of essence aims at resisting their conflation, at any gesture that would make of essence an origin, an *essentia.* But more particularly, it allows us to register the kind of distance that Heidegger is taking from Herder's text. Herder's express aim is to refuse a conception of a "divine origin" of language, and to establish in its stead a conception of origin oriented entirely to the context of human life, its needs, its drives. The question of "origin," then, will be directed toward a description of a structure of causal determination (*kausal denkende Erklärungsfrage*) (*He* 81). It will be a question of genesis, of an establishing, an *Entstehungsfrage.* In framing his approach as a question of essence, Heidegger does not seek to withdraw from the question of origin, but on the contrary, to explore the full consequences of an engagement with language in terms of origin: to speak, in other words, not about the origin *of* language, but of language *as* origin. This will require that the two notions, essence and origin, be detached from one another—hence the shift in the title. But they must be detached in such a way as to allow them to address one another reciprocally: this mode of keeping-apart while holding-in-play *is* precisely what Heidegger means by "question." The "question" here, in this sense, will be the question of language, and it will be engaged in the form of a reflection on the central axes of Herder's investigation.

For Herder, language retains the merest trace of the cry, the indices of joy and suffering. But these "remains" are, crucially, "not the roots, but the juices that enliven [*beleben*] the roots of language." There is no mechanism, no route that the spontaneity of an affective cry might take to emerge into language. The residue of the affective will haunt the word, but can never cross the gulf that separates them. Such a possibility emerges only within Herder's very particular notion of *Besonnenheit* ("awareness"), which does not so much operate as the *differentia specifica* of the human, as lay the ground for such a differentiation from the animal to take place.

The human, then, is determined for Herder in and as lack, as deficiency (*Lücken und Mangeln*) in relation to the animal. The latter is understood in terms of its "sphere" of operation, its "circle" (*Kreis*)—one could almost say its "world"—which both responds to and determines its needs and drive-capacities (*Kunsttriebe*). It is precisely the lack of specificity of such a "circle" that opens the possibility of the human. Instead of the limit of adaptive cooperation, the human experience is one of dispersion: "his forces of soul [*Seelenkräfte*] are distributed over the world. There is no direction of his representations toward one thing" (*He* 79/94). It is this dispersive lack that Herder understands as *Besonnenheit,* which for that reason cannot be correlated with "consciousness."

It is within this field of dispersion, this zone of deficiency, that Herder will uncover the central axes that link his account of language to the question of origin. The word, for Herder, will be torn out of this dispersive field: a mark, scarring the indifferent surface of sensation. It is this breaking-off, this stoppage that marks the movement from the indistinct zone of *Besonnenheit* to the more properly human specificity of *Besinnung.* And it is this movement, too, that grounds the origin of the word. The marking, the halting occurs, says Herder, "when the power of his soul operates so freely, that in the whole ocean of sensation, flooding through his senses, it can separate off, can stop, so to speak, a single wave" (*He* 103/87). From out of what Herder calls the "hovering dream" (*schwebenden Traum*), a mark (*Merkmal*) is articulated, differentiated, split off. And with this splitting, with this incision, language will emerge.

It is difficult, at this point, not to pause and take note of the remarkable similarities between this passage and one of the decisive moments in Novalis's thinking, a moment in which thoughts

> seem to be nothing but emanations and effects which each I calls forth in that elastic medium, or the breaking apart of the I in that medium or, above all, a strange game that the waves of the ocean play. (*WI*: 220/ *NS* 95)

We saw earlier that, for Novalis, the word is the transitory inhibition, the crystallization of an indefinite drive to liquefaction. Herder, we can say, will invoke the same transience, the same sense of the interruptive, but will engage it from an entirely different direction. The word, once again, for Herder, will be ripped from out of the dispersive field in which the disorientation of the human unfolds. But it is precisely this event of breaking that will mark the difference between Novalis's thinking and those aspects of Herder's work toward which Heidegger is oriented: where Novalis will think of the word as crystallization and temporary inhibition, Herder will think the "mark" of the word as break, as irruptive incision.

What is initially most striking about Herder's notion of the "mark," the marking with which language is initiated, is that it is fundamentally aural, acoustical: a silence rent by sound provides the paradigmatic image of the "mark-word." To express the origin of the word in its sounding suggests immediately a centralization of listening; and indeed, listening becomes, for Herder, not merely a perceptual starting-point, but rather the nexus around which the entire possibility of human experience will gather and coalesce. *Besinnung*, in this sense, *is* precisely a listening. It is precisely at this juncture, though, at the point of the emergence of the mark-word and its concomitant listening, that Herder must develop his text in ways that will draw Heidegger's attention powerfully. In making the "mark" not merely the sign of an external phenomenon but the index of a coming-to-awareness, Herder's "mark" must necessarily push beyond the limits of the sounded: it must be more than the rending of silence. Neither the pure irruption of sound, nor yet mimetic inscription, the notion of the "mark" will hover in a space sufficiently indeterminate to release the question of the origin of language in such a way that it can begin to play, too, within the field of its essence. Such a development of the notion of the mark will imply an equally intensive elaboration of the question of listening. If the mark is not purely or exclusively sounded, then how are we to develop and extend an understanding of listening that embraces the mark beyond its acoustical instantiation? Furthermore, if the mark hovers in a zone of indeterminacy between external manifestation and internal correlate, inseparable from both and yet belonging to neither, it would no longer be possible to maintain the opposition between mark as sounded event and listening as its perceptual registration. Instead, mark and listening will appear in Herder's text to coalesce, almost to merge, as if—and this will be the direction in which Heidegger will want to push Herder—the two belong equally, co-originarily to the event of language. Indeed, one might say that the movements of Heidegger's reflections on Herder are oriented toward this intersection of origin and listening—toward the place where listening becomes an origin, and origin a listening.

"We creatures that hear, stand in the middle," says Herder (*He* 104/109). It is the manifold complexity of this "middle" that will enable Heidegger to appropriate Herder's project to a new sense of "origin." In an effort to elaborate the notion of "mark" as the primary event of language, but beyond the constraints of an acoustical model, Herder develops a conception of the human as *sensorium commune.* The sensorium is the arena, the space in or toward which the multiplicity of sense gathers. What will be decisive for Herder is precisely this gathering: it will be his insistence on the "middle"—the point of coalescence, the drawing-in of the multiplicity—that allows him to elaborate a concept of hearing that, for Heidegger, opens his text onto an experience of language that breaks free of the representational.

Heidegger describes the domain of the sensible in Herder's treatise as the domain of "the interwoven, dark, blurring, manifold, capturing, pressing afflicting [*drängende Bedrängnis*]." And indeed, for Herder, for whom "originally [*ursprünglich*] the senses are only feeling [*Gefühl*]," the centrality of hearing—its status as the "middle" sense—has nothing to do with any newly discovered clarity or transparency that would usurp the traditional dominance of the visual. On the contrary, for Herder, hearing gathers the sensorium by virtue of its indistinction, hovering between dazzlement and obscurity, immediacy and indifference. Hearing gathers from out of an inadequacy, a lack that at one and the same time determines, in relation to the other senses, both its specificity and its dependence. Heidegger, however, understands that the middle ground in which Herder's sense of hearing hovers is precisely what will tend to draw his sensorium away from a model that might be fully assimilated within a traditional framework of perception. What, for Heidegger, will mark out the limits (*Grenzen*) of Herder's account is his express intention "to explain in which way that which is *non-sonorous* comes to language. How that which is non-sonorous can gather itself in a middle region, how this middle is of such a kind as to mediate everything that is felt into a sounding" (*GA* 85: 117/101). If, then, hearing is to be of the *non-sonorous* as much as of the *sonorous*, one must wonder again about the middle ground, the zone of indistinction that is to determine hearing as such. Heidegger observes that, given Herder's insistence that the sensible is interwoven with an obscurity that sets its origin within the domain of "feeling," such a "middle"—a zone of indistinction, a lack—might be seen to be determinative of all forms of sensible experience, not merely hearing. Furthermore, if "hearing," for Herder, is to gather both the sounded and the non-sounded, then it is clearly being thought beyond the limits that would determine it as a "perceptual function." Here is what Heidegger says:

> With this consideration of limit, it is overlooked that if the senses are taken in their full essence (vibrating in awareness [*schwingend in der Besonnenheit*]), the corresponding possibilities (e.g. the dulling and spreading out) still subsist overall. The fact that here the sense of hearing as perceiving with the ear has in no way priority, but only insofar as it is grasped as perceiving *in the sense of being attentive [Aufmerken], of listening, of being-silent.* (*GA* 85: 123/105, emphasis added)

Aufmerken, here, is engaged in a very particular sense, one that will enable Heidegger to draw Herder's thinking toward an acknowledgment of the belonging-together, the *Zugehörigkeit*, of the "mark" (*Merkmal*) and the listening that attends to it. What Heidegger does is take up the "middle" (*Mitte*) with which Herder reaches for an understanding of the sensible as gathered into and around hearing, and recast it not as the "middle," but rather as the *in-between* (*das Inzwischen*): "What Herder intimates with the 'middle' character of 'hearing' is the in-between and in-the-midst-of the *clearing*" (*GA* 85: 96). *Aufmerksamkeit* will indicate a double movement, one that gathers, draws in, but also simultaneously "spreads out" and "displaces" (*Entrückt*). The "middle" toward which sensibility is gathered is not, then, the originary *punctum* of consciousness that Herder's account might be taken to imply. Rather, as Heidegger says, that which hearing gathers toward is "insistence" in the "there." What is heard, what marks and is marked, what is attended to, *is* this insistence; an elliptical moment in Heidegger's text reads just "attunement [*Gestimmtheit*] as insistence in the in-between" (*GA* 85: 93/80), and elsewhere, "hear-ing of an insistence" (*Er-hörung einer Inständigkeit*) (*GA* 85: 71/61).

If hearing, if listening (and Heidegger's text might allow us to slip between the two) no longer recoils upon the intensities of the subject, but rather indicates a gathering from and toward a "there," such a "there" cannot constitute a ground of experience. Rather, the "there"—fragile, tenuous—comes to pass in and as *mark*. How, though, is such a mark to be understood, if not as the registration of a givenness, as the index of an exchange between sensibility and understanding? Heidegger returns insistently to Herder's first insight: the mark, writes Herder, is "the tone that *breaks free*." But we have already seen how Herder pushes the "mark," and its hearing, beyond the limit of the sounded; and for Heidegger, too, "sound can never for itself and firstly become that which sets the measure; if this happens, then everything would lapse into error." If the mark, in other words, were to be understood exclusively from out of the sounded, this would entail falling back upon a classical symmetry of opposition, in which the sounded word takes place as the registration, or expression, of the silent plenitude of the given. It is not thus that silence is to be understood. The notion of "mark" will avoid restaging this metaphysical opposition of sound and silence by virtue of its functioning *between*, as a crossing, moving seamlessly along the borders that would seek to demarcate these poles. If listening, for Heidegger, gathers in and around what he calls a "clearing," it will do so as "mark," but a mark that *carries silence in and as its breaking*. The "there," for Heidegger, is thus—properly thought—not silent, but is precisely the index of this movement, the crossing that the mark effects.

At this point a question intrudes, disarming in its simplicity. It is this: can one *listen* to a *clearing*? The question is far more than a matter of mixed metaphors. It is, in fact, a fundamental question, as it is precisely here, within this question, that the intertwinement of sounded and non-sounded, silent and resounding is to be experienced. Listening, which gathers itself as an insistence, is, as Heidegger puts it, "the dominance of ex-pectation" (*Die Herrschaft der Er-wartung*) (*GA* 85:61/51), the place which both marks and is marked by silence and its sounding. If we are speaking here of the essence, or of the origin of language, it is because it is the word which carries most completely this intertwinement. The word is the marking of silence, not just as sounded utterance, registering silence in its interruption, but also equally as inscription, as writing: "Decisive: the essence of sound and of the sounding as *Sage*. Script, the written, the legible" (*GA* 85:133/114). And it is this, too, that leads Heidegger to note, without elaboration, without explanation, almost in passing: "The silence of beyng itself, *is* the word" (*GA* 85: 76/66).

But what, then, is one to say of a philosophical discourse that would attempt to engage this intertwinement? Heidegger writes: "'Listening'—

diffusion that takes hold (νοῦς), displaced gathering (λόγος)" (*GA* 85: 137/119). A philosophical *logos* will be one that takes up this listening in the form of the inscriptive silence of the word, a *ratio* that no longer displaces the sensible, but rather thinks itself as the intertwinement of silence and sound, the marking that traverses their in-between: "the sensible not lesser, essentially, than 'reason'; indeed *both here the same*" (*GA* 85: 131/113, *emphasis added*). The *seynsgeschichtlich* treatises will work through this sameness, crossing always toward an origin in which such a sameness might be grasped. If the works of this period speak in a language which is fragmentary, elliptical, opening onto interruption, onto silence, such a language in no way represents the abandonment of philosophical discourse. Rather, it is its fulfillment: a language that pursues the paradoxical project of remaining, of insisting in a "crossing" which can itself not be understood or grasped other than as "*the transitory*, the incidental—what, barely thought, shall be abandoned" (*GA* 85: 61/51).

In-Conclusion

Word is the mark that, bearing in it its silence, brings forth something like a "there." So, if we can understand the occurring of a "there" as event, then we can, at least speculatively, come close to seeing the intimacy of being, conceived as emergent event and as inception, with the irruptive emergence of language. Once again, it is not a matter of a fullness of the given that language will step in to describe: for Heidegger, this would be the lure of representational thinking, and "every representational order is superficial here." Instead, the "there" will *be* the event of language. This is why Heidegger will say—later, once again in his work on Trakl—that "the event gathers the *Aufriß* of saying and unfolds it as the joining [*Gefüge*] of a manifold showing" (*GA* 12: 247/128). So, the event of/as language embraces the rupturing mark, the tear of the word (*Aufriß*), but at the same time gathers it together, conjoining and connecting.

It is this conjoining and gathering that we must explore now, if we are to engage fully the philosophical work that the *seynsgeschichtlich* treatises, and the *Contributions* in particular, undertake. In the passage just cited, Heidegger writes of a movement (a "gathering" and an "unfolding") in which the irruptive mark of the word will coalesce into what he refers to as "joinings." However we are to understand this sense of "joining" in the *Contributions*, it will clearly be in a way entirely different from the simple question of "continuity." The joining of the text must be of a sort that embraces the interruptive and the fragmentary, that gathers it toward a whole, but without eliding the cut or smoothing across the fragmentary incision. The whole will be a gathering of such a nature as to include its own breaking, a totality that becomes complete in refusing its completion.

In considering the question of the whole, we are, as Heidegger says, engaging a project that is "precarious inasmuch as it will be very tempting to slip from there into a systematics of an earlier style." Something new, then, will be enjoined in this joining; something to which the event of the word belongs in a decisive and wholly integrative sense. But the gathering of this order will play on the edge of a "systematics of the old style," will run, always, the risk of lapsing into a mode of static construction. It will operate an insistent deferral of that risk, and in so doing will find itself reentering a domain that we saw occupied by Novalis as he struggled with his "Encyclopaedia" project. It is thus indeed that, in order to approach the question of "joinings," we find ourselves—strangely enough—back in the vicinity of the "system," which we find exerting a pull not entirely distinct from that experienced by the Jena Romantics. It will be, then, within the question of system as it emerges in these texts of the *seynsgeschichtlich* period that the kind of reenvisioning of gathering-together and "ordering" that Heidegger envisions can come into view.

That the thought of system was, after all, not far from Heidegger's mind at the time he was commencing work on the *Contributions* can be established by the following striking claim, from Heidegger's 1936 lecture series on Schelling's "Freedom" essay:

> System, in the true sense, is one of, indeed *the* task of philosophy. (*GA* 42: 46/24)

The context of this surprising declaration is, of course, a discussion of Schelling, which goes some way toward explaining a particular investment in the notion of system. However, the date of these lectures again gives us pause, especially when we engage the *Contributions*, whose opening pages declare categorically: "the time of systems is over." Indeed, scattered through this latter work, and through the other treatises of the *seynsgeschichtlich* series, are clear indications that a thinking of event was to discard, firmly, the notion of system, as being a necessity that is no longer ours. An experience of inceptive thinking would be, Heidegger claims here, "in its essence without system, unsystematic." However this thinking was to unfold, then, it would be with a rigor entirely other than that of the system, whose historical moment belongs to what Heidegger calls "mathematical thought."

From such a vantage point, Heidegger's preoccupation with system in his Schelling lectures might seem determined, simply, by interpretative concerns—by the fact that it is Schelling's *own* work that responds to the historical exigency of the system. But this reduction would run roughshod over Heidegger's explicit insistence that the past claims us in an active and dynamic sense. So too, when Heidegger calls for a "decision" as to whether history is to be "degraded into an arsenal of confirmations and precursors, or rise up as a chain of strange and un-climbable mountains" (*GA* 65: 188/147), he is insisting that we must allow the historical necessity of the system to claim us as it claimed Schelling. A necessity, a historical exigency, is our own to the extent that we are capable of its access; and to think through such an exigency is precisely to place ourselves in its midst—to undergo it, as it were, creatively. Thus, when Heidegger writes that "a legitimate renunciation of system can only originate from an essential insight into it" (*GA* 42: 46/24), what he is requiring of us is an experience that fully acknowledges the necessity of system before it can move beyond it.

What will be asked here, then, is: what might happen if we were to consider the *Contributions* as an explicit address to (and this also means a questioning of) the exigency of the system? What will be suggested, in response, is that while the language of the *Contributions*—fragmentary, dispersive, repetitive—appears very distant from any kind of systematic presentation, even of the sort that still governs the course of *Being and Time*, this distance would not represent the manifestation of an effort to abandon the system or to relinquish the systematic. Rather, it would be an attempt to understand and engage the system from within. Indeed, that very distance, and the writing to which it gives birth, can be seen to belong intrinsically to that engagement. Heidegger will claim, in the lecture course *Basic Questions* from 1937, that in inceptual thinking, "a deeper necessity will rule thinking and questioning . . . because their inner order and rigor will be concealed to the seemingly unsurpassable (because transparent) completeness of system." The claim here is that this new order, this "rigor," can be seen to play, always, in and around that same completeness.

The question, then, will be one of gathering, of binding-together, of seams and articulations, joins and jointures: these are the fault lines within which the "unsystematic rigor" of this writing unfolds. And it will once again be a question of language. Not merely in terms of a homology in the vocabulary—*Fuge, Fügung, Gefüge*—that courses through his descriptions of the systematicity of Schelling's project as much as it does through the *Contributions*, but because the very articulations, the jointures of Heidegger's text, will render themselves visible in a particular way in and as language—as a kind of writing. The rigor, then, will be that of the fragment; the order, that of the interruption.

Posing, in the Schelling lectures, the question: "what, in general, is a system?" Heidegger answers by making his familiar gesture of recursion to Greek etymology. What the Greek *sunistemi* teaches Heidegger is contained in its simplest translation: "I place together" (*stelle zusammen*) (*GA* 42: 46/24). But this "togetherness" conceals a question: how is the collecting, the gathering of this "together," to be understood? And what is the sense here of the "placing" of this togetherness? The sense of "placing together" has two senses, Heidegger shows: on the one hand, it can mean an arbitrary conjoining of indiscriminate elements, in which *systema* means "mere accumulation and patchwork." On the other hand, it can mean placing together "in such a way that the order is thereby first projected"; in a way, in other words, that presents in an originary manner an articulation of different elements. And such a projecting, Heidegger writes, "throws beings apart [*wirft das Seiende auseinander*] in such a way that they precisely now become visible in the unity of their inmost jointure" (*GA* 42: 47/25). Such a *systema* would be one which, engaging togetherness, makes explicit the very articulations, the seams of this gathering. Divergent possibilities are engaged, then, by the system at its point of etymological origin. What is significant here, though—and radically so—is that this diremption of possibilities belongs to system *at its very core*; any "gathering together," then, will both produce, and be sustained by this split; "joining" will be both arbitrary *and* essential, indiscriminate *and* originary, extrinsic *and* intrinsic.

System is beset with, and determined at its root by this tension, and is described precisely in this manner by Heidegger: "*Between* these extreme opposites of meaning—inner jointure and mere manipulation—stands that which gives system its name." And he goes on: "This shows that this inner possibility of wavering [*Schwanken*] between jointure and manipulation and framework always belongs to system, that every genuine system always remains threatened by ruin [*Verfall*]" (*GA* 42: 46/24). System, then, is neither extrinsic nor intrinsic, but occurs in the unstable oscillation of the in-between, hovering in the zone of the neutral, neither one nor the other, as Blanchot might express it. What is clear, too, is that this conception of system is one penetrated by its own failing; that, far from an ever more complete unfolding of an inner necessity, the system is driven and determined by lines of fracture, by points of failure.

It is this movement of instability that is most keenly at play in the *Contributions*, a movement of oscillation and indeterminacy. Heidegger himself repeatedly describes the work as "transitional," by which he means not a "work in progress"—unachieved, incomplete—but rather a "work in motion"—mobile, fluid. Thus, when he writes: "these 'contributions' are *not yet* able to join the free conjuncture [*freie Fuge*] of the truth of Beyng out of Beyng itself," this "not yet" must be understood as a constitutive instability, one which belongs to the paradoxical logic of the "transitional structure." We have already explored the extent to which this sense of transition—of crossing, or *Übergang*—can be understood as the in-between in which the "there" of Da-sein is discovered in the midst of inceptions. The figure, then, is one of crisis, of indeterminacy, and of possibility: "the openness of the *Übergang* . . . is the abyssal in-between amid the 'no longer' of the first inception and its history, and the 'not yet' of the fulfillment of the other inception." A thinking of transition, then, is one that finds itself pitched into a radical uncertainty, hovering between recollective energies, on the one hand, and the paradoxical projection of the possibilities of an "other inception" on the other.

The question will now be: how do we understand a transition of this kind, a transition that does not merely constitute the passage from one stable point to another? What kind of "structure," or order, must pertain to this transition? It is in this light that we can see the composition of the *Contributions* itself, with its structural division into six "joinings" (*Fügungen*), to which Heidegger gives names often expressive of a gesture or movement: "Echo," or resonance ("Anklang"), "Interplay" ("Zuspiel"), "Leap" ("Sprung"). Heidegger says of these that "every joining stands in itself, and yet there exists a hidden oscillation between them [*Ineinanderschwingen*]." These gestures are the modes of articulation of instability, moving in and around one another, completing and undoing, maintaining the spectral presence of an expository unfolding while refusing the consistency of a developmental logic: "The most difficult is to effect, purely *conjuncturally*, an abiding with the same," he warns. In this play of simultaneity and difference, then, each gesture of thinking is complete, whole in itself, and yet entirely dependent on the others. They unfold, on the one hand, necessarily in sequence, each adding to the force, the urgency (*Eindringlichkeit*) of the others, while at the same time, each says always "the same of the same." The risk is immediate, and powerful, to see these "joinings" as either pushing toward or growing out of a larger conceptual unity; but a project of overarching unity would render their sameness mere repetition, their difference mere "conceptual elaboration." What is at stake, rather, is a structure that *refuses to surrender its motility*, a "systematic unfolding" that is precisely determined in and as a fluid *in*determinacy.

The interplay of these six "joinings" does not arise from the singularity of a conceptual directive, but in relation to what Heidegger calls a *Grundstimmung*, or "fundamental attunement" of thinking. This attunement, as we have already seen, does not merely "underpin" the structure of the "joinings" as an affectivity that precedes and makes possible a conceptual elaboration. Rather, it sets in motion the entire tension between the demands of the progressive unfolding of structural cohesion and the unstable play of the "joinings," the gestures of thought. It is in this sense that Heidegger describes the *Grundstimmung* as diffusive—a "diffusion of the trembling of the event," but a diffusion which, nonetheless, rather than dissipating, "preserves the spark" (*GA* 65: 21/19)—which *holds in place,* as it were, what is intrinsically and radically evanescent.

The *Grundstimmung,* says Heidegger, "attunes thinking as a projection . . . in word and concept." The fundamental attunement, then, in a certain way precedes and enables the movement of thought in language. But it is itself in a tense relation with that "coming to word": there is, says Heidegger, no word for the *Grundstimmung* itself. It hovers in a play of verbal determinations within the movement, the oscillation of other attunements that can themselves be "only distantly named" (*GA* 65: 14/14). We have already seen how the originary multiplicity of inception is guided and grounded in a structure of contradictory attunements: "wonder" and "foreboding." As we saw, these can in no way be seen as some static "mixture" of different elements. Fundamental attunements arise instead *within* their oscillation and interweaving. This resistance to the cohering of name, then, is something other than an accidental inaccessibility, an elusiveness of expression. Rather, it occurs and takes shape *in and as* a failing of the word, as a silence that is not an originary plenitude, but a lack generated in a movement that cannot be stabilized. This relation of these "distantly named" attunements, then—this movement of unstable play that *is* the namelessness of the *Grundstimmung*—is accessible only to a thinking that belongs in a primary way to silence, to the breaking, the failure of the word.

"All essential thinking," writes Heidegger, "demands that its thoughts and sentences be extracted each time anew, like ore, from out of the fundamental attunement" (*GA* 65: 21/19). The word, the utterance, the determinations of thought are to be "mined"—forced out, and this at each and every moment—from the element of silence. And the language that will mark out this deficit, that will articulate lack as structural necessity, is a language of the fragment, of fragmentation. This is why *Verhaltenheit*—holding back, restraint—becomes the "style" of inceptual thinking: its hesitations, its erasures, its collapse, ensure the circulation of a silence that "holds the measure" (*Maß-halten*), that measures out the limits of a structural unfolding. Remaining entirely within the rhetorical exigency of the fragment, Heidegger writes: "restraint as the origin of stillness and the law of gathering." *Verhaltenheit* is such an origin and such a law because only a "holding-back" can engage the tensions that drive an expository unfolding; only a "holding-to-silence," an *Erschweigung*, as Heidegger calls it, can play out fully the demands of the systematic.

Once again, we return to the claim: "The word fails . . . not as an occasional occurrence . . . but *originarily*." The *Contributions* respond to this sense of a "failing language" by initiating a kind of writing that opens in particular ways onto silence, onto the spaces and interruptions in which this originary failing can appear: a fragmentary writing. If, then, as Heidegger claims, "system, in the true sense, is . . . *the* task of philosophy," it is precisely within the writing of the *Contributions* itself that this sense is most fully realized. Neither a "new logic" nor an "anti-logic," the domain of this writing, which Heidegger himself, with a kind of terminological irony, names the "sigetic," is a domain that circulates in and around silence, around interruption. Not a silence that can be appropriated to the demands of a dialectic, but one whose peculiar rigor allows the full reach of the systematic, while attending—always—to its limits.

Epilogue

> For it was late now; and everything was dark.
> —Robert Walser

It is in relation to Heidegger's recasting of the thought of system in the *Contributions* that we return to the following, which emerges, once again, as a crucial axis of thought:

> The Greek word for joining [*Fügung*] sounds as *harmonia*. In this word we think right away of the joining of tones, and grasp "harmony" as concord [*Ein-klang*]. Only, what is essential in *harmonia* is not the domain of ringing or of tones, but rather *harmos*, that whereby one fits to another, the join in which both are joined, so that the joining *is*. (*GA* 55: 141)

The *Fügungen* that bind together and articulate Heidegger's "contributions" are, then, to be conceived, and explicitly so, in relation to the thought of Heraclitean *harmonia* which has sustained this study from the outset. And just as these thought-gestures undergirding the composition of the *Contributions* echo and reinforce this presence, so, too, does the thought of being as multiple inception; so, equally, do the thinking of the human as the crisis of a "there," and the complex agonistics of affective attunements evolve from the same tensed logic of splitting-apart and gathering-together that lies at the heart of this thought of *harmonia*. In each case, says Heidegger, it is the join itself, the bringing-together, which is to be thought: not the concordance that appropriates and resolves the tension of difference, but the very rift of the join, its point of fracture.

This, then, is the "between" whose lineaments we have attempted to descry, uncovering its operation as it drives forward the thinking of Novalis as of Heidegger. It is the figure of an abyssal join, the non-space of a meeting articulated only in a static tension of gathering. To think this meeting, this join, in itself—outside and beyond the forces that gather and separate around it—is to think *nothing*, and thus to think in the mode of the *alogon* that so alarmed Eryximachus in respect of Heraclitus. The nothingness of the between—the seam itself, the join of *harmonia*—is, and can only be radical, absolute: the abyssal point of gathering and separation that can in no wise slip into the language of place, of space, nor into the language of the negative.

It is indeed this, and only this, that can obviate the risk that a study such as this must necessarily run. This risk is as follows: a tensional *harmonia* of gathering and holding-apart, whose entry into what will become Western thought we ascribed to Heraclitus, has been seen to emerge in many ways, in multiple different configurations and at different historical junctures. The danger that lurks, and that lurks precisely in this multiplicity, is that this *harmonia*, and with it the between of which we have tried to speak, might in turn reveal itself to be just another metaphysical structure, a form that underpins or overlays the multiple modes of its encounter: a schema, in other words, whose outline would be apparent in its manifestations, all of which would thereby be reduced to the status of "instantiations."

But it is here that the importance of the radical nothingness of the between becomes clear: the between, to repeat, is the join—the seam, which is nothing other than the join itself. It is this "nothing other" that allows a *harmonia* of difference to become apparent in multiple contexts without coalescing into a uniform conceptual structure, or frame. *Harmonia* can be nothing but the multiple occasions of its appearance, because the between—the seam of relation—is *nothing but* the seam itself, in all its tension. If Fichte conceives the abyssal nothing of the between as *Anstoß*—the seam of I and not-I—whereas Heidegger discovers it in the temporality of the "there," there is no sense in which these can be understood as "the same"—exemplars of a singular conceptual structure. If the "between" is nothing, then all is in the conjoining, the bringing-together, the harmonic join itself. What brings Heidegger and Novalis into the same orbit is an understanding of the fundamentally generative and productive force of this tensional conjoining—of the bow, of the lyre. In invoking the working of this *harmonia*, they invoke, too, its history, and thus its recurrent strangeness, of which the strangeness of the between, of the join, is the most apparent aspect.

Nothing is unsayable: and to imagine that one can circumvent the paradox of this locution by writing of "the" nothing would not allay its strange force. This, of course, is precisely the scene of Heidegger's investigation of *Der Satz vom Grund*, which is equally that of his most significant direct engagement with Novalis. The proposition "*Nichts ist ohne Grund*" must be given time, says Heidegger, must be allowed to resonate in a strange and ambiguous space in which the "*Nichts*" can come to the fore: not as bearing a newly acquired positivity, but precisely in its polyvalence, its *Vieldeutigkeit.* The unsayability of the nothing, then (imposing upon it, temporarily, the definite article by means of which it becomes sayable), is the silence that makes possible, for Heidegger, word: "the silence of beyng, itself, *is* the word," we recall from the notes on Herder. And whether word is thought as irruptive mark, or as pain, it is—for Heidegger—in the abyssal join of the between that the possibility of speaking begins. But for Novalis, too, word emerges in this way, as the fragile and transient crystallization of a play of forces, a *harmonia* whose work is generated in and as this same abyssal nothing of the between. And yet it seems as if the mode in which Heidegger and Novalis are able to address themselves to this figure is quite different. For Heidegger, the between of *harmonia* is primary dissonance, a tension in which word erupts from the pain of the gathering and sustaining of difference. For Novalis, this same tension appears as a fertile energetics, a fecundity in which the word emerges as the creative space of engagement and belonging.

This difference, to be sure, is one of historical possibility, of the historical moments in which these thinkings of the between are able to come to the fore. But for us, perhaps, the resonance of their work is best felt together, conjointly. This is because, in the end, if Heidegger and Novalis both understand the abyssal nothing of the between of *harmonia* as a generative possibility, it is always in view of the human, in view of human life, that such a possibility presents itself. To the extent that, for the human, being present—being-there—means always and also being-with, these human possibilities must engage concrete modes of relation, and issue in concrete configurations. And whether it is within the thought of community, in which respect the complexities of our belonging-together—our difficult *harmonia*—become daily more evident, or in the matter of our connection with what remains of a natural world, the question of the between—of relation, of relationality—presses upon us in new, unprecendented, and urgent ways.

The proposal of this study, then, is that if we are to go on, if we are to continue, if we are to rescue our distraught communities and restore our devastated landscapes, it may well be by embracing a different kind of harmony: not a harmony that seeks to absorb difference, but one for which the tensional dynamism of difference is originary, constitutive, irreducible. Such a harmony of original difference involves an absence, an acceptance of loss. But it is in that acceptance that we can recover the fertility of the differential spaces in which we dwell and that we are. It is not merely in mourning our loss, but in retrieving the productive energy of our primal dissonance that something like a future might still unfold.

* * *

If, one day, wandering through the Museum of Fine Arts in Boston, you were to find yourself in the room devoted to ancient coins, you might, as you wander, discover a drawer filled with coins that hail from the most distant provinces of the Roman Empire, minted in its desperate, waning years. Among these, you could chance upon a small coin from the deeply corrupt reign of Elagabalus, a coin which, depicting the emperor and his *mater castrorum* on the obverse, displays on its reverse the goddess Concordia. The coin was found at the empire's outermost edge, in an area destined to be lost within a century of the coin's minting. The goddess of harmony, then, as the Romans saw it, seemed to have taken up residence even in the furthest and most dubious reaches of the empire, as if insisting on the absorption of every inch of its vast hegemonic enterprise. The goddess rules all: harmony is concordance, agreement, synthesis. And insistently so: not infrequently, one finds the inscription *Concordia militus* printed on the obverse of coins. Resolving—forcibly—all dissonance, *Concordia militus*, militant concord, insists upon harmony, absorbing all difference and uniting even the conflict-ridden extremes of the empire under one law, one smiling and beneficent center of governance.

The disarming ease with which Erixymachus "corrects" Heraclitus, informing us of what the Ephesian sage "must have meant" by a harmony which "in variance from itself . . . agrees with itself," should give us pause. Is it the case that the only way togetherness can be understood is as a harmony of concordance? Is an ecstatic D major resonance truly an image in which we can still see ourselves reflected? Of course we could, like Beethoven, see concordance as an achievement, a hard-won triumph (the word is telling) over the forces of dissonance. And if we do this, we are in agreement with Erixymachus, for whom "what is first at variance later came to agree." The possibility of a linear history emerges here, of course, one whose outline Beethoven's Enlightenment ear was not slow to discern. But for us? Surely the spectacle of our own "G-10 leaders" being driven through the restless, angry streets of Hamburg in armored vehicles to attend a special performance of the "Ode to Joy" cannot but fill us with a sense of gloomy and despairing irony. For us, the music will have ended before it has even begun, the dissonance of the streets surging forth to drown out the euphony. Like Elagabalus, we can today barely imagine a harmony that does not operate under the sign of *Concordia militus*, a militant concord.

If our energies at this moment are consumed with the excluded, with what has been left out, left behind, with what seeps out of the edges of our concordant histories, then it may not be without importance that we attempt to allow a different experience of harmony to reemerge. If Erixymachus's assurances can even begin to strike us as platitudinous, we might be in a position to catch sight of what it is that his blandishments conceal: the operation of a harmony of difference, an experience of dissonance as a primary and productive energetics—the *harmonia* of Heraclitus, a harmony whose tensions are originary, irreducible, and unresolvable. It is to this restless wellspring of energy that the foregoing pages are committed. In them, the thinking work of two individuals, remote in time and historical context, is seen to revolve, in a certain aspect, around an energetics of separative gathering, in which what is fissured and entropically dispersive is *at the same time* subject to a force of gathering. Whether it is in a writing that, like Novalis's, pursues to the point of speculative collapse the oppositional structures by which a thinking of the primacy of consciousness is held in thrall; or whether, like Heidegger, it is in the agonistic disconcertment of being that such a figure may be intimated, it is the dynamic double-pull of this figure that is, always, the fertile source of productive energies.

Thought thus, *harmonia* would reside in the meeting-point of these conflictual energies: it is this *harmonia* which requires us to think of a "between" that is not a mediation, that is not an absolute, that is not even nothing. For Novalis, it is in this "between" that the word crystallizes that sustains the tensions of our engagement with the natural world; for Heidegger, it is in and as this "between" that an affectivity becomes possible and courses through our tension of belonging. In both cases, the *harmonia* of separative-gathering challenges the linearity of thought and language, leading them into difficult avenues of expression. And indeed, as Erixymachus intimated, it may well be that Heraclitus's *harmonia* requires and necessitates for its emergence an engagement with the *alogon,* that the possibilities it affords can be glimpsed only anamorphically. In operating, insistently, at a remove from expository or discursive modes of reason, the thinking of Novalis and of Heidegger opens a seam long-buried, one that runs deep through our history. It could be that, if we listen, we will hear it too.

Notes

Introduction

1. At this point, let me take note of a recent book by Pol Vandevelde, *Heidegger and the Romantics* (New York: Routledge, 2012), which, to my knowledge, is the first book in English to focus specifically upon this connection. Vandevelde attends principally to the aspects of Heidegger's work that take up hermeneutic principles initiated in Jena, in particular by Schlegel and Schleiermacher. More germane to this inquiry, though, is the work of Giampiero Moretti, *La Segnatura romantica: Philosophia e sentimento da Novalis a Heidegger* (Cernusco: Hestia, 1992). My book owes a good deal to Moretti's discussion of the question of analogy, particularly in terms of the relation between Herder and Novalis, and to his account of the relation of Novalis's work to that of the early Schelling.

2. It is important to note here that Heidegger did not have access to the monumental critical edition of Novalis's works, *Historische-Kritische Ausgabe – Novalis Schriften*, which did not begin publication until 1960. Heidegger quotes from an earlier and much less complete edition from 1923, by J. Minor. Although this edition is only partial, and not correctly organized, the quotations that Heidegger uses are nonetheless in accord with the *Historische-Kritische Ausgabe*. However, it is certainly interesting to speculate that the possibility for a fuller reading of Novalis might have engaged Heidegger's attention had a more complete text been available to him.

3. It is Andrew Mitchell, the translator of the volume, who points out in a footnote the origin of the unattributed quotation "*Schlüssel aller Kreaturen*." The context is interesting here: Heidegger acknowledges that "since long ago and once again, measure number and figures have become the 'key to all creatures.'" The full irony of the passage emerges in relation to the poem from which this quotation is taken, since this description of the "key" operates under a negative sign. The poem is to be found in Novalis, *W*I: 406.

4. Eva Brann, *The Logos of Heraclitus* (Philadelphia: Paul Dry Books, 2011), 15–28.

5. See the discussion of this issue in Charles H. Kahn, *The Art and Thought of Heraclitus* (Cambridge: Cambridge University Press, 1979), 195–97. However, Kirk, Raven, and Schofield do provide strong arguments for an alternate reading of the fragment, one that brings it somewhat closer to Erixymachus's version. See Kirk, Raven, and Schofield, *The Presocratic Philosophers* (Cambridge: Cambridge University Press, 1983), 192.

6. Brann, *Logos*, 90.

7. In an important essay, Nicole Loraux develops an understanding of what she argues is the hidden centrality of Heraclitean *harmonia* precisely in terms of the multiple meanings of the Greek *stasis*. It is more than a historical accident, she claims, that this word comes to indicate both a kind of motionlessness and a kind of violent conflict: rather, Loraux claims that it is in this tension of meanings that is installed the secret Heraclitean heart of Athenian conceptions of the political. See N. Loraux, "The Bond of Division," in *The Divided City: On Memory and Forgetting in Ancient Athens* (New York: Zone Books, 2002), 93–123.

Chapter 1

1. For a thorough and engaging account of the details, both psychological and historical, surrounding Hardenberg's adoption of his nom de plume, see Donehower, *The Birth of Novalis* (Albany: State University of New York Press, 2007). See also the commentary by Hans-Jürgen Balmes in Novalis, *W*III: 249.

2. Goethe, trans. Miller, *The Metamorphosis of Plants* (Cambridge, MA: MIT Press, 2009), 10. Dalia Nassar sees the importance of Goethe's text for an understanding of Novalis's metamorphic process, and considers it at length in *The Romantic Absolute* (Chicago: University of Chicago Press, 2014), 59–61. Nassar is following the lead of Frederick Beiser, who has repeatedly insisted on the importance of *Naturphilosophie* for a proper understanding of Novalis's work. See, for instance, F. Beiser, *German Idealism: The Struggle against Subjectivism, 1781–1801* (Cambridge, MA: Harvard University Press, 2002), 428–31; and his "Romanticism and Idealism," in *The Relevance of Romanticism: Essays on German Romantic Philosophy*, ed. D. Nassar (Oxford: Oxford University Press, 2014), 30–43, esp. 41–42.

3. According to the *Oxford English Dictionary*, "anastomosis" is the "intercommunication between two vessels, channels, or distinct branches of any kind, by a connecting cross branch."

4. Goethe, *Metamorphosis*, 102.

5. See J. Neubauer, *Bifocal Vision: Novalis' Philosophy of Nature and Disease* (Chapel Hill: University of North Carolina Press, 1971), for a thorough account of the development of these interests and their relation with contemporary experimentation. See also David Farrell Krell, *Contagion* (Bloomington: Indiana University Press, 1998), for an exhilarating account of Novalis's investments in the question of disease, and the stakes of that engagement.

6. Elsewhere, in a related passage, Novalis will say: "The visible clings to the invisible—the inaudible to the audible—the felt to the unfelt—perhaps the thinkable to the unthinkable" (*W*II: 423). It is this sense of a "clinging" of opposites, of phenomena constituted in a dynamic of exchange, touched and haunted by what is other, that will permeate and mark every aspect of Novalis's writing.

7. David Farrell Krell has drawn attention to the frequency and significance of Novalis's use of the word *mannigfach*. See D. F. Krell, *The Tragic Absolute: German Idealism and the Languishing of God* (Bloomington: Indiana University Press, 2005), 62.

8. It is the *Fichte Studies* that have largely formed the core of philosophical inquiry into Novalis's work: in general, the relations between these studies and his later writings have been less fully explored. Nonetheless, work of crucial significance has been done with regard to these early notes, in particular by Manfred Frank, who takes up the question of the reciprocal formation of consciousness, in particular as Novalis explores this in the early segments of his notes. Frank importantly discovers in Novalis a form of ontological realism that is at odds with more conventionally Fichtean approaches to his work, such as that of Gezá von Molnár (see *Novalis' Fichte Studies: The Foundations of His Aesthetics* [Stanford, CA: Stanford University Press, 1970]). An interesting dispute has subsequently arisen (well-documented by Dalia Nassar in her valuable recent study *The Romantic Absolute*) between those who, like Frank, insist on this form of ontological realism and those who, like Frederick Beiser, appear to want to situate Novalis's work closer to the mainstream of German idealism. Beiser has recently offered an interpretation of this dispute that comes close to closing the gap, insisting on a distinction between a subjective idealism (Fichte) and an objective idealism that comes close to the version of ontological realism that Frank articulates (see Beiser's essay "Romanticism and Idealism" in *The Relevance of Romanticism*). The debate, then, hinges on the status of the absolute, which Frank would like to see as both regulative idea in the Kantian sense and as ontologically real. Dalia Nassar's important work pushes beyond the limitations of this dispute by insisting on broadening the scope of inquiry into Novalis's work beyond his early notes on Fichte, a move that allows for a vision of "Novalis's absolute as an internally differentiated, active and dynamic unity" (*Romantic Absolute*, 23). For Frank's reading, see his *Einführung in die frühromantische Ästhetik* (Frankfurt am Main: Suhrkamp, 1989), 248–87; *Philosophical Foundations of German Romanticism*, trans. Millán-Zaibert (Albany: State University of New York Press, 2004), 151–77; and "What Is German Romantic Philosophy?" in *The Relevance of Romanticism*, 15–29.

9. Fichte, trans. Breazale, *Foundations of Transcendental Philosophy: Wissenschaftslehre Nova Metodo (1796/99)* (Ithaca, NY: Cornell University Press, 1992), 132.

10. Fichte, *Foundations*, 133.

11. Fichte, *Foundations*, 126.

Chapter 2

1. For a valuable account of this appropriation, see Lore Hühn, "Das Schweben der Einbildungskraft: Zur frühromantische Überbietung Fichtes," *Deutsche Vierteljahrsschrift für Literaturwissenschaft und Geistesgeschichte* 70, no. 4 (December 1996): 569–99.

2. David W. Wood studies the decisive importance of geometrical proofs to Fichte's method in *Mathesis of the Mind: A Study of Fichte's Wissenschaftslehre and Geometry* (Amsterdam: Rodopi, 2012). Wood has, in addition, discussed the connection of this quasi-mathematics to aspects of Novalis's thinking in "The 'Mathematical' *Wissenschaftslehre*: On a Late Fichtean Reflection of Novalis," in *The Relevance of Romanticism*, 258–73.

3. For a useful account of this reciprocity, and the dynamics of mutual limitation, see the essay by Christian Klotz, "Fichte's Explanation of the Dynamic Structure of Consciousness in the 1794–95 Wissenschaftslehre," in *The Cambridge Companion to Fichte* (Cambridge: Cambridge University Press, 2016), 65–92.

4. Klotz, "Fichte's Explanation," 80.

5. C. Jeffery Kinlaw writes, helpfully, that the "imagination must reconcile the irreconcilable, unite what cannot be united, and give representation to what cannot otherwise be represented" (C. Jeffery Kinlaw, "Imagination and Time in Fichte's Grundlage," in *New Essays in Fichte's "Foundation of the Entire Doctrine of the Science of Knowledge,"* ed. Daniel Breazale and Tom Rockmore (Amherst, NY: Humanities, 2001), 122–37.

6. For a valuable account of the function of different forms of circularity in Fichte's early work, see Daniel Breazale, "Circles and Grounds in the Jena *Wissenschaftslehre*," in *Fichte: Historical Contexts, Contemporary Controversies,* ed. Daniel Breazale and Tom Rockmore (Amherst, NY: Humanities, 1994), 43–70. Breazale distinguishes between what he calls "intra-systematic" and "extra-systematic" circularities, the latter "a consequence of the synthetic unity of consciousness itself" (54). The circle we are describing must presumably be said to belong to this latter category, though it cannot be said to sit comfortably and unambiguously *within* the system.

7. For an alternative, and highly influential account of these early stages of Novalis's thinking, which revolves around the dynamics of limit and reflection, taking the *reversal* involved in reflexive mirroring as central, see Frank, *Philosophical Foundations of German Romanticism,* 151–77; and his *Einführung in die frühromantische Ästhetik*, 248–62.

8. On the significance of the notion of "sign" here, see Frank, *Philosophical Foundations of German Romanticism,* 165–66; and, more broadly, William Arctander O'Brien, *Novalis: Signs of Revolution* (Chapel Hill, NC: Duke University Press, 1994).

9. On the emergence of a conception of feeling in Novalis, see Frank, *Philosophical Foundations of German Romanticism,* 166–69.

10. The reference here is to the *hen kai pan* that had been Lessing's motto, and which was taken up in Tübingen by the youthful Hölderlin, Schelling, and Hegel.

11. More than anything, it is the strangeness of this term—"absolute relation"—which suggests that it is possible to take distance from versions of Novalis's thought which insist on locating and describing a conception of the absolute in his work (see, for instance, the accounts of Manfred Frank, Frederick Beiser, and more recently Dalia Nassar). If it is the relation itself that is absolute, the question becomes one not of determining the nature of this between-space, but rather of trying to understand the dynamics of reciprocity and tensions of exchange without recourse to a middle space, however understood. In this sense, the question, once again, becomes that of *harmonia.*

12. The crystal, and processes of crystallization, will become crucial later on, when questions of language are engaged (see the following chapter). On the significance of the notion of crystallization in Novalis's thinking, in relation to

language, see Franziska Struzek-Krähenbühl, *Oszillation und Kristallisation: Theorie der Sprache bei Novalis* (Paderborn: Ferdinand Schöningh, 2009).

Chapter 3

1. It seems important, in passing, to note that, at stake here, is not the usually presumed opposition of speech and writing, but rather a difference in potentialities, a difference in the kinds of productivity operative within words.

2. See Émile Benveniste, "The Notion of Rhythm in Linguistic Expression," in his *Problems in General Linguistics*, trans. Mary Meek (Miami, FL: Miami University Press, 1971), 281–88.

3. This thought evidently is one that arches across the history of philosophy, if in ways that necessarily lack the clarity of an open space, remaining in a certain way obscure, covert: it is an arc that reaches out from *Phaedo* 61a and resurfaces in Merleau-Ponty's exhortation to "sing the world." I am suggesting only that Novalis's thinking belongs to the moments of the trajectory in which the intimacy of music and philosophy is given voice.

4. Maurice Blanchot, *The Infinite Conversation*, trans. Susan Hanson (Minneapolis: University of Minnesota Press, 1993), 359.

5. Philippe Lacoue-Labarthe and Jean-Luc Nancy, *The Literary Absolute* (Albany: State University of New York Press, 1988), 46.

6. See chapter 8.

7. Rodolphe Gasché examines the concept of the Romantic fragment from the perspective of a reading of Kant, and finds that the form responds more to the exigency of the Aesthetic Idea in Kant's *Critique of Judgment* than to Fichte. To the extent that the Aesthetic Idea itself involves a kind of lacuna, a gap in which the concept remains constitutively inaccessible, this point of view seems entirely germane, though different from the approach adopted here. See R. Gasché, "Ideality in Fragmentation," published as the foreword to Schlegel, *Philosophical Fragments* (Minneapolis: University of Minnesota Press, 1991).

8. Blanchot, *Infinite Conversation*, 353, emphasis added.

9. Abraham Gottlob Werner, *Von der Äußerlichen Kennzeichen der Foßilien* (Leipzig, 1774), trans. Carrozzi, *On the External Characters of Minerals* (Urbana: University of Illinois Press, 1982).

10. "I have also pointed out that those external characters hitherto employed by mineralogists lack much in precision, and how the latter is indispensable in describing them" (Werner, *Von der Äußerlichen Kennzeichen*, xxi).

11. An insightful account of Novalis's ideas concerning mineralogy is given by Laurent Margantin in his *Système minéralogique et cosmologie chez Novalis, ou Les Plis de la terre* (Paris: L'Harmattan, 1998).

12. See Werner's preface to his treatise *Von der Äußerlichen Kennzeichen*, xxi–xxii.

13. Werner writes: "the word oryctognosy originates from ορυκτος, defossus, and γνωριξω, notum facio. Oryctognosy is thus the science of the determi-

nation of minerals" (*Von der Äußerlichen Kennzeichen,* xxiii, n.1). Novalis will adopt and appropriate Werner's unusual vocabulary in his own project, transforming it from a descriptive articulation of a limited domain to a field of much broader concerns. Thus, for example, Novalis will write that "the poet is the oryctognostic analyst . . . who finds the unknown from out of the known" (*W*II: 587/89).

14. Werner, *Von der Äußerlichen Kennzeichen,* 110 (Werner's emphases).

15. Michel Foucault, *The Order of Things* (London: Tavistock Books, 1974), 153.

16. Foucault, *Order,* 154.

17. The original French title of Foucault's book is *Les Mots et les choses* (Paris: Gallimard, 1966).

18. Novalis was personally acquainted with Schelling from his period of study in Jena earlier in the decade, and read—repeatedly, it would seem, and with enthusiasm—Schelling's early publications. He was equally fascinated by the *Ideas for a Philosophy of Nature,* and wrote a series of notes on *Von der Weltseele* of 1798 while he was studying in Freiberg. The most striking confluence of their thinking, however, is certainly in Schelling's *First Outline of a System of the Philosophy of Nature* (to be considered here), which, interestingly enough, Novalis could not have read despite the clear parallels with developments in his thinking at exactly the same period (it was not published until after his death). It seems likely, though, that there is far more than serendipity involved here: Schelling's *First Outline* was written for courses that he was teaching in Jena in 1799. Novalis, following his graduation from Freiberg, became once again a frequent visitor to Jena as a guest of the Schlegels: it is possible, then—though regrettably undemonstrable—that he would at the least have been exposed to elements of Schelling's thought of the moment.

Chapter 4

1. It was indeed Novalis's teacher Reinhold who formed the conduit for this image into Jena in the 1780s. For an extensive account of the reception and proliferation of the image of the temple of Saïs, see J. Assmann, *Moses the Egyptian* (Cambridge, MA: Harvard University Press, 1997). On the potency and significance of the representation of the veiled goddess, see the important and fascinating discussion in Pierre Hadot, *The Veil of Isis* (Cambridge, MA: Harvard University Press, 2006).

2. "Poetics: If the novel is of a retardant nature [*retardirender Natur*], so is it truly poetic, prosaic, a *consonant*" (*W*II: 384).

Chapter 5

1. On the question of nearness in Heidegger, see Krzysztof Ziarek, *Inflected Language: Toward a Hermeneutic of Nearness* (Albany: State University of New York Press, 1992), especially 46–55.

2. "Das Ding," repeated as a public lecture in 1951, slightly altered, and published in *Vorträge und Aufsätze* (*GA* 7). The lecture "Das Ge-Stell" transforms itself into Heidegger's ongoing discourse on technology, notably "Die Frage nach der Technik," 1962.

3. Andrew Mitchell helpfully translates the verb *be-stellen* as "to beset with positioning."

4. The disturbingly casual nature of this invocation has been commented upon at length, especially by Philippe Lacoue-Labarthe in *Heidegger: Art and Politics* (Oxford: Blackwell, 1990) and elsewhere. It is not at all my intention to revisit the rhetoric of condemnation that this passage inevitably unleashes. It seems conceivable, though,, at least in this particular instance, that the difficulty of the passage has much to do with a certain rhetorical poverty in Heidegger's own writing, a poverty perhaps occasioned by the very proximity of the events in question, rather than to any willful elision or dismissal.

Nevertheless, a harsh and difficult question does remain—a question both inconvenient and intransigent—that gathers itself in relation to the proximity of these two corpses. This is the question of "*who?*" The inconvenience of this question has to do with its refusal to allow the corpse to relinquish the historicity of its dying. An involvement in this question would entail a full exploration of the discursive conditions that make such a relinquishment possible. This cannot be attempted here.

5. By way of taking the measure of Heidegger's extremely curious sense of the "flourishing" of death here, we could refer to the extended etymological description of *gedeihen* in Grimm's dictionary, which revolves around the "flourishing" of plants: "the fundamental meaning is to grow, to intensify in healthy growth and thereby reach its goal."

6. By far the most complete and significant account of the dynamics of thinghood in Heidegger is that given by Andrew Mitchell in his book *The Fourfold: Reading the Late Heidegger* (Evanston, IL: Northwestern University Press, 2015). Any attempt to engage this thematic will necessarily find itself indebted to and grateful for Mitchell's research. The current work is no exception.

7. Schürmann contends that the "four constituents . . . matter less than the way in which they transmute the *hen*," and that what is primarily at stake is the "plurification of the *hen*." However, there seems to be a risk in abandoning the specificity of Heidegger's terminology in favor of what comes to resemble more an abstracted function related to the question of "One and Many." This danger would have to do with a reduction of Heidegger's language to a kind of metaphorics, in which the very precise coordination of conceptual pairs in the text becomes flattened out and reduced to the status of analogy. See R. Schürmann, *Heidegger on Being and Acting: From Principles to Anarchy* (Bloomington: Indiana University Press, 1987), 223. It is this danger that Andrew Mitchell's work avoids by engaging the fourfold in terms of a structure which is similar to Schürmann's, but which insists on the specific content of the elements of the fourfold. The tensions between these approaches fuel the energies of Mitchell's remarkable and comprehensive endeavor. See Mitchell, *The Fourfold.*

8. This is a central and productive tension in Andrew Mitchell's account,

where the elements of the fourfold are described in terms of two incommensurate sets of metaphorics: on the one hand, a vocabulary that emphasizes agonistic difference—a vocabulary of the "cut"—and on the other hand a vocabulary of absorption, of concordance.

9. The notes reference a letter (unpublished) to Prof. Reisner dated November 3, 1950. The lectures were composed and delivered toward the end of 1949, and delivered again in March 1950.

Chapter 6

1. See Gerhard Richter, *Afterness: Figures of Following in Modern Thought and Aesthetics* (New York: Columbia University Press, 2011). See, in particular, the introduction, 10ff., in which the etymology that Heidegger broaches here is elaborated and explored in an exemplary manner. Richter cites three sources for this etymology, including Grimm's *Wörterbuch*, where the development of the proximity of "nearness" to what he calls "afterness" is explored. The discussion here is indebted to suggestions in Richter's work. Of this confluence of terms, and of his neologism "afterness," Richter writes: "The concept of afterness and its double figure of *nah* and *nach* also invites us to reconsider, among many things, the logic and movements of mourning and melancholia; the experience of loss, trauma and recovery; and the inexplicable emotions connected with living on." In a somewhat different register, one that engages the affective intensities of the echo, the work to be done in chapter 7 of this book reflects and can in some ways be measured by the terms of this confluence.

2. It should be clear that the sense of a crisis at the center of Dasein being argued here is quite a different sense than that of Gregory Fried who, taking as his central thought the understanding of *polemos* as war, finds the agonistic tensions of Dasein to revolve exclusively around this confrontational dynamic (Gregory Fried, *Heidegger's Polemos* [New Haven, CT: Yale University Press, 2000]). The sense of *harmonia* we are trying to engage here would seek to embrace *polemos* as part of a broader tensional dynamic, and not capitulate to the altogether too easy translation of the term as "war." "Polemos is Dasein and Dasein is Polemos," writes Fried (87), polemos being "usually translated as war" (4). The assumptions at work behind this "usual translation" have been beautifully interrogated by Claudia Baracchi in "The Polemos That Gathers All: Heraclitus on War," *Research in Phenomenology* 45 (2015): 267–87.

3. E. Jünger, "Über den Schmerz," in *Blätter und Steine* (Hamburg: Hanseatische Verlagsanstalt, 1934), 155. Translated by David C. Durst as *On Pain* (New York: Telos, 2008), 1–2 (translation modified).

4. Jünger, *Blätter und Steine*, 211; Jünger, *On Pain*, 45.

5. F. Nietzsche, *The Will to Power,* trans. Walter Kaufmann (New York: Vintage Books, 1968), 549–50.

6. See the "Analysis" by David Farrell Krell in his translation of Heidegger's Nietzsche lectures in *Nietzsche,* vol. 1 (San Francisco: Harper Collins, 1984), 274–77.

7. In an interesting turn in the Nietzsche lectures of 1937, it is the students in Heidegger's seminar who appear to want to push him to discuss the figure of Dionysus, remarking upon its neglect. In response, Heidegger maintains that the figure of Dionysus can be grasped only in "thinking together" the will to power and the eternal recurrence. On Heidegger's neglect of the figure of Dionysus, see Krell's "Analysis" in Heidegger, *Nietzsche,* 1: 274–77. Heidegger writes, for example, that "at the time of *The Birth of Tragedy* the opposition [between Apollonian and Dionysian] is still thought in the sense of Schopenhauerian metaphysics," and that this opposition "all too often becomes a vacuous catchword" (*Nietzsche,* 102). However, in the same text there are indications of a less monolithic reading: on this point, see John Sallis, *Crossings: Nietzsche and the Space of Tragedy* (Chicago: University of Chicago Press, 1991), 60 n.16. Sallis quotes, for instance, a reaction of Heidegger's to a note written in relation to *The Birth of Tragedy*: Heidegger writes that "the statement is reminiscent of Schopenhauer, but is already thinking against him."

It may well be, as Krell suggests, that the deferral of the figure of Dionysus in Heidegger's Nietzsche lectures has to do with a distaste for a certain kind of writing that was in vogue at that time in Germany, a writing that envisioned Nietzsche's figure of Dionysus as the paradigm of a kind of ecstatic "philosophy of orgiastics." In this regard, Krell points in particular to Ludwig Klage's *Der Geist als Widersacher der Seele* of 1932. (See his "Analysis" in Heidegger, *Nietzsche,* 1: 242.) This interpretation is all the more convincing in that it places this deferral entirely in line with Heidegger's quite explicit rejection of Wagner, in whose music he was apparently only able to see a "plunge into frenzy and the disintegration into sheer feeling as redemptive," and so on. In this narrow misunderstanding, Heidegger appears to be placing himself, unquestioningly, on the ground of Nietzsche's own dismissal of his earlier allegiance to Wagner. Nietzsche's reaction against Wagner clearly needs to be thought better and more fully than from the ground on which he himself placed it; but this reaction, and Heidegger's easy endorsement, does go some way to explaining the deferral we are considering, in that it sets up a line of development that would link, clearly, the Dionysian with Schopenhauer, and thence with Wagner, or at least with a certain kind of Wagnerianism evident in the fashionable literature of the time, such as Klage's. This is a mode of thinking, one might add, that was thoroughly endorsed by the political regime of the time. Indeed, given the common currency and fashion of this appropriation of Wagner in the Germany of the late 1930s, it seems to me that the visceral and non-thoughtful rejection of Wagner in Heidegger's texts is by no means the least significant sign we have of an active political dissent in his lectures of the period.

8. Sallis, *Crossings,* 57.

9. See, for example, *GA* 71: 235/203, or 211/181.

10. Heidegger, *Erläuterungen zu Hölderlin's Dichtung, GA* 4. See also the full-length courses on Hölderlin's "Andenken" (*GA* 52), "Der Ister" (*GA* 53), and on "Germanien" and "Der Rhein" (*GA* 39).

11. J. W. von Goethe, "Wonne der Wehmut," in Goethe, *Werke,* ed. Betsch, vol. 1: *Dichtungen* (Leipzig: Bibliographisches Instituts, 1926), 52.

12. For an example from Schiller, we might cite the poem "Das Mädchen's Klage," which speaks of "the sweetest joys of the sorrowing breast."

13. Friedrich Hölderlin, *The Death of Empedocles: A Mourning-Play,* trans. David Farrell Krell (Albany: State University of New York Press, 2008), 144.

14. This pair, and in particular the term "aorgic," presents a puzzle for readers, but one which David Farrell Krell has elucidated with great clarity. *Organisch,* says Krell, is not to be thought of in the familiar sense of "organic," but somewhat closer to the Greek sense of *organon*—he thus translates the term with cognates of the "organizational." "Aorgic," by contrast, is to be understood in terms of the privative "a-," "suggesting those elements of nature that escape or at least resist the human organization of them." Hölderlin, *Death of Empedocles,* 257, n.7.

15. See "The Fatherland in Decline" ("Das Werden im Vergehen"), in Hölderlin, *Death of Empedocles,* 155.

Chapter 7

1. This has tended to be the direction taken by even the most aware commentators on Heidegger's work of this period. See, for instance, Daniela Vallega-Neu, who, despite her sensitivity to this question, nonetheless appears to think the in-between of inceptions as an "on-the-way" from one to another. For example: "meditating on what happened in the first [Greek] beginning of the history of beyng leads to understanding this abandonment of beings by being. . . . This in turn brings into play the intimation of another beginning." In this way, the narrative is presented in chronological form, a linear sequence, which effectively turns the "history of beyng" into a very ordinary history indeed. See Vallega-Neu, *Heideggger's Poietic Writings: From Contributions to Philosophy to The Event* (Bloomington: Indiana University Press, 2018), 22. Richard Capobianco is aware of the complexity of thinking the unity of inceptions, though he contents himself with insisting that "the account of 'first' and 'other' beginnings is not fully worked out," and hence does not elaborate the problem. R. Capobianco, *Engaging Heidegger* (Toronto: University of Toronto Press, 2010), 42.

2. Michel Haar, *Song of the Earth: Heidegger and the Grounds of the History of Being* (Bloomington: Indiana University Press, 1993), 55.

3. The pleasure invoked would have to do with the experience of reciprocity, a pleasure in the intertwinement and play of the "mutual surpassing" of beginnings, in their insistent opening onto one another. Especially given the sense of play in the "Zuspiel" of this section, it seems to me of great interest to dwell upon this strange, and indeed (within the *seynsgeschichtlich* texts, at least) unique invocation of "pleasure" as a mode of encounter, a mode of thinking transitionally. It would be necessary to interrogate vigorously the status of this pleasure that, occurring from within something like a "play," cannot help but suggest a Kantian frame of reference. This connection cannot be pursued here.

Chapter 8

1. Relatively little attention seems to have been paid to the text of this seminar, although there is a brief but valuable account in David Nowell-Smith, *Sounding/Silence: Martin Heidegger at the Limits of Poetics* (New York: Fordham University Press, 2013), 86ff. By contrast with this scarcity, a far greater emphasis has tended to be placed on the influence of Humboldt in the development of Heidegger's thinking of language. While in no way disputing the significance of Humboldt's presence, I would like to suggest that the particular mode of engagement with language that occurs in the texts of the late 1930s is forged more directly out of the confrontation with Herder than in relation to Humboldt's thinking. For an invaluable account of the significance of Humboldt for Heidegger's thinking of language, see G. Figal, *Objectivity: The Hermeneutical and the Philosophical,* trans. T. George (Albany: State University of New York Press, 2010), especially 191–97.

There are important accounts of Herder's work on language to be found in K. Terezakis, *The Immanent Word: The Turn to Language in German Philosophy, 1759–1801* (New York: Routledge, 2007); C. Taylor, "The Importance of Herder," in *Isaiah Berlin: A Celebration,* ed. E. Margalit and A. Margalit (Chicago: University of Chicago Press, 1991); and M. Forster, *After Herder: Philosophy of Language in the German Tradition* (Oxford: Oxford University Press, 2012). The first two of these, in particular, discuss the question of the relation between Herder and Humboldt's conceptions of language. For a valuable account of this and other controversies surrounding the reception of Herder's work on language, see J. Zammito, "Herder, Sturm und Drang, and Expressionism," *Graduate Faculty Philosophy Journal* 27, no. 2 (2006): 51–74.

Bibliography

Works by Novalis

References to the works of Novalis are from the three-volume edition by Richard Samuel and Hans-Joachim Mähl (1978). References are given parenthetically as *W* followed by the volume number, with the German pagination provided first, and followed by a slash and the pagination of relevant English translations where available.

W *Werke, Tagebücher und Briefe.* 3 volumes. Edited by Richard Samuel and Hans-Joachim Mähl. Munich: Hanser Verlag, 1978.

AB *Notes for a Romantic Encyclopaedia: Das Allgemeine Brouillon.* Translated by David W. Wood. Albany: State University of New York Press, 2007.

FS *Fichte Studies.* Translated by Jane Kneller. Cambridge: Cambridge University Press, 2003.

NS *The Novices of Saïs.* Translated by R. Manheim. New York: Archipelago Books, 2004.

PW *Philosophical Writings.* Translated by M. M. Stoljar. Albany: State University of New York Press, 1997.

Works by Martin Heidegger

References to the works of Martin Heidegger are provided in the text parenthetically by volume number of the complete works (*Gesamtausgabe*, abbreviated *GA*), with the German pagination provided first, followed by a slash and the English pagination of published translations where available. Where emphasis has been added, the words *emphasis added* follow the reference.

Heidegger, Martin. *Gesamtausgabe.* 102 volumes projected. Frankfurt am Main: Vittorio Klostermann, 1975–.

GA 1 *Frühe Schriften.* Edited by Friedrich-Wilhelm von Herrmann. 2018. Partial translation by John Van Buren in *Supplements.* Albany: State University of New York Press, 2002.

GA 2 *Sein und Zeit.* Edited by Friedrich-Wilhelm von Herrmann. 1977. Translated by Joan Stambaugh as *Being and Time*, revised by Dennis J. Schmidt. Albany: State University of New York Press, 2010.

GA 4 *Erläuterungen zu Hölderlins Dichtung.* 2nd edition. Edited by Friedrich-Wilhelm von Herrmann. 1991. Translated by Keith Hoeller as *Elucidations of Hölderlin's Poetry.* Amherst, NY: Humanity Books, 2000.

GA 5 *Holzwege.* 7th edition. Edited by Friedrich-Wilhelm von Herrmann. 1994. Edited and translated by Julian Young and Kenneth Haynes as *Off the Beaten Track.* Cambridge: Cambridge University Press, 2002.

GA 6.1 *Nietzsche I.* Edited by Brigitte Schillback. 1996.

GA 6.2 *Nietzsche II.* Edited by Brigitte Schillback. 1997. Both volumes translated by David Farrell Krell as *Nietzsche,* 4 vols. San Francisco: Harper and Row, 1979.

GA 7 *Vorträge und Aufsätze.* Edited by Friedrich-Wilhelm von Herrmann. 1994.

GA 8 *Was heißt Denken?* Edited by Paola-Ludovika Coriando. 2002. Translated by J. Glenn Gray as *What Is Called Thinking?* New York: Harper and Row, 1968.

GA 10 *Der Satz vom Grund.* Edited by Petra Jaeger. 1997. Translated by Reginald Lily as *The Principle of Reason.* Bloomington: Indiana University Press, 1998.

GA 12 *Unterwegs zur Sprache.* Edited by Friedrich-Wilhelm von Herrmann. 1994. Translated by Peter Hertz as *On the Way to Language.* San Francisco: Harper and Row, 1971.

GA 15 *Seminare.* Edited by Kurt Ochwadt. 1986. Partially translated by C. H. Seibert as *Heraclitus Seminar.* Evanston, IL: Northwestern University Press, 1993.

GA 29/30 *Die Grundbegriffe der Metaphysik: Welt—Endlichkeit—Einsamkeit.* Edited by Friedrich-Wilhelm von Herrmann. 1992. Translated by William McNeill as *The Fundamental Concepts of Metaphysics: World, Finitude, Solitude.* Bloomington: Indiana University Press, 1995.

GA 32 *Hegels Phänomenologie des Geistes.* 3rd edition. Edited by Ingtraud Görland. 1997. Translated by Parvis Emad and Kenneth Maly as *Hegel's Phenomenology of Spirit.* Bloomington: Indiana University Press, 1988.

GA 39 *Hölderlins Hymnen "Germanien" und "Der Rhein."* 2nd edition. Edited by Susanne Ziegler. 1989. Translated by Julia Ireland and Will McNeill as *Hölderlins Hymns: "Germania" and "The Rhine."* Bloomington: Indiana University Press, 2014.

GA 42 *Schelling: Vom Wesen der Menschlichen Freiheit.* Edited by Ingrid Schüßler. 1988. Translated by Joan Stambaugh as *Schelling's Treatise on the Essence of Human Freedom.* Athens: Ohio University Press, 1984.

GA 53 *Hölderlins Hymne "Der Ister."* 2nd edition. Edited by Walter Biemel. 1993. Translated by William McNeill and Julia Davis as *Hölderlin's Hymn "The Ister."* Bloomington: Indiana University Press, 1996.

GA 55 *Heraklit.* 3rd edition. Edited by Manfred S. Frings. 1994. Translated by S. Montgomery Ewegen and Julia Goesser Assainte as *Heraclitus: The Inception of Occidental Thinking and Logic.* London: Bloomsbury Academic, 2018.

GA 65 *Beiträge zur Philosophie (Vom Ereignis).* 2nd edition. Edited by Friedrich-Wilhelm von Herrmann. 1994. Translated by Daniela Vallega-Neu and

Richard Rojcewicz as *Contributions to Philosophy (Of the Event)*. Bloomington: Indiana University Press, 2012.

GA 66 *Besinnung*. Edited by Friedrich-Wilhelm von Herrmann. 1998. Translated by Parvis Emad and Thomas Kalary as *Mindfulness*. New York: Continuum, 2006.

GA 68 *Hegel*. Edited by Ingrid Schüßler. 2009. Translated by Joseph Arel and Niels Feuerhahn as *Hegel*. Bloomington: Indiana University Press, 2015.

GA 70 *Über den Anfang*. Edited by Paola-Ludovika Coriando. 2005.

GA 71 *Das Ereignis*. Edited by Friedrich-Wilhelm von Herrmann. 2009. Translated by Richard Rojcewicz as *The Event*. Bloomington: Indiana University Press, 2013.

GA 74 *Zum Wesen der Sprache*. Edited by Thomas Regehly. 2010.

GA 79 *Bremer und Freiburger Vorträge*. Edited by Petra Jaeger. 1994. Translated by Andrew Mitchell as *Bremen and Freiburg Lectures: Insight into That Which Is and Basic Principles of Thinking*. Bloomington: Indiana University Press, 2012.

GA 85 *Seminar: Der Metaphysik der Sprache und die Wesung des Wortes*. Edited by Ingrid Schüßler. 1999. Translated by W. Torres Gregory and Y. Unna as *On the Essence of Language: The Metaphysics of Language and the Essencing of the Word*. Albany: State University of New York Press, 2004.

GA 90 *Zu Ernst Jünger*. Edited by Peter Trawny. 2004.

Abbreviated Works by Other Authors

DK Diels, Hermann, and Walther Kranz, eds. *Die Fragmente der Vorsokratiker*. 19th edition. 3 vols. Zurich: Weidmann, 1996.

EE Schelling, Friedrich Wilhelm Joseph. *Erster Entwurf eines Systems der Naturphilosophie*. In volume 1, part 3 of *Sämmtliche Werke*, edited by K. F. A. Schelling, 14 vols. Stuttgart: J. G. Cotta, 1856. Translated by Keith R. Peterson as *First Outline of a System of the Philosophy of Nature*. Albany: State University of New York Press, 2004.

GT Nietzsche, Friedrich. *Die Geburt der Tragödie: Schriften zu Literatur und Philosophie der Griechen*. Frankfurt am Main: Insel Verlag, 1994. Translated by Walter Kauffman as *The Birth of Tragedy*. New York: Vintage Books, 1968.

H Hölderlin, Friedrich. *Hyperion, oder der Eremit in Griechenland*. Tübingen: Cotta, 1799. Translated by Erich Santner as *Hyperion and Selected Poems*. New York: Continuum, 1990.

He Herder, Johann Gottfried. *Werke*, vol. 5: *Abhandlung über den Ursprung der Sprache*. Berlin: Aufbau-Verlag, 1964. Translated and edited by Michael N. Forster in J. G. Herder, *Philosophical Writings*. Cambridge: Cambridge University Press, 2002.

KGW Nietzsche, Friedrich. *Werke: Kritische Gesamtausgabe*. Edited by Giorgio Colli and Mazzino Montinari. Berlin: de Gruyter, 1967– . VII–3: *Nachgelassene Fragmente*; *KGW* 4: *Also Sprach Zarathustra*; *KGW* 1: *Die Geburt der Tragödie: Unzeitgemäßige Betrachtung I–IV*.

MA Kant, Immanuel. *Metaphysische Anfangsgründe der Naturwissenschaft.* Translated by James W. Ellington as *Metaphysical Foundations of Natural Science* in I. Kant, *Philosophy of Material Nature.* Indianapolis: Hackett, 1985.

SW I Fichte, Johann Gottlieb. *Sämmtliche Werke,* vol. 1, *Grundlage der gesammten Wissenschaftslehre.* Berlin: Veit, 1845. Translated by Peter Heath and John Lachs as *The Science of Knowledge.* Cambridge: Cambridge University Press, 1982.

Other Works Cited

Aristotle. *Metaphysics.* Translated by J. Sachs. Santa Fe, NM: Green Lion Books, 2002.

Assmann, Jan. *Moses the Egyptian.* Cambridge, MA: Harvard University Press, 1997.

Baracchi, Claudia. "The Polemos That Gathers All: Heraclitus on War." *Research in Phenomenology* 45 (2015): 267–87.

Beiser, Frederick. *German Idealism: The Struggle against Subjectivism, 1781–1801.* Cambridge, MA: Harvard University Press, 2002.

———. *The Romantic Imperative.* Cambridge, MA: Harvard University Press, 2006.

Benveniste, Emile. *Problems in General Linguistics.* Translated by Mary Meek. Miami, FL: Miami University Press, 2003.

Blanchot, Maurice. *L'Entretien infini.* Paris: Gallimard, 1969. Translated by Susan Hanson as *The Infinite Conversation.* Minneapolis: University of Minnesota Press.

Brann, Eva. *The Logos of Heraclitus.* Philadelphia: Paul Dry Books, 2011.

Breazale, Daniel, and Tom Rockmore, eds. *Fichte: Historical Contexts/Contemporary Controversies.* Amherst, NY: Humanities, 1994.

———, eds. *New Essays in "Fichte's Foundation of the Entire Doctrine of Scientific Knowledge."* Amherst, NY: Humanities, 2001.

Calasso, Roberto. *The Marriage of Cadmus and Harmony.* New York: Knopf, 1993.

Capobianco, Richard. *Engaging Heidegger.* Toronto: University of Toronto Press, 2010.

Derrida, Jacques. *La Bête et la souveraine,* vol. 2. Paris: Éditions Galilée, 2010. Translated by Geoffrey Bennington as *The Beast and the Sovereign, Vol. 2.* Chicago: University of Chicago Press, 2012.

Donehower, Bruce. *The Birth of Novalis: Friedrich von Hardenberg's Journal of 1797, with Selected Letters and Documents.* Albany: State University of New York Press, 2007.

Eckermann, Johann Peter. *Conversations of Goethe.* New York: Da Capo, 1998.

Fichte, Johann Gottlieb. *Foundations of Transcendental Philosophy: Wissenschaftslehre Nova Metodo (1796/99).* Translated by D. Breazale. Ithaca, NY: Cornell University Press, 1992.

Figal, Günter. *Objectivity: The Hermeneutical and the Philosophical.* Translated by T. George. Albany: State University of New York Press, 2010.

Forster, Michael. *After Herder: Philosophy of Language in the German Tradition.* Oxford: Oxford University Press, 2012.

Foucault, Michel. *Les Mots et les choses*. Paris: Gallimard, 1967. Translated as *The Order of Things*. London: Tavistock Books, 1974.

Frank, Manfred. *Einführung in die Frühromantische Ästhetik*. Frankfurt am Main: Suhrkamp, 1989.

———. *Philosophical Foundations of German Romanticism*. Translated by E. Millán Zaibert. Albany: State University of New York Press, 2004.

Fried, Gregory. *Heidegger's Polemos: From Being to Politics*. New Haven, CT: Yale University Press, 2000.

Gasché, Rodolphe. "Ideality in Fragmentation." In K. W. F. Schlegel, *Philosophical Fragments*. Minneapolis: University of Minnesota Press, 1991.

Goethe, J. W. von. *The Metamorphosis of Plants*. Translated by J. Miller. Cambridge, MA: MIT Press, 2010.

Haar, Michel. *Song of the Earth: Heidegger and the Grounds of the History of Being*. Bloomington: Indiana University Press, 1993.

Hadot, Pierre. *The Veil of Isis*. Cambridge, MA: Harvard University Press, 2006.

Hegener, Johannes von. *Die Poetisierung der Wissenschaften bei Novalis*. Bonn: Bouvier Verlag, 1975.

Heraclitus. *Fragments*. Edited by T. M. Robinson. Toronto: University of Toronto Press, 1987.

Hölderlin, Friedrich. *The Death of Empedocles*. Translated by D. F. Krell. Bloomington: Indiana University Press, 2010.

———. *Essays and Letters*. Translated by C. Louth and J. Adler. London: Penguin Books, 2009.

Hühn, Lore. "Das Schweben der Einbildungskraft: Zur frühromantische Überbietung Fichtes." *Deutsche Vierteljahrsschrift für Literaturwissenschaft und Geistesgeschichte* 70, no. 4 (December 1996): 569–99.

James, David, and Günter Zöller, eds. *The Cambridge Companion to Fichte*. Cambridge: Cambridge University Press, 2016.

Jünger, Ernst. "Über den Schmerz." In *Blätter und Steine*. Hamburg: Hanseatische Verlagsanstalt, 1934. Translated by D. Durst as *On Pain*. New York: Telos, 2008.

Kahn, Charles H. *The Art and Thought of Heraclitus*. Cambridge: Cambridge University Press, 1981.

Kant, Immanuel. *Critique of Judgment*. Translated by W. Pluhar. Indianapolis: Hackett, 1987.

———. *Critique of Pure Reason*. Translated by W. Pluhar. Indianapolis: Hackett, 1996.

Kirk, Geoffrey S., John E. Raven, and Malcolm Schofield. *The Presocratic Philosophers*. Cambridge: Cambridge University Press, 1983.

Kneller, Jane. *Kant and the Power of Imagination*. Cambridge: Cambridge University Press, 2006.

Kompridis, Nikolas, ed. *Philosophical Romanticism*. London: Routledge, 2006.

Krell, David Farrell. *Contagion: Sexuality, Disease and Death in German Romanticism and Idealism*. Bloomington: Indiana University Press, 1998.

———. *The Tragic Absolute: German Idealism and the Languishing of God*. Bloomington: Indiana University Press, 2005.

Lacoue-Labarthe, Philippe. *Heidegger: Art and Politics*. Oxford: Blackwell, 1990.

Lacoue-Labarthe, Philippe, and Jean-Luc Nancy. *The Literary Absolute*. Albany: State University of New York Press, 1988.

Loraux, Nicole. *The Divided City: On Memory and Forgetting in Ancient Athens*. New York: Zone Books, 2002.

———. *The Mourning Voice: An Essay on Greek Tragedy*. Ithaca, NY: Cornell University Press, 2002.

Margantin, Laurent. *Novalis, ou L'Ecriture romantique*. Paris: Éditions Belin, 2012.

———. *Système minéralogique et cosmologique chez Novalis, ou Les Plis de la terre*. Paris: L'Harmattan, 1998.

Mitchell, Andrew. *The Fourfold: Reading the Late Heidegger*. Evanston, IL: Northwestern University Press, 2015.

Molnár, Géza von. *Novalis' Fichte Studies: The Foundations of His Aesthetics*. Stanford, CA: Stanford University Press, 1970.

———. *Romantic Vision, Ethical Context: Novalis and Artistic Autonomy*. Minneapolis: University of Minnesota Press, 1987.

Moretti, Giampiero. *La Segnatura romantica: Philosophia e sentimento da Novalis a Heidegger* Cernusco: Hestia, 1992.

Nancy, Jean-Luc. *Dis-Enclosure: The Deconstruction of Christianity*. New York: Fordham University Press, 2011.

Nassar, Dalia, ed. *The Relevance of Romanticism*. Oxford: Oxford University Press, 2014.

———. *The Romantic Absolute*. Chicago: University of Chicago Press, 2014.

Neubauer, John. *Bifocal Vision: Novalis' Philosophy of Nature and Disease*. Chapel Hill: University of North Carolina Press, 1971.

Nowell-Smith, David. *Sounding/Silence. Heidegger at the Limits of Poetics*. New York: Fordham University Press, 2013.

O'Brien, William Arctander. *Novalis: Signs of Revolution*. Durham, NC: Duke University Press, 1995.

Plato. *Lysis, Symposium, Gorgias*. Translated by W. Lamb. Cambridge, MA: Harvard University Press, 1925.

———. *Phaedrus*. Translated by N. Fowler. Cambridge, MA: Harvard University Press, 1914.

Richardson, William. *Heidegger: Through Phenomenology to Thought*. New York: Fordham University Press, 2003.

Richter, Gerhard. *Afterness: Figures of Following in Modern Thought and Aesthetics*. New York: Columbia University Press, 2011.

Sallis, John. *Crossings: Nietzsche and the Space of Tragedy*. Chicago: University of Chicago Press, 1991.

———. *The Force of Imagination: The Sense of the Elemental*. Bloomington: Indiana University Press, 2000.

———. *The Gathering of Reason*. Albany: State University of New York Press, 1980.

———. *The Logic of Imagination: The Expanse of the Elemental*. Bloomington: Indiana University Press, 2012.

Schürmann, Reiner. *Broken Hegemonies*. Bloomington: Indiana University Press, 2003.

———. *Heideggger on Being and Acting: From Principles to Anarchy*. Bloomington: Indiana University Press, 1987.

Struzek-Krähenbühl, Franziska. *Oszillation und Kristallisation: Theorie der Sprachebei Novalis*. Paderborn: Ferdinand Schöningh, 2009.

Taylor, Charles. "The Importance of Herder." In *Isaiah Berlin: A Celebration*, edited by E. Margalit and A. Margalit. Chicago: University of Chicago Press, 1991.

Terezakis, Katie. *The Immanent Word: The Turn to Language in German Philosophy, 1759–1801*. New York: Routledge, 2007.

Trzaskoma, Stephen, R. Scott Smith, and Stephen Brunet, eds. *Anthology of Classical Myth: Primary Sources in Translation*. Indianapolis: Hackett, 2004.

Vallega-Neu, Daniela. *Heidegger's Poietic Writings*. Bloomington: Indiana University Press, 2018.

Vandevelde, Pol. *Heidegger and the Romantics*. New York: Routledge, 2012.

Werner, Abraham Gottlob. *Von der Äußerlichen Kennzeichen der Foßilien*. Leipzig, 1774. Translated by C. Carozzi as *On the External Characters of Minerals*. Urbana: University of Illinois Press, 1982.

Wood, David W. *Mathesis of the Mind: A Study of Fichte's Wissenschaftslehre and Geometry*. Amsterdam: Rodopi, 2012.

Ziarek, Krzysztof. *Inflected Nearness*. Albany: State University of New York Press, 1989.

———. *Language after Heidegger*. Bloomington: Indiana University Press, 2016.

Index